D0592248

A SCATTERING OF JADES

Stories, Poems, and Prayers
of the Aztecs

TRANSLATED BY

THELMA D. SULLIVAN

EDITED, COMPILED, AND INTRODUCED
WITH COMMENTARY BY

T. J. KNAB

A TOUCHSTONE BOOK
PUBLISHED BY SIMON & SCHUSTER

New York   London   Toronto   Sydney   Tokyo   Singapore

SIMON & SCHUSTER/TOUCHSTONE
Rockefeller Center
1230 Avenue of the Americas
New York, New York 10020

Translations from Nahautl copyright © 1994 by Rita Wilensky
Original material copyright © 1994 by T. J. Knab

Designed by Irving Perkins Associates
Manufactured in the United States of America

10 9 8 7 6 5 4 3 2 1
10 9 8 7 6 5 4 3 2 1   PBK

Library of Congress Cataloging-in-Publication Data

A Scattering of jades : stories, poems, and prayers of the Aztecs /
translated by Thelma D. Sullivan ; edited, compiled, and introduced
with commentary by T.J. Knab.
        p. cm.
Translated from Aztec and Spanish.
"A Touchstone book."
Includes bibliographical references and index.
1. Aztecs—Folklore.   2. Aztec literature.   3. Aztec poetry.
    I. Sullivan, Thelma D.   II. Knab, T. J.
            F1219.76.F65S27   1994
398.2'089974—dc20   93-31321
                                                               CIP

ISBN 0-671-86414-9
0-671-86413-0 (PBK)

For I. F.

Ontetepeoac, on chachayaoac
There was a sowing, there was a scattering.

> This was said of a royal orator
> who counsels the people well. After he spoke,
> after the oration had been delivered,
> they understood its truth, they told him:
>
> > "The people have been well informed,
> > they have been enriched.
> > There has been a sowing,
> > there has been a great scattering of jades."
>
> > (FLORENTINE CODEX, VI, 205v)

Contents

◻️🔲🔲🔲🔲🔲🔲🔲◻️

The Manners of Speech of the Elders in Their Ancient

Acknowledgments

THE FIRST OUTLINE for this book was sketched by Thelma Sullivan and myself shortly before her death. Unfortunately the outline and most of the materials remained in my files as I moved from Mexico to the United States and turned my attention from academics to being a full-time chef and innkeeper at the Auberge des 4 Saisons. Late in the winter of 1989 a cold snap burst the pipes above my office in our inn, destroying much of my professional library. In the process of salvaging my books and papers, I came upon the outline for this book and some of the materials that Sullivan had given me for it. A search later that year of Sullivan's files at Dumbarton Oaks pre-Columbian research center in Washington, D.C., revealed that most of the materials for this book were in fact there among her voluminous notes and drafts.

Thelma D. Sullivan was my first professor of Nahuatl, the Classic Aztec language. She taught at the National School of Anthropology and History (ENAH) in Mexico. Her constant counsel and encouragement of my own work was always invaluable. Thelma was far more than a professor and colleague for us, often celebrating holidays and vacations with our family. She was our "godmother" in Mexico, and her loss was deeply felt by all who knew and loved her.

Thanks to our staff at the inn, Alain Raybaud, Claude Revatier, and many other fine chefs who have worked with me, I could take off the time to compile the materials for this book. Elizabeth H. Boone and her staff at Dumbarton Oaks merit special thanks. They took in this wandering scholar and provided a superb and stimulating environment in which to compile this book. Bridget Toledo in the library and all the staff were especially helpful as were the fellows John Pohl, Barbara Mundy, and Xavier Urcid. In the process of editing this material Doris Heyden, Karen

Dakin, Nick Hopkins and J. Kathryn Josserand, Johanna Broda, H. B. Nicholson, Rita Wilensky, Arthur J. O. Anderson, Wayne Rewet, and many others provided encouragement and considerable aid in locating the materials that Sullivan had left at the time of her death. Janine Pommy Vega provided a stimulating environment in which to finish the book and without Peter Shotwell's sagacious advice it would have never been completed. Davíd Carrasco was perhaps the most enthusiastic promoter of this book, and his commentaries, along with those of Willard Gingerich, B. J. Price, B. J. Isbell, Jill Furst, and Jorge Klor de Alva have all helped make this a better book. Doris Heyden, a close friend of Thelma Sullivan, the nurturing mother to generations of anthropologists, ethnohistorians, and art historians in Mexico, was perhaps my most thorough critic. Dennis and Barbara Tedlock's advice and counsel have been invaluable and greatly influenced my view of Aztec literature. Peter and Jill Furst's commentaries have also been invaluable.

Finally the encouragement of my family has been what made this book possible.

—T. J. KNAB
Auberge des 4 Saisons
Shandaken, New York

THE AZTEC WORLD
OF ANCIENT MEXICO

THE AZTECS WERE A WANDERING TRIBE of barbarous refugees when they entered the lush Valley of Mexico at the end of the twelfth century, but within the space of a little over two hundred years they came to dominate the entire valley. By the time of their conquest by the Spanish in 1521 they controlled most of central Mexico and territories well into Central America. Their capital was Tenochtitlan in the center of Lake Texcoco at the heart of present-day Mexico City. The cities of Europe paled in comparison to its splendor. The odyssey of the Aztecs, as well as their precipitous downfall brought about by the Spanish conquest, is a tale of blood, power, and opportunism. Theirs was an empire unlike anything the Spanish conquerors had ever known. Yet the Aztec empire fell in but two years to a small band of intrepid conquistadors.

How was it that one of the great civilizations of ancient Mexico could fall so suddenly and with such finality? Disease introduced by the Spaniards as well as the foreigners' genocidal disregard for the lives of their Aztec subjects played a part, but there was far more to the lightning conquest of the Aztec empire than the inhumanity of its conquerors. The Aztecs horrified the Spaniards with their sanguinary practices: skull racks in front of their temples and dismembered human bodies in their plazas. The Aztec gods were devils in the eyes of the Spanish. In Europe serious debates were held to determine whether or not the natives of the New World were even human. They were the prototypical "others," a civilization so shocking to Western traditions that it was surely never understood by its conquerors.

The Aztecs never knew what to make of the strange Spanish

conquerors either. Traditionally, Aztec warriors fought on the
battlefield until death. If captured, Aztec warriors were sacrificed on the altars of their gods. The Aztec warriors believed
the ultimate glory of battle and a place with the gods was found
in death. The conquistadors, on the other hand, fought only to
win, or at least to live to fight another day. Puzzled by this odd
behavior, Motecuzoma[1] bestowed rich gifts befitting gods on the
Spaniards in the hope that these strangers would take his offerings and leave the empire in peace. Any Mesoamerican native
would have easily understood that this was the purpose behind
the presents. Instead Motecuzoma's gifts only whetted the
Spaniards' appetite for more gold and their lust for further conquest. The collision of these two uncomprehending worlds re-
sulted in one of the greatest cataclysms in human history.

Much of what we know about the ancient world of Mexico
comes from Classic Aztec[2] texts written down shortly after the
conquest. These texts constitute the most extensive single body
of Native American literature in existence. Unfortunately much
of this vast corpus has remained in scholarly circles where the
material is inaccessible to most readers. The superb translations
in A Scattering of Jades allow us to glimpse the beautiful and
terrifying world of the Aztecs as they experienced it. It also
helps to build an understanding of the ancient world of Mexico
and its modern descendants.

Today over one hundred thousand people in Mexico still speak
dialects of Modern Aztec. Millions are descended from the
union of the peoples of the empire and their new rulers. Mexico
is a nation of mestizaje, or mixing. The language and literature,
art and aesthetic, metaphors and meanings of the descendants
of the Aztec empire provide us with new vantage points on the
Aztec world of ancient Mexico and the modern nation.

Our present understanding of the Aztec world may in fact be
no better than the understandings of the Aztec priests and diviners who used obsidian "smoke mirrors," their crystal balls,
to peer into the worlds of their ancient deities. Theirs was a
world of extreme aesthetic refinements sharply contrasted with
macabre rituals for bloodthirsty deities. It was a world of harmony and chaos, a world whose origins are lost in myth and
whose histories are constantly being rewritten. Through the

smoke and mist of time translations allow us to re-create a dialogue with the historical remains of the Aztecs not lost to the conquest.

Mesoamerican Origins

The Valley of Mexico was one of the cradles of civilization in Mesoamerica. The central Mexican highlands at over seven thousand feet in altitude have a pleasant climate, almost springlike year-round, that varies between wet and dry seasons. The valley is a huge bowl surrounded by high snow-capped volcanic peaks. Before the conquest the basin floor contained five lakes that provided water. The volcanic soil of the valley was highly productive. The lakes and the migratory waterfowl that they attracted provided an ample base of food and water for the peoples of the valley. Irrigation networks and other ingenious techniques for agriculturally exploiting the lake shores extended the bounty of the land. Compared to the arid reaches of northern Mexico that were the original home of the Aztecs, the valley was truly a promised land.

Other major Mesoamerican civilizations rose and fell in the Valley of Mexico before the Aztecs entered the region. The ancient urban center of Teotihuacan—the city of the pyramids just outside Mexico City—dominated Mesoamerica's Classic period, 100–800 C.E. (common era). From there, the urban elite of this period extended their trade networks and promulgated their art forms, architecture, and ideology throughout Mexico and Central America long before the Aztec time.

The Valley of Mexico has always been a tapestry of different ethnic groups and languages. Archaeological evidence shows that there were most certainly Otomí speakers and people from the coast of Veracruz living in and about the city of Teotihuacan. *Barrios,* or neighborhoods, in the city were inhabited by people from the southern highland states of Oaxaca, as well as Mayan lowlanders, and perhaps there were even Mayan highlanders from Guatemala in Teotihuacan. Though we do not know who the rulers were of this first great Mesoamerican city, we do know that Teotihuacan was a multilingual multiethnic city.

The Toltecs

The Toltecs, who dominated the post-Classic period, 900–1200 C.E., were the last great civilization in the Valley of Mexico before the rise of the Aztec empire. The Aztecs viewed the Toltecs as the developers of high culture, and claimed to be their descendants. The Aztecs knew little of civilizations that had preceded the Toltecs and used the Toltec legacy to legitimize their bloody reign. In the eyes of the Aztecs, Toltec artists and builders had been the most accomplished, and their fields had produced the richest bounty. Their city Tollan, located in Tula in the state of Hidalgo on the northern edge of the Valley of Mexico, is memorialized in Aztec poetry and song. Though Tula was quite a bit smaller than Teotihuacan, the Aztecs simply assumed that all ruins in Mexico were attributable to the Toltecs, whom they considered the founders of the greatest urban civilization the world had ever known.

The Toltecs were guided by the god/king Quetzalcoatl. According to myth (see Part I, Chapter 1), Quetzalcoatl was both a deity and a real personage. He was an ascetic priest who eschewed the practice of human sacrifice and built the great temples of Tollan, the House of the Precious Feathered Serpents, the Turquoise House, and the House of the Dawn. He was also known as Ce Acatl Topiltzin, Our Lord 1-Reed. All the major events concerning his life occurred at cycles in the ancient calendar in the year 1-Reed, which recurred only once every fifty-two years. Quetzalcoatl was a culture hero, the hero with a thousand faces, with supernatural powers, who brought learning and knowledge to the world. He brought bountiful harvests of corn and cotton of various colors to his people. He controlled vast wealth measured in turquoise and precious stones, feathers and fine clothing, all of which disappeared after the fall of the Toltecs.

Quetzalcoatl's downfall was brought about by the deity Tezcatlipoca, the Mirror's Smoke, also known as the Enemy of Both Sides. Tezcatlipoca was one of the most powerful members of the Mesoamerican pantheon. He was an evil sorcerer who tricked Quetzalcoatl into becoming drunk on pulque, a native beer, and sleeping with his sister (see I, 1). Quetzalcoatl left

Tollan in disgrace and shame. Fleeing Tollan he proceeded to the east to search for Tlillan Tlapallan, the Place of the Black and the Red, the Place of Knowledge.[3] He set out on this pilgrimage to find atonement and in his repentance he sought the Place of the Burning, Tlatlayan, on the shores of the Gulf of Mexico. There, arraying himself as the god, he set himself afire. The conflagration produced all the birds of precious feathers, feathers that for the Aztecs were historically far more valuable than gold, or even gemstones.

> And they say that while he was burning,
> his ashes ascended, and there appeared,
> they saw, all the birds of precious feathers ascend into the
>   heavens . . .
> And when his ashes were consumed,
> then they saw the heart of the Quetzal bird,
> Quetzalcoatl, ascend, thus they knew
> that he had gone to the heavens,
> that he had entered the heavens.
> The ancients said that he was transformed
> into the star that appears at dawn.

From that time forward Quetzalcoatl was the Lord of the Dawn, the morning star, forever associated with the planet Venus. Quetzalcoatl was also the Sky Serpent and the Lord of the Winds; thus his temple in the center of the sacred precinct of the Aztec capital was rounded so that the winds should flow around it more freely. Quetzalcoatl was both god and man, an integral part of the mythic ontology of the Aztec world. Quetzalcoatl's demise and departure from the eastern shores was what for many presaged the coming of Cortéz and the conquest from the east.

The Gods

Spirits, gods, and demigods inhabited the entire Aztec world. Some like Quetzalcoatl merged real historical personages with myth and divinity. There were household gods and there were gods that pertained to neighborhoods and lineages. There were gods of the fields, forests, and streams. State cults at the time of the conquest included scores of deities and literally thousands of priests who ministered to the gods and goddesses. The priests were keepers of the highly sophisticated and complex knowledge of the deities. They were diviners, seers, soothsayers, astrologers, and sorcerers. This was the basis of their power within the empire. Religion was a part of daily life and the natural order of things that kept the universe a harmonious whole. The Aztecs easily adopted new deities into their pantheon from other peoples. As the empire grew so did the Aztec pantheon. Aztec religion was, and still is, essentially pantheistic.

The deities were often seen as related to one another, great families of kindred spirits. Toci was the grandmother of the gods, Teteo Inan was the mother of the gods. Tlazoteotl Ixcuina, a sister of the goddesses and the Eater of Filth, the goddess of carnal love, was the gods' great spinner and weaver of the threads of life. There were also Cihuacoatl, the Snake Woman; Coatlicue, the Snake-Skirted Goddess; Chalchiuhtlicue, the Jade-Skirted Goddess of the waters. They were the sisters of the gods. All the goddesses, ferocious though some of them were, shared the fundamental feminine characteristics of the earth. They were worshipped and feared as the mothers of all, the source of growth and renewal of life.

Most deities had male and female counterparts—such as Xochipilli, the Flower Prince, and his counterpart, Xochiquetzal, the Flowered Quetzal Feather Princess. Many gods were dualistic. Deities also had multiple aspects and attributes. Tlaloc, the god of earth and rains, was, and still is, addressed as "Our Mother/Our Father." Tlaloc is the provider of mankind's sustenance on the earth as well as an embodiment of the earth.

Today the three hearthstones, Mixcoatl, Tozpan, and Ihuitl (see I, 1), who guard the old fire god Huehueteotl, are a part of daily life in the Aztec world. Women in present-day Aztec villages can still be seen feeding the old god, tossing a bit of food into the fire as they toast tortillas on the griddle balanced atop the three hearthstones. Chronicles of the empire tell us that women and children likewise fed the fire god in ancient times and that even Motecuzoma danced a princely dance at celebrations before the temple of Huehueteotl in the sacred precinct of Tenochtitlan.

The range and variety of Aztec gods and goddesses is astonishing. Often a single deity had several names. Tezcatlipoca, for example, was also known as the Night Wind, the Keeper of Men, and He by Whom We Live. Tezcatlipoca, who caused the downfall of Quetzalcoatl, was everywhere. He was all powerful and capricious. He was sometimes seen as the dark counterpart of Huitzilopochtli, the Aztecs' titulary deity, about whom more will be said later. This Warrior of Darkness was opposed to Huitzilopochtli, the Warrior of the Sun. Another god with many faces was Xipe Totec, the flayed god, who was always represented wearing the skin of a sacrificial victim. He was able to bring death back to life; thus he was the embodiment of the spring and the renewal of life.

Many of the gods were potentially malevolent. It was thus essential that they be kept placated with lavish offerings and vast celebrations. Each month of the Aztec year was punctuated by immense celebrations and sacrifices officiated over by the priesthood. This was an important part of the priests' duties. These rituals integrated the nobility, the priesthood, and the commoners in the single purpose of honoring the deities and staving off the chaos that could result from malcontent gods.

For the Aztecs at the time of the conquest, myth and religion were the basis for philosophy, history, science, and the arts. Myth, history, theology, cosmology, and politics all played a role in the Aztecs' own saga. It was a tale of biblical proportions, an epic of empire.

The Aztec Quest

According to their own tales the Aztecs were the people of Aztlan, Place of the Heron Feathers, in a lake, reminiscent of the site of their great city to be, Tenochtitlan. The location of Aztlan has long been a subject of considerable scholarly debate and has been placed everywhere from California to the Valley of Mexico. Promising candidates for Aztlan are to be found among the lakes of the states of Michoacan and Jalisco, northwest of Mexico City; and even a little further north in the state of Nayarit.

The Aztecs themselves were not sure of the city's exact location. The first Motecuzoma, ruler of the Aztec empire in the fifteenth century as it began to dominate all of Mesoamerica, sent out his most adept magicians and diviners to find Aztlan. To begin the search they were transformed into wild beasts. Their mission was to carry news of the great successes of the Aztecs to their kin who had remained behind. However, the sorcerers returned with dire warnings for the empire, leaving the location of Aztlan lost in the clouds of myth. When the Spanish friars inquired about the origins of the Aztecs after the conquest in the sixteenth century they received contradictory information. Aztlan was, and still is, a homeland that remains in unknown realms. From there it exerts its greatest power as a paradise from which a people emerged.

The road from Aztlan to the empire was a long one according to Aztec myth. The god Huitzilopochtli commanded the Aztecs to set out in search of their destiny. He guided them in their wanderings that eventually led to the site where they founded their great city, Tenochtitlan, the hub of the empire. Huitzilopochtli was the titulary deity of the Aztecs, the Warrior of the Sun, the consumer of human hearts. He was the ultimate warrior deity, who, like Quetzalcoatl, was seen as both human and divine.

The god may have been an actual personage, perhaps someone of great wisdom or power who upon his death was transformed into a deity. When the priests left Aztlan they carried Huitzilopochtli's mummy bundle with them. The bones would speak to them in dreams and prophesy their destiny. After the conquest Christian friars burned many such mummy bundles in their efforts to convert the heathens of Mesoamerica. Today the Huichol in northwest Mexico, who speak a language closely related to Aztec, may well still keep mummy bundles like that of Huitzilopochtli hidden from view in sacred caves.

From Aztlan Huitzilopochtli commanded his people onward to Chicomoztoc, the Place of the Seven Caves, a mythical place in the far northern deserts. Caves have always been highly charged with meaning in Mesoamerica. They are entries to the underworld of the ancestors, the dark womb of mother earth. Chicomoztoc was the place where all of the wandering tribes of the northern borders of Mesoamerica—the Chichimeca, the Teochichimeca, and other groups—mustered. They came together and set out from there (see I, 2).

Under the Pyramid of the Sun in pre-Aztec Teotihuacan is a cave with seven chambers, a symbolic Chicomoztoc. Perhaps this sanctuary was the original earth womb that was to become the model for the Chicomoztoc of the Aztecs. Clearly the notion of emergence from a cave antedated the Aztecs by a considerable period. The Tepaneca, the Acolhua, the Chalca, and numerous other groups in the region around the Valley of Mexico also emerged from Chicomoztoc. The Aztecs were the last to depart from Chicomoztoc, and thus were latecomers to the splendors of the Valley of Mexico.

The third place the Aztecs encountered in their early wanderings was Culhuacan, the Curved Mountain. Here they shed their rough animal skins and began to plant crops. Culhuacan was where the Aztecs began to take on the traits of the more civilized peoples of Mesoamerica. It is often even referred to as Culhuacan-Tollan, implying that this was the source of high Toltec culture that the Aztecs were imitating. The Aztecs stayed there for some time. The actual location of Culhuacan may have been in the northern deserts, or on the edges of the more civilized Valley of Mexico. Like Aztlan and Chicomoztoc, Culhuacan has also been lost in time and space, yet these three places are of paramount importance in understanding the Aztec world. The myths surrounding these sites were potent motivators of peoples like the Aztecs and played a huge role in their unfolding histories.

Founding the Center of the Aztec World: Tenochtitlan

An integral part of the Aztecs' tale is the epic battle of celestial proportions in which Huitzilopochtli, the Warrior of the Sun, defeated Coyolxauhqui, the Goddess of Moon and Stars. This battle is called the birth of Huitzilopochtli and it may well have been the birth of the Aztecs as a warrior state. The tale, which is something between myth and history, is one of power, politics, battles, and blood. The Warrior of the Sun destroyed his opponents, the moon and her followers, the Centzonahua, the Four Hundred Southerners, who were the stars, on the Hill of the Serpents, Coatepec, a place of paramount importance for the Aztecs (see I, 2). This was a battle between the forces of day and night, light and darkness, but it's possible that this engagement was an actual political conflict as well.

Huitzilopochtli utterly defeated his opponents, the forces of darkness, and possibly also dissent within the Aztec world. When the enemy, Coyolxauhqui, was overpowered, her head was cut off. Her body was ripped asunder and rolled down the slope, where she fell to pieces. Massive sacrifices at the site of Coatepec followed the battle just as there were to be later at the Great Temple in the heart of Tenochtitlan. The massive Coyolxauhqui stone depicting the defeated and dismembered goddess was found by telephone workers excavating a new line in 1978 in downtown Mexico City at the base of the remains of the *Templo Mayor*. Thus began the modern process of rediscovery of this ancient world axis, the Great Temple of the Aztec world.

In another episode in the epic of the Aztec quest for their promised land, Huitzilopochtli's sister Malinalxoch was abandoned while sleeping. She was considered an evil sorceress (see I, 2). She founded Manalco, which still contains one of the most impressive Aztec shrines in Mexico. It features eagles and jaguars carved into solid rock. The Aztecs, meanwhile, had settled near Coatepec, a rich and watery world that seemed a paradise, but this was not to be their promised land. Huitzilopochtli commanded his people onward and he destroyed the dam that held the waters. The Great Temple of the Aztecs erected there was called Coatepec. This place memorialized an entire series of seminal episodes in the founding of the Aztecs' great capital.

The Aztecs, now called the *Mexica*, or the Mexicans, for Huitzilopochtli had declared his followers such, then settled near Chapultepec. Having slain Coyolxauhqui, the moon, *meztli* (which is probably the basis of the name *Mexica*, which the Aztecs now called themselves), they entered the Valley of Mexico in the twilight of the Toltec empire. They settled within sight of what was to become their great city, but these nomads were expelled twice from this place. They were not welcome intruders in the Valley of Mexico and were relegated to marginal and menial positions as vassals of other groups, yet they multiplied and prospered, much to the consternation of their neighbors. These were a bloody and barbarous people not yet accustomed to the ways of the more civilized inhabitants of the valley. They were attacked by neighboring groups on all sides, but the most devastating part of the attack came from Copil, the son of Huitzilopochtli's spurned sister Malinalxoch. This tale is both mythological and blatantly political (see I, 2). Copil set out to destroy the Aztecs in order to avenge his mother. His goal was to usurp the destiny promised the Aztecs by Huitzilopochtli. The Aztecs were expelled from the precincts of Chapultepec, but they were not completely defeated. According to tradition, Huitzilopochtli captured Copil during the battle.

Huitzilopochtli's final victory, followed by the sacrifice of Copil, set in motion the process by which Tenochtitlan was founded. When Huitzilopochtli defeated Copil he cut off his head and tore out his heart. He gave the heart to one of his "idol bearers," his priest, to be cast among the reeds and rushes of the lake. From this heart, which looks like the red fruit of the nopal cactus, grew the nopal that had been prophesied by the gods as the site of the Aztecs' great city. The name of the city, Tenochtitlan, means "the place among the nopals."

The Aztecs managed to return to Chapultepec, but not for long. Soon they were driven out again. Their leader, Huitzilhuitl, was captured and sacrificed in the city of Culhuacan. Leaderless, they then became the supplicants and vassals of the lords of Culhuacan. Eventually at the behest of Huitzilopochtli, who spoke through his priests, the Aztecs convinced the Culhua lords to give them a small tract of land. Anxious to be rid of these barbarous nuisances, the Culhua lords sent them to Tizaapan, a useless bit of marginal land located on the edge of Mexico City near where the National University of Mexico is located today in the area known as the Pedregal. The area was, and remains, a rocky and inhospitable region, which at that time was full of venomous snakes. The Aztecs were delighted with the place, as they found the snakes delicious, and they prospered, much to the dismay of the Culhua lords.

The Aztecs soon fought on the side of Culhuacan and distinguished themselves as ruthless and resourceful warriors. They became in effect mercenaries for the Culhua lords and were quite successful. They were then instructed by their god to ask Achitometl, the Culhua lord, for the hand of one of his daughters, who was sent as a sign of their new status. Huitzilopochtli, however, commanded his people to sacrifice the bride and dress a priest in her skin. The Aztecs invited Achitometl to the festival to celebrate their new goddess. When Achitometl became aware that the priest was arrayed in his daughter's skin he became furious and again drove these barbarous Aztecs from their homes on the shore of Lake Texcoco onto the low swampy islands of the lake.

There among the reeds and rushes the Aztecs saw the sign that Huitzilopochtli had predicted. The site was significant for it recalled the great city of the Toltecs, Tollan, the place of the reeds and rushes. There they saw, perched on the nopal cactus, sprouted from Copil's heart, an eagle eating a serpent. It was just as Huitzilopochtli had prophesied. This occurred in the year 2-House according to the ancient calendar, 1325 by our calendar. The Aztecs had finally found the place that was to be the seat of their empire, the site of their capital, Tenochtitlan. The eagle and serpent remain the national symbol of Mexico.

The eagle consuming a serpent perched atop a nopal cactus is also a symbol of the Aztecs' triumph over adversity. For a wandering tribe of crude barbarians like the Aztecs to become rulers of most of the known world was an astonishing feat. The Aztecs were wily opportunists and shrewd players in the politics of the Valley of Mexico. They also knew full well how to make the most out of their reputation as the most ruthless, sanguinary, and barbarous people in the valley.

The Empire

With the founding of Tenochtitlan the history of the Aztecs as a formally constituted people begins. Tenochtitlan was, despite the fact that it was originally little more than a small group of muddy islands, the perfect capital for the Aztecs. Strategically

it was easily defensible. The land in the lake was highly productive, and there were plenty of waterfowl, fish, frogs, and
snakes to trade with the inhabitants of the lake shore. Another
advantage to the lacustrine location for the Aztecs was that this
was marginal territory, and thus they could escape being vassals
of any of the lords of the lake.

They built their city on Lake Texcoco by constructing artificial
islands called *chinampas*. The construction of *chinampas* on the
lake shore antedated the Aztecs by easily a thousand years. To
construct *chinampas* they would anchor debris and reed mats in
the muddy lake bottom with sturdy poles, which would usually
sprout into trees. Then they would dredge the rich mud from
the lake bottom, heaping it on top of the debris and reed mats
until it reached a height a few feet above the water level of the
lake. *Chinampas* are among the most highly productive agricultural devices in the world. Crops can be grown, planted, and
harvested all year long on these little islands, given the climate
of the Valley of Mexico.

The Aztecs thus had a wealth of resources, but no building
materials, no wood and no stone. They had to trade for these
things. Their wise leaders easily saw the advantage of trading
with all the peoples of the lake, eschewing the protection of one
or another of the great lords of the valley. Their ruler, or *Tlatoani*,
at this time was Tenoch. Though called kings by the invading
Spaniards, the role of the *Tlatoani*, the Speaker, was in fact quite
different. The *Tlatoani's* function was to see that the interlocking
network of rights and obligations of his people functioned
smoothly. The people were seen as a lord's burden, his charge,
but the lord's primary role was not so much to rule as to maintain the necessary relationships for harmony and prosperity.

Upon the death of Tenoch the Aztecs sought a ruler who
would legitimize their position in the valley. Naturally they
looked to the ruling families of Culhuacan who could trace their
heritage to the Toltecs. Having a direct link to the Toltecs was
of paramount importance for the Aztecs. Since the Toltecs were
the most prized line of descent for the peoples of the Valley of
Mexico, a Toltec ancestor provided the ultimate link to legitimacy. Even at this early stage the Aztecs were fiercely oppor-
tunistic in their drive toward empire. They needed Toltec

legitimacy to achieve their lofty goals. Acamapichtli was chosen
as the Aztec's new *Tlatoani*.

Shortly after Tenochtitlan was established, a sister city called
Tlatelolco was founded on nearby islands. The inhabitants chose
a Tepanec ruler, the son of Tezozómoc the elder. Tlatelolco was
to become the city of the merchants and an integral part of the
empire. Eventually it was incorporated into Tenochtitlan. The
rulers of the two cities in the lake balanced their allegiances
between the two major dynasties of the valley, thus creating an
interlocking network of rulers. This provided them with pa-
tronage and protection as well as legitimacy.

The Aztec leaders who followed Acamapichtli—Huitzilhuitl,
Chimalpopoca, and Itzcoatl—expanded the city and its territories into the Valley of Morelos, where such luxury goods as
tropical cotton could be obtained. Before this the Aztecs had
dressed in clothes made from the rough fibers of the agave, a
relative of the century plant. Having a source of fine cotton was
an important step on the road to empire for the Aztecs. They
were integrating themselves into Mesoamerican trade networks.

Itzcoatl, the Obsidian Serpent, became ruler of Tenochtitlan
in the early part of the fifteenth century. His rule was the turning
point for the empire, for it was Itzcoatl who forged the triple
alliance freeing the Aztecs from domination by the Tepanecs of
Azcapotzalco. This alliance united Tenochtitlan, Texcoco, and
Tlacopan (Tacuba in present-day Mexico City), but from the very
beginning the Aztecs controlled the association. It was at this
time that the histories were rewritten to fit the aims of the
empire. Through deft political maneuvering the Aztecs had become the dominant force in the valley and extended their rule
through both ruthless warfare and statecraft. By the middle part
of the fifteenth century the Aztecs were lords of a region that
reached out like a spiderweb embracing a wide area of Mesoamerica from its capital in Lake Texcoco.

After the death of Itzcoatl, the first Motecuzoma, Motecuzoma
Ilhuicamina, became the leader of the empire. Motecuzoma I
expanded the empire far beyond the Valley of Mexico, mobiliz-
ing every man and boy available for his armies to assist in the
domination and conquest of new territories. With each battle
the stock of the Aztecs rose. They became well known as the

fiercest, most ruthless, most valiant warriors of the region. Motecuzoma I instituted the practice of the Flower Wars. These were continuous ritual wars that sought fresh captives for sacrifice, rather than an absolute political victory on the battlefield, further feeding the Aztecs' bloodthirsty reputation. These wars marked the beginning of a period of continuous warfare and massive human sacrifice that served the empire well.

Motecuzoma I used the *Pochteca*, an independent class of traders with their own customs and laws, both as ambassadors and spies. When they perished on their dangerous missions for the empire the Aztecs considered them warriors killed in battle who went to live with the sun. Motecuzoma retaliated for such affronts to his rule and used their deaths as excuses to expand his empire further. The Aztec armies often had only to use the threat of warfare to attain victory, so ruthless was their reputation. The empire was not like European or Asian empires. It was strictly a military construct with little direct political control. Tribute, and in its wake trade and commerce, was at its heart. Rich goods flooded into Tenochtitlan along with sacrificial victims.

Tenochtitlan

The city of Tenochtitlan appeared to function flawlessly, partially because the rights and obligations of its residents were rigidly fixed. The *pipiltin*, the nobles, concerned themselves with the empire, its leadership and administration, warfare and religion. Lavish feasts punctuated with stirring and profound orations were celebrated to remind these upper classes of their roles and obligations to the people.

The *Tlatoani*, or Speaker, together with the Commander of the Armies, the *Cihuacoatl*, or Snake Woman, oversaw the empire and convened its councils of nobles. The courts were administered by a tribunal headed by the *Tlailotlaca*, or Chief Justice. This supreme tribunal handled both civil and criminal matters that could not be adjudicated elsewhere. Usually disputes and criminal cases were resolved by local administrative groups and the elders of each region. The supreme tribunal was the court of last resort. As Aztec metaphors show (see IV, 1), bringing a matter before the royal court was risky business. Frivolous suits could result in death. Justice was swift and severe. The nobles acted for the ruler and at his pleasure.

From childhood the sons of the nobility were trained in special schools (the *calmecac*) by the priests. They were taught to pray and to do penance before the gods. They were also taught the arts of rhetoric and song, and the narratives and myths of their people. It was in the *calmecac* that youths learned to read the painted manuscripts, the books of dreams and the books of the years and the books of songs. They learned to count the days according to the ancient calendar and to understand their divinatory meaning. It was in the *calmecac* that they also learned the essential obligations to the people and to the gods. These were rigorous lessons that were essential to maintain harmonious order in what was perceived as a chaotic world. The training received in the *calmecac* was scrupulous and severe.

The commoners, *macehualtin*, were the backbone of the empire. These lower classes were organized into *calpullis*, residence- and kinship-based organizations. Each *calpulli* had its own warders and elders who assured that festivals were celebrated, justice was done, and duties carried out. The *calpullis* were the basic social, political, and economic units of the Aztec world, organizing schools, work parties, and temple and social services. They participated in the lavish festivals for the gods and worked the land. They were protected by their leaders in exchange for their services. Every major aspect of life—birth, death, marriage, coming of age, and betrothal—was celebrated by *calpulli* members with feasting and elaborate oratory (see II, 1 and 2). They were the beneficiaries of the empire.

Axayacatl, who followed Motecuzoma I after his death, ascended to the leadership of the empire very early in his life. The empire he inherited was quite different from that of his predecessor. Axayacatl expanded the role of human sacrifice in Tenochtitlan to unheard-of proportions, although he continued to maintain trade and commerce as the principal function of the empire. By dominating Tlatelolco, the city where the merchants lived, he redistributed the vast new wealth on the basis of both political and economic priorities. The vast stores of wealth that came into the city as tribute were released through the great market of Tenochtitlan, making it a thriving center for commerce with what were probably artificially low costs. Additional merchandise was also granted to the *Pochteca* on the extensive journeys they undertook to seek out the finest and most luxurious goods available throughout Mesoamerica.

Tizoc followed Axayacatl in 1481, and then in 1486 Ahuizotl followed Tizoc. Both added to the empire's reputation for ferocity. During the reign of Ahuizotl as many as eighty-four thousand victims were sacrificed on a single occasion for the rededication of the Great Temple at the heart of Tenochtitlan.

Such ceremonies were not just bloody festivals of human carnage. They were both political and religious events. Rulers from throughout the empire were invited to these events, friend and foe alike. To refuse such an invitation was to invoke the wrath of the Aztec war machine. Ceremonies were accompanied with great pomp and endless orations, dances, and songs to the gods. Great feasting and rich gifts were lavished on visiting dignitaries, who were flattered with elegant and florid speeches. The temple precincts were festooned with fresh flowers, and lavish viewing areas were reserved for special guests. All the splendor and ferocity of the Aztec world was on display during such occasions. Massive human sacrifice was a vast spectacle, and an essential means of controlling the empire.

By the end of Ahuizotl's reign in 1502, when Motecuzoma II acceded to the Eagle and Jaguar Mat, the throne of the Aztec Empire, the death knell for the empire could already be heard. The Spanish were on the island of Hispaniola and their lust for the riches of the New World had just begun to be aroused.

For the Aztecs, the wider the extent of their empire, the more difficult it was to control. The empire was never a solidly centralized hierarchical system administered from Tenochtitlan, but rather a loose confederation held together by trade and the ferocious Aztec reputation. But fear of the Aztecs was no substitute for direct political control. Huge tracts even within the empire remained unsubdued, and many of the tributary states chafed under the yoke of Aztec domination. The Aztecs relied on the allegiance of diverse local rulers whose loyalty could switch at any time. Whether an empire such as this could have survived the test of time without considerable modification is questionable.

The Conquest

Omens of the empire's impending disaster had been seen by the Aztecs long before the first contacts with the Spanish. A comet and a meteor had appeared in the skies. The temple of Huitzilopochtli had burned and another temple had been struck by lightning. Then the first Spanish expedition, headed by Francisco Hernández de Córdoba, set sail from Cuba early in 1517. Though they reached the coast of the Yucatan, they were defeated by the native Mayans and the expedition was a failure. They retreated toward Florida and Hernández died there. In 1518 Juan de Grijalva set out. The group also landed on the coast of the Yucatan and then proceeded along the Gulf coast of Campeche onward as far as the river Pánuco. Motecuzoma heard about these strange invaders almost immediately. He informed his council, but did nothing. Whether this was indecision or an astute political calculation we shall never know.

A third Spanish expedition set out February 10, 1519, led by Hernán Cortéz under the pretext of finding Grijalva, who had not yet returned. Cortéz's contingent of men and armaments was certainly more than was needed to find Grijalva. Clearly, he planned more than a rescue mission. When the expedition landed on the coast of the Yucatan they received word that there were two captured Spaniards in the region, Jerónimo de Aguilar and Vicente Guerrero. Guerrero had married a native and become a local leader and was not interested in returning to Europe, but Aguilar, living in virtual slavery, was overjoyed to hear of the Spaniards' arrival. Aguilar spoke Yuacatec Maya with proficiency and was able to serve as Cortéz's translator. Shortly thereafter in Tabasco, the local lords gave Cortéz twenty women, all of whom were immediately baptized before being given to Cortéz's men. Among them was a woman who took the name María. She spoke both Nahuatl, the Aztec language, and Maya. Thus, through Aguilar and Marina, as she was also called, Cortéz had a direct channel to the *lingua franca* of the empire, Nahuatl. Doña María, whose name was corrupted to *Malintzin* in Aztec, became a symbol of treachery and treason to her people. To call someone in Mexico a *Malinche* in Spanish today is still a terrible insult.

When Motecuzoma's spies reported all of these events the emperor sent envoys with elaborate gifts befitting a god to Cortéz. The envoys quickly returned to Tenochtitlan reporting to Motecuzoma every detail of their visit. The ruler then sent another embassy replete with sorcerers, but their powers were of no avail against the Spaniards. Cortéz demanded gold, and when he received a helmetful of it, as well as figures of golden ducks and other animals, the fate of the empire was sealed.

Cortéz quickly found that there was dissension in the ranks of the empire and moved to exploit this lack of unity to his advantage. In Cempoala he found his first ally in the person of a local Totonac leader known to us only as the Fat Chief. Cortéz was an astute politician and assured the loyalty of his new ally by having him seize Motecuzoma's tax collectors. Faced with the wrath of Motecuzoma, the Fat Chief and his people were thus bound to Cortéz for protection. Cortéz on the other hand released the tax collectors so that they could return to Motecuzoma and tell him of Cortéz's own benevolence.

Before leaving Cempoala for the long march inland, Cortéz sent fifty of his men to destroy the Aztecs' idols and set up a church on top of their temples. The priests of the temples were appropriated as acolytes. Their matted locks shorn to clerical fashion, they were outfitted with white surplices. Cortéz thus declared war on the gods of the Mesoamerican world, his lust for gold and his religious fanaticism serving to fuel the conquest. Cortéz was resolved to capture this foreign land as a rich prize for his king and his holy mother church.

Cortéz was also set upon circumventing the authority of his superiors, such as Velázquez, the governor of Cuba. He now communicated directly with the king of Spain through his famous self-serving letters, which were clearly aimed at establishing before the crown an independent basis for his enterprise.

As Cortéz marched inland, Motecuzoma was now faced with the prospect of the disintegration of his empire. He vacillated, sending more emissaries. After pitched battles in the eastern highlands Cortéz was welcomed by the Tlaxcalans, the longtime enemies of Motecuzoma. At all costs Motecuzoma tried to avoid letting Cortéz into his own capital. He sent ever more lavish gifts in the hope that this strange invader would take them and leave. Motecuzoma even offered to pay tribute to King Charles of Spain if only Cortéz would proceed no further. But Cortéz knew that there was a rich prize just within his grasp and he had no intention of turning back.

From Tlaxcala Cortéz marched to Cholula and then onward and upward between the two snowcapped volcanoes, Popocatépetl and Iztaccihuatl, into the Valley of Mexico. The sight that greeted him was astounding, as it was unlike anything Cortéz or his men had ever imagined. The heavily populated valley was alive with towns and villages, each more impressive than the next. At its center was the imperial city. The soldiers thought they were dreaming when they beheld the splendor of Tenochtitlan. These were not sophisticated men but they had seen the great cities of Spain and were nonetheless in awe of what they saw.

The city itself was immense, with its *chinampas* extending far out into Lake Texcoco. A regular lattice of canals linked all parts of the city to the center of the sacred precinct, which was filled with tall and elegant temples, palaces, and schools. Causeways linked the city to the mainland and fresh water was brought over the brackish lake waters by aqueducts stretching well beyond the shores. This was the Venice of the New World.

At the heart of the city was the sacred ceremonial precinct surrounded by a high wall, the central axis of the Aztec world. The area was crammed with tall stuccoed pyramids with steep stairs leading up to temples for the various deities. There were vast plazas and areas for viewing the festivities associated with the gods of the Aztec world. The entire sacred precinct was covered with brightly colored paintings and murals. Buildings were elaborately decorated with the signs and symbols of the empire. These glyphs spelled out the manifest destiny of the Aztecs to rule their world.

As Cortéz approached the city Motecuzoma sent more legations, each more elegant than the last. The lords wore elaborate woven capes, embroidered breechcloths, and headdresses crowned with valuable feathers. Labrets and earplugs were essential adornments. Women wore *quechquemitls*, triangular pullovers often stretching below the waist, over *huipiles*, long flowing gowns, and skirts.

Although he was surely impressed by this lavish display, Cortéz would not halt his drive into the heart of the Aztec world. Finally Motecuzoma realized he had no choice but to meet the intruders on the causeway leading into Tenochtitlan. Ultimately he not only allowed the Spaniards into his capital but he let them take him prisoner virtually without resistance. The relationship of Cortéz and Motecuzoma was indeed a curious one. These were two astute and ambitious men and yet they had no comprehension of each other. To our eyes Motecuzoma may appear bewildered, vacillating, and inept. However, his actions were clear and comprehensible in terms of the Aztec world in which he lived. The omens that had presaged the downfall of the empire had led him to seek refuge in the land of the dead. But he found no solace there. His fate was sealed. He was alone. He acted in a way that he thought would preserve his people.

According to Spanish sources, Motecuzoma was finally killed by his own people in an attempt to prevent the final confrontation and siege of Tenochtitlan. According to indigenous sources it was the Spaniards who brought about his death. Whatever actually occurred, Motecuzoma's death forced the Spanish to flee Tenochtitlan with heavy losses. Had the Aztec armies continued their assault, perhaps events would have been different, but Cortéz escaped to the protection of Tlaxcala. It took nine months for Cortéz's reinforcements to arrive from Cuba and to prepare for the final siege of Tenochtitlan.

The final assault on the Aztec capital was a protracted and bloody battle, but with the capture of Cuauhtémoc, heir of Motecuzoma II, the empire of the Aztecs ended. In their final surrender (see I, 3) the Aztecs attempted to explain how their empire functioned to the uncomprehending Spaniards, who sought gold. Unfortunately the true nature of the Aztec empire was never understood and the Aztec world passed into oblivion. Today anthropologists are still hard at work reconstructing this complex society.

Once the Aztecs were successfully subdued, Cortéz set about

destroying the temples of their bloody gods with fanatical fervor. He demolished their books, schools, and libraries. The Aztec priests were among his most fearsome opponents. They would fight to the death for their gods, for they could foresee their diminished role in society destroyed with the coming of a new order. The images of Huitzilopochtli and Tlaloc were toppled from their seats high on the top of Tenochtitlan's Great Temple. The great sanctuaries of the gods would no longer be the sites of elaborate ceremonies, songs, and dances. Everywhere the Aztec pantheon was eclipsed by the Christian cross. The old gods were now devils and their worshippers were considered deluded heathens. But the spiritual conquest of the New World was never quite as successful as its political domination. Even today in remote Aztec-speaking areas at planting time one can hear the name of Tlaloc whispered in prayers to the holy earth.

The Spiritual Conquest and the Preservation of Classic Aztec Culture

The stormtroops of the spiritual conquest began arriving almost immediately. Pedro de Gante and two other Flemish priests were the first clerics to arrive in the wake of the conquest in 1523. In 1524 the first twelve Franciscans arrived. These early apostles of the church were to have immense impact on the way that the New World developed. The twelve friars walked barefoot from Veracruz to Mexico City wearing rough monk's cloth. They were conquerors who sought souls rather than gold, and their humble ways much impressed the native populations, who were beginning to suffer from the ravages of Western diseases and the cruel treatment of their new masters.

The Franciscans saw the New World as a millennial kingdom of God and the Indians as a lost tribe of Israel. They were men of the Renaissance and so set about founding the institutions necessary for a good and just kingdom where faith, learning, and humanity could exist hand in hand. Although they had some early successes with mass conversions among the Indians, the friars realized that the old ways were still alive and well.

The Spaniards' destruction of the Aztecs' idols did not make these peoples of the New World into easy converts. Thus the friars had to learn everything they could about these people in order to guide them into the fold of Christianity. They had to know the ancient ways, the idolatries and diabolical beliefs, of these strange new peoples in order to win their loyalty. This was essential for the establishment of their millennial kingdom.

The friars set about seriously learning languages and converting the idolaters. They built churches, founded schools and monasteries. Pedro de Gante established the first school shortly after his arrival in 1524. This school and those that followed formed the backbone for learning and faith in the New World. The friars also managed to quickly reduce the Classic Aztec language to an alphabetic script.

The Franciscans were instrumental as well in training the sons of the nobility. They instilled within these young men not simply religious devotion, but a dedication to learning and the preservation of knowledge. The sons of Aztec lords were trained in Spanish, Greek, and Latin, as well as in the reading and writing of their own language. These young assistants were essential to the spiritual conquest of the New World. They were the friars' bridge to the Aztec community. It became their job to seek out the few surviving elders to recount the ancient songs, "read" the ancient histories from their painted books, perform the narratives of their peoples, and deliver the elegant florid discourses that were once a part of everyday life under the empire.

The friars recorded what information they could glean from these few survivors. The Augustinians, Dominicans, and Jesuits followed the Franciscans, and advanced the learning of native languages by writing dictionaries and grammars, as well as religious tracts, to further the spiritual conquest. The body of writings that the friars, their students, and a few native historians have left us constitutes most of what we know about the Aztecs. Much of this work has unfortunately been lost or destroyed, but of what remains, no work on the Aztec world is as complete or systematic as that of Fray Bernardino de Sahagún.

Sahagún was an erudite Renaissance scholar. He was born in Spain circa 1499 and died in 1591 in the convent of San Francisco in Mexico City, where he was interred. In 1529 Sahagún set out for the New World as a member of the Franciscan order, having studied in the great Spanish university of Salamanca. His first task in the New World was to learn the Classic Aztec language. Having perfected his Nahuatl he began in 1547 to compile materials for his monumental *Historia general de las cosas de Nueva España*. At first he wrote exclusively in Classic Aztec. This work was intended as an encyclopedia of all things in this new and wondrous world. It was also intended as a compilation of the heathen practices of the natives to aid the friars in stamping out all vestiges of the Aztecs' past religion.

From 1547 until 1570, when his works were impounded, Sahagún gathered materials and organized them along the lines of medieval encyclopedias. He used sophisticated interviewing techniques, and with the aid of his native assistants produced the most extensive, lucid, and elegant account we have today of the Aztec world. Around 1575, when his works were returned, Sahagún wrote the accompanying Spanish text to his *Historia*. The Spanish version is a separate text for a Spanish audience rather than simply a translation and differs significantly from the Classic Aztec text upon which it is patterned.

Between 1577 and 1578 Sahagún produced two bilingual copies of his work. One was sent directly to the king of Spain. This, as well as innumerable other works concerning the peoples and cultures of the New World, is now lost. Perhaps it was in the crown's best interest that these manuscripts disappear, as the idea of a Franciscan millennial kingdom in the New World was not welcome at court. Debates at the time concerning the nature of the inhabitants of the New World and crown policy toward them were shrill, pitting religious and secular authorities against one another, and religious order against order. These discussions were not simply about souls, but also about power, politics, and control in the New World. They centered on whether the church or the crown had authority over the peoples of newly discovered lands and how these territories were to be ruled.

The other copy of Sahagún's *Historia*, sent via Rodrigo de Sequera, who was openly sympathetic to Sahagún and the Franciscan enterprise, found its way by a curious and poorly understood course of events to the Laurentian Medici Library in Florence. This is the copy that is today known as the Florentine

Codex. It was not until over two hundred years later in 1793 that this copy of Sahagún's work was rediscovered by Bandini, a bibliographer at the library. Even in the nineteenth century few scholars knew of the existence of this work, and far fewer had access to it. All but four selections in this book are from the Florentine Codex.

Throughout the process of compiling the *Historia*, Sahagún's assistants actively sought out the elders, who could adequately describe the lost splendor of the Aztec world. Many of the narrations and performances were read from the few pre-Conquest books that survived the fanatic burnings of the conquerors. The Aztec hieroglyphic scripts and pictorial manuscripts were both read and performed. The writing system, which is actually far more intricate than the simple rebus writing systems that it has been compared to, formed a complex set of mnemonics keyed to the performance of well-learned texts. Of the vast corpus of pictorial manuscripts pertaining to the Aztec world that exist today, only one could be pre-Columbian in origin, yet almost all are surely derived from the traditions and performances of the pre-Columbian world. Even the late lengthy histories and *relaciones* by native historians such as Tezozomoc, Chimalpahín, and Ixtlixochitl, though written in a tedious Westernized style, show flashes of the original true narrative styles. Such rich and vibrant tales can be heard performed today in remote regions by the descendants of the empire. The themes may differ, but Aztec oral tradition is not dead.

"A Polished Eye": Understanding the Aztec World

The Aztec world was so far from our own that one must understand the culture that produced these texts in order to understand the actual material. The Aztecs were fundamentally agriculturalists concerned with the seasons, winds, and rains. They understood their own world in its own terms. Its contradictions and inconsistencies were what in fact defined the texture of everyday life.

The process of understanding this society is a process for one "possessed of good eyes and possessed of good ears"—a metaphor for one who is knowledgeable in the Aztec world. *Ixpetz* (see IV, 1), having a "polished eye," is how the Aztecs defined one who was astute, skilled at finding or discovering the essential nature of things, of seeing the difficulties of an enigma. For many people the entire Aztec world is an enigma. Understanding what made that world work requires a penetrating look at its fundamental contradictions. The translations in this book provided a basic set of texts to build understanding. Thelma Sullivan spent much of her life polishing the translations here. During that process she came to understand the enigmatic nature of the Aztec world better than most scholars in the field. Through her work she also discovered several fundamental threads running through the Mexican world that have become our keys to understanding this strange other.

Human Sacrifice

Human sacrifice and ritual cannibalism practiced by the Aztecs on an unprecedented scale exemplify just one of the many contradictions of the society. These were a people who spoke of their children as "precious jades, precious feathers," their most valued objects, yet continually sacrificed crying newborns to Tlaloc (see III, 1). Other rituals involved ripping the beating hearts from the breasts of thousands as sustenance for their gods. Sacrificial victims with bladeless weapons were pitted against armed warriors in gladiatorial combat. Other victims were beheaded or burned alive or shot with arrows. For the gods Xipe and Toci, victims were flayed and priests danced in the victims' skins. How are we to understand such profound inhumanity?

   Human sacrifice and ritual cannibalism are perhaps the most problematic and widely analyzed aspects of the Aztec world.[4] This gruesome part of Aztec society has been interpreted, misinterpreted, and reinterpreted since the first contact. Human sacrifice was an instrument of empire, as the horrified Spaniards found when they entered the first villages on the Gulf coast of Mexico. The villages were strewn with the dismembered bodies of sacrificial victims. Were the natives offering the ultimate sacrifice of human life to their gods, or showing the ultimate disregard for humanity? What could the European mind make of such practices?

In the sixteenth century human sacrifice was used both as a pretext for wars on native peoples, accompanied by merciless exploitation of these supposedly barbarous Indians, and as demonstrating the natives' deep, though misguided, capacity for religious devotion that would make them potentially faithful Christians.[5] The courts and academies of Europe echoed with vociferous debates about the nature of these peoples of the New World. Scholars actively questioned the Aztecs' humanity.

Modern scholars have devised some occasionally rather whimsical interpretations of Aztec practices, including the notion that sacrifices and ritual cannibalism provided an essential source of protein in an environment lacking domestic animals for food. Another theory can be termed "socioeconomic thermodynamics" as applied to human culture. This theory maintains that the offerings of blood, hearts, and victims, which the Aztecs believed help to keep the sun on its course, also maintained social and economic stability in the empire. Another theory views sacrifice as a type of "calculated brutality" designed to inspire devotion and terror as a means of social control. Human sacrifice has even been viewed as an effective method of population control.

One of the more cogent modern views of these macabre rituals of empire belongs to Inga Clendinnen, who believes human sacrifice is rooted in a deep-seated need for human violence stemming from an unstable worldview, something that was pervasive in Aztec society. This notion introduces one of the fundamental threads that Sullivan saw woven through Aztec society.

The most penetrating analysis of this practice of the Aztecs is Sullivan's. In her work on rulers and rulership, she finds that "to feed the gods was to feed man." By feeding the gods sacrificial victims from an expanding empire, Aztec rulers were attempting to stave off the chaos caused by capricious spirits and rulers. War, drought, famine, and disease, the chaotic events that disrupt the fabric of everyday life, were perceived as caused by the whimsy of both rulers and deities. The deities

of pre-Columbian Mexico were quite definitely unpredictable.
Tezcatlipoca, the Mirror's Smoke (also called Ipalnemoani, Giver
of Life; Teimatini, Knower of People; and Telpochtli, the Youth,
or Young Warrior) was one such capricious lord. Aztec rulers
acted as his surrogate. In the Florentine Codex it is said:

> He thinks as he pleases,
> does as he pleases;
> he mocks us.
> As he wishes, so he wills.
> He puts us in the palm of his hand, he rolls us about;
> like pebbles we spin and bounce.
> He flings us this way and that,
> we make him laugh; he mocks us.

(F.C. VI, 51v)

With so much dependent on the whims of the deities, and by
extension the rulers, it was an obligation to ensure by any means
possible that balance and harmony were maintained and that
the continuing cycles of renewal—life and death—remained
unbroken.

The Balance of Life

The perpetual cycle of life-growth-death and renewal is an essential part of the nature of Mesoamerica, where the changing
climate goes through a never-ending cycle of wet and dry seasons. The Aztecs believed that the holy earth must constantly
be nourished with offerings to maintain mankind's sustenance
and life.[6] Aztec rulers bore the ultimate responsibility for their
people. They were the mother/fathers of both the people and
the gods. To maintain harmony and balance they had to provide
the human sustenance required by their deities to keep the
eternal cycles of the universe in motion. Each individual and
each deity had a function. If either man or god should cease to
fulfill their role, they risked throwing an essential cycle out of
balance. This would spell disaster for life on the earth.

Sullivan traced this concept of maintaining balance between

mankind and nature from at least as far back as the first great urban centers, such as Teotihuacan, in the Classic period and perhaps even the pre-Classic period, 600 B.C.E.–200 C.E. According to Sullivan, "This symbolic rejuvenation and nourishment of the ruler with human blood . . . was a way of legitimizing his powers."[7] The sacrificial victim—slave, commoner, captive, or noble—was deified. Sacrificial victims became one with the deity, and rode with the sun on its celestial journey, as did the warriors killed in battle and women who died in childbirth. Eventually they became the swarms of butterflies that to this day brighten the Valley of Mexico.

The human body in the Aztec world was a model of the cosmos and it contained the cosmic forces associated with the soul.[8] By offering human life to their gods the Aztecs were returning these essential powers to their ultimate source. Offerings of sacrificial victims returned the heat, movement, and life that were necessary to maintain the cosmic cycles of the gods. This process was also a way of sharing with the deities these powerful forces that animate all life. In the Aztec world the human soul was tripartite. It consisted of the heart, *yollotl*, which was equated with movement and life. The *tonalli* was equated with heat, the sun, the breath, that spark of life that animated man and the universe. The third, more obscure and less-well-understood, aspect of the soul was the *ihiyotl*. This is a dark and sinister part of personality associated with an individual's animal alter ego, the *nagual*.

Women in Aztec Society

The role of women, at least ideologically, in Aztec society was equivalent to that of men. For the Aztec woman the glories of battle were to be found in the renewal of life. A successful birth was considered the equivalent of taking a captive on the field of battle. Women who died in the battle of giving birth were afforded the same position in the hereafter as warriors. When they were with child it was said that they held within their wombs a "precious feather, a precious jade." What they held was the jewel of life and renewal for their people, their lineage, sprouted from the seed of their ancestors (see II, 2).

It was the women who assured the constant renewal of Aztec society. Functioning primarily as the keepers of hearth and home, women were also often referred to as precious jewels. Metaphorically they were guarded, "kept in a box, a coffer." At as early an age as three or four women began to learn to weave, to carry out the duties of the household, and to follow the ways of the deities. Though many of the powerful goddesses of the Aztec pantheon were fearsome and terrifying, they all harbored the basic principle of life and renewal. This was a part of their essentially dualistic nature. Women were not often sacrificed, but at ceremonies celebrating some of the goddesses they were required victims. In general women were not politically active, but in most cases their role in the dynastic lineages was a key to understanding both the ideology and politics of the empire.[9] Though they effectively had little to do with the administration of the empire they were the motivating force for much of the complex political life surrounding their communities.

The Warrior's World

In the Aztec world the birth of a boy was greeted by war cries, and from that time on he was considered a warrior of the sun (see II, 2). A successful warrior was richly rewarded. The umbilical cord of the newborn was ritually interred on the field of battle. Today the male child's umbilical cord is planted in the family fields in many Aztec communities. This symbolizes the child's link to the land and earth of his ancestors, as well as to his ultimate destiny as a planter of fields.

Warriors were educated from an early age. They slept and were trained in the schools called *telpochcalli*, the house of youths. They were educated not only in warfare but rhetoric, song, and dance. Virtuosity in the verbal arts was highly regarded among warriors. Around the great fires in the houses youth men sang, danced, and told tales of valor through the night. The most successful warriors were the taskmasters of the houses, who oversaw the training of younger men. Upon marriage men no longer resided in the house of youths, though many bachelors remained with their houses throughout their lives. All remained a part of the close-knit warrior society, however, and were available during the remainder of their lives should the empire require their services. Most Aztec men were farmers as well as warriors. This was a warrior society founded on agriculture.

Contradictions of the Aztec World

The Valley of Mexico was a complex network of diverse peoples and beliefs, a chaotic jumble of competing interests and ethnic groups—not a single harmonious entity, as the Aztecs portrayed it. As Alfredo López Austin, perhaps the most incisive contemporary interpreter of the Aztec world, has observed, "It appears from our present point of view as if all of the ancient Nahuas had participated in the same conceptual world [but] . . . it is in fact our own shortsightedness that produces such limitations."[10] The variety of beliefs held in the ancient Aztec world was probably even wider than it is in the modern world. The notion of homogeneity is in fact a result of limited sources and limited research and doesn't represent the reality of the empire.

Neither the Aztecs nor the Toltecs remained a dominant group in the Valley of Mexico for more than a relatively short period and there were dozens upon dozens of other groups vying with them for both political and ideological power. The chronicles and histories of the various ethnic groups that have come down to us show perplexing differences and variations. Even the mythic tales of the origin of the Aztec world vary significantly. The tales of the *Anales de Cuauhtitlan,* for example (see I, 1),[11] are quite different from the versions of the same histories recorded by Sahagún and Diego Durán. The Aztecs themselves had no qualms about rewriting their history to legitimize their own empire.

This Aztec rewriting of their own history made their world seem more homogenous than it actually was. The Aztecs did more than just embroider on the text of history—they ripped it apart under Itzcoatl, burning their original books and histories under his rule in 1431. Both the Aztec scholars Rudolph Van Zantwijk and Susan Gillespie have written extensively about the Aztec tendency to reinterpret the past.[12]

Histories among the Aztecs were, and remain even today among their descendants, explanations of present realities. If history doesn't fit new realities, it is changed. This allows the Aztecs to view the contradictions in their own past as a harmonious drive toward a predestined empire and a dominant position in their world. The actual history of the Aztecs' rise to power is a "tale of the victorious"[13] that has been edited and rewritten to reflect their own overly glorified views. In fact, it was not the singular rise to power that they claimed.

Therefore it should come as no surprise that in the Aztec world the discontinuities and contradictions of life cause little problem. Among contemporary Aztec-speaking peoples individuals have little problem integrating disparate beliefs within their traditional ethos, even beliefs that to us would seem contradictory and incongruous. A traditional shaman and curer devoted to the world of the Aztec ancestors, for example, may be sympathetic to Jehovah's Witnesses and a member of Catholic Action. In a pluralistic society this adaptability is a distinctive advantage. The Aztecs easily adopt new deities into their pantheon, even Christian ones. They consistently extract unity and harmony from the chaos and contradiction of everyday life just as they rewrite and reinterpret their roots.

World-Centering

Tenochtitlan has been called an exquisite "parasite feeding on the lives and labour of other peoples and casting its shadow over all their arrangements."[14] The city was the Aztec world's *axis mundi*, the social, political, and symbolic center that fed off the life of the empire.

With the sacred precinct of the Aztec empire at its heart, the city was built to mirror the cosmos. Originally designed on a quinquepartite plan that in 1473 added a sixth precinct with the incorporation of Tlatelolco and the great marketplace, it reflected the quincunx pattern typical of Mesoamerica since before the

Classic period. Mesoamericans recognized five directions—north, south, east, west, and the center, or *axis mundi*.

The process of world-centering, that is, making the social, political, and religious center of a community a conscious reflection of the cosmological order, is one that was carried out throughout Mesoamerica. Each town had its sacred center modeled after the heavens. Today in many villages the pattern remains.[15] Tenochtitlan was without doubt "the largest and most highly urbanized of all Mseoamerican cities,"[16] and as such it dominated the social, political, and symbolic discourse of the Aztec world. By re-creating at its very heart, and by its very design, a fundamentally Mesoamerican *axis mundi*, the "Aztec state validated itself by expressing its indissoluble connection with the sacred universe."[17]

The center of Tenochtitlan (see I, 2), the *Templo Mayor*, was a place of immense political and ideological power. This site was located at the physical and spiritual core of the Aztecs' world. Though they ruled a diverse and disparate empire, the Aztecs saw themselves as the zenith of a harmonious world, its most powerful force. When the appearance of the other, who did not fit into their world, occurred in 1519, the entire edifice of unity and harmony began to crumble in chaos, doubt, and bewilderment (see I, 3).

Tlaloc and Huitzilopochtli

In the sacred precinct of Tenochtitlan high atop the Great Pyramid, the *Templo Mayor*, sat the twin temples of Huitzilopochtli and Tlaloc. The union of these two temples in fact united older traditional Mesoamerican beliefs with the resurgent warrior deity of the Aztec world. It represented the melding of agricultural society with a city of warriors.

Today Huitzilopochtli has fallen into obscurity, but Tlaloc (or his/her equivalent) remains the embodiment of the most holy earth, and this deity is the center of covert cults in remote regions throughout modern Mexico. In contrast to Huitzilopochtli, Tlaloc had universal appeal to all elements of the empire.[18] This was extremely important since the imperial myths were predicated on unity and harmony of disparate peoples. Ritual, pomp, and ceremony were focused on making the diverse aspects of the empire seem a harmonious whole.

The Aztec ritual calendar was filled with vast ceremonies involving hundreds of individuals and innumerable sacrificial victims, such as *Atl Cualo*, where weeping children were sacrificed to Tlaloc; *Ochpaniztli*, "the sweeping of the roads," where the women skirmished and an impersonator of the mother of the gods was sacrificed; and *Panquetzaliztli*, "the festival of the banners," where hundreds of victims were "given their paper banners and heron feather headdresses," to use the standard Aztec metaphor for sacrifice (see IV, I). These vast rituals brought people from all over the empire to watch, to trade in the great market, and to participate.[19] As Clendinnen points out, "The Mexica leadership was intent on a very difficult feat: the transformation of a politics of remorseless competition into one of effortless, cosmically prescribed supremacy, sacred order focused on and displayed in Tenochtitlan."[20] The coming of the conquest, the confrontation with the other, was the final dissolution of the myth of cosmic order that the Aztecs had built around themselves.

A Scattering of Jades: Classic Aztec Literature

When the Aztecs saw the conquest looming over them, their world disintegrated in chaos along with much of their art and aesthetic achievement. The great majority of the Aztec aesthetic achievement was lost along with many of the elaborately constructed myths that the Aztecs cherished.[21] The Spanish destroyed Aztec art and culture along with the empire.

The Aztecs referred to their classic poetry by the metaphor *in xochitl, in cuicatl*, "the flower, the song," both aspects of which represent ultimate ephemeral aesthetic achievements.[22] The more complex, metaphorical, and formulaic a piece was in Nahuatl literature, the greater the literary value the Aztecs placed on it. Men such as Fray Bernardino de Sahagún clearly recognized the aesthetic achievement of the Aztecs in the verbal arts.

In the prologue to the sixth book of his monumental encyclopedia, *The Book of Rhetoric and Moral Philosophy*, he states:

> That which is written in this book is not within the capacity of man to invent, nor is there a man alive who could devise such language.

Until the begining of this century little was known of the vast corpus of Classic Aztec literature. A few scholars in the United States, Mexico, and Europe had glimpsed the range of Classic Aztec materials hidden in libraries, archives, and private collections, but good translations were mostly unavailable, and the majority of interest in Classic Aztec was for historical purposes only. One notable exception was Daniel G. Brinton, the first American anthropologist, who in 1887 and 1890 published in his collection of Aboriginal American Literatures[23] the first volumes of Classic Aztec translations. Brinton clearly recognized Classic Aztec as one of the great Native American literatures, but unfortunately there were few individuals trained to translate this language.

Thelma Sullivan's translations provide a view of a broad cross section of the Aztec world. They range from the mythic tales of the origins of the Aztec peoples to prayers and poems that rank among their highest achievements in the verbal arts. This book is arranged in four sections, beginning with the narratives, myths, and histories of the origin of the Aztec peoples and their ultimate downfall with the Spanish conquest. These myths not only recount the origins of the Aztecs, but constitute their primordial sacred history, embodying the ethos and ontology of the Aztec people.

The second section consists of a selection of Sullivan's translations concerning life, death, rulership, and the wisdom of the ancients, as well as her translations of the elegant words of the Aztec matriarchs and midwives concerning pregnancy, childbirth, and new life. These elegant performances provide the most important and moving statement in existence on the role of women in Aztec society. They constitute the essential moral teachings and human spirit of life, death, and birth in the Aztec world and especially the world of women.

The elaborate "songs" and prayers to the gods of the Aztec tradition comprise the third section. These constitute the poetics of the Aztec world. These are moving, complex, and highly esoteric poems with multiple layerings of metaphor and meaning.

And finally, the fourth section consists of the metaphors, proverbs, and riddles that illustrate the major themes of Aztec thought, and provide us with a window on this ancient world like no other. These metaphors are pictures in words from the Aztec world, the gems with which they bejeweled floral rhetoric and luminous songs.

This arrangement follows the Aztec view, which was shared by Sullivan, of the progression from language to literature in Classic Aztec. All of these pieces are based on the florid and elegant verbal performances, punctuated with luminous metaphors, that were part of the skill required of any well-educated member of Aztec society. The metaphors of the final section are truly the precious jades of Aztec language, jewels the Aztecs considered more valuable than gold. Among the ancient Aztecs an elegant turn of a word was a precious stone, "polished and burnished" to perfection (see IV, 1). The title, *A Scattering of Jades*, is an Aztec metaphor for elegant and erudite speech. These selections are the jewels of the Aztec world.

TRANSLATING THE AZTEC WORLD: THELMA D. SULLIVAN

THELMA SULLIVAN WAS A PIONEERING SETTLER in the village of San Jerónimo in the mountains on the edge of Mexico City. I remember that as a student on my first visit to her home I was admitted at the main gate by her impeccable majordomo, Salvador, and her ever-present dogs. They accompanied me to her study, which was set off from the main house amid lush gardens. There, where Sullivan did most of her translations, she had a panoramic view of the entire valley and the surrounding snow-capped volcanoes. Her study was a perfect place to contemplate the Aztec world that had once dominated the Valley of Mexico.

Thelma Sullivan was always a brilliant and dedicated student. Born Thelma Dorfman on August 18, 1918, to a well-to-do family on the Upper East Side of Manhattan, she attended Hood College, receiving a degree in English literature. Immediately upon completing her degree she began graduate work at Columbia University, and started to write professionally for radio and the theater.

After her marriage to Dennis Sullivan, the couple left for Mexico City. There she plunged into the life of Mexico with the same dedication and rigor that she had applied to her studies. She wrote on cultural affairs and literature for Mexico City's English language daily *The News*, contributing over forty book reviews, and, working with the American embassy, she was responsible for visits by numerous artists, performers, and lecturers throughout Mexico. Sullivan was a member of the pres-

tigious *Circulo de Escritores*, to which all the major writers in
Mexico belonged. She also worked for the Mexican government
translating presidential communications into English.

Sullivan began her studies of Nahuatl in 1959 at forty years
of age, and became one of the world's foremost Aztec scholars.
Amparo de Parres first brought her to a class being given as
part of the National University of Mexico's *Seminario de la Cultura
Náhuatl* by Dr. Miguel León-Portilla. She had already begun a
translation of the Spanish text of Sahagún's *Historia general de
las cosas de Nueva España* when she began her study of the Aztec
language. She became an exemplary student and went on to
study with Padre Angel María Garibay K., the dean of Nahuatl
studies in Mexico.

Father Garibay became Sullivan's mentor and guide in the
Aztec world. They shared a common literary background, as
well as a view that Classic Aztec literature was a vibrant part of
Mexico's national heritage that should be made available to the
widest possible public. They also shared a fundamentally hu-
manistic orientation in the study of pre-Columbian cultures.
Sullivan constantly repeated Garibay's counsel that a good translation must stand on its own as literature. She could not tolerate
the choppy, awkward, bulky, and ungrammatical translations
so typical at the time in scholarly works.

Sullivan came to the study of Nahuatl through a vital interest
in the languages, literature, art, and cultures of her adopted
country, Mexico. As a hostess Sullivan received the political,
literary, and artistic elite of Mexico at her San Jerónimo estate
on the edge of Mexico City. Her salon was one of the most
stimulating and congenial of meeting places for anyone with an
interest in Mexico. She came to her study of the Aztec world
with a passion, interest, and literary background that was
unique among modern scholars. She was also the only woman
to become a major translator of Classic Aztec literature. Her
work was strongly influenced by the work of Ezra Pound, Robert
Duncan, and others. Long before her death she had contemplated preparing a volume of her translations and an anthology
of Nahuatl literature for a popular audience. Most of her translations have remained unpublished, or can be found only in
obscure journals. This is the first time Sullivan's translations

have been brought together in a single volume on the Aztec world.

Sullivan's colleagues Doris Heyden and Karen Dakin, in editing a memorial volume dedicated to her, mentioned her intention to write an anthology of Nahuatl literature. In 1979 Sullivan presented at Dumbarton Oaks a paper entitled *A Scattering of Jades* that was to be a version of her anthology in miniature.

Her presentation was a masterful selection of readings from her translations that elicited great praise, even from Don Wigberto Jiménez Moreno, the doyen of Mexican ethnohistorians. Jiménez Moreno rarely praised anything, and usually commented, with extensive oral footnotes, on further research needed. Sullivan was justifiably fearful when Don Wigberto began his comments on her work. Jiménez Moreno was, however, effusive in his praise.

While editing the Dumbarton Oaks paper, Sullivan and I drafted a book proposal for this anthology of her translations and made a short outline of the materials she would want to include in the volume. She had not been feeling well for some time, but could not find anyone in Mexico to diagnose her condition. Shortly thereafter she left for treatment in Houston.

On the morning of August 8, 1981, Doris Heyden called to let us know that Thelma had died. It was a devastating shock, as she had let almost no one know that she was terminally ill with an inoperable cancer. A few weeks later Sullivan's dear friend Rita Wilensky, who had accompanied her to Houston, returned to Mexico with the task of disposing of Sullivan's estate. Her library and papers were donated to Dumbarton Oaks Pre-Columbian Research Center, where they remain.

Form and Style in Aztec Literature

In her notes on specific texts Sullivan clearly distinguished rhetoric, oral narrative, prayer, and "song" from description, explanation, exposition, instructions, and historical accounts. The other major dimension of Aztec literature that Sullivan saw was that the more complex, metaphorical, elegant, and at times ob-

scure in its meaning a text was, the closer it was to what the
Aztecs called a song, or what we would call a poem. The songs
of the Aztec world were their highest achievement in the verbal
arts. The fundamental orality of Classic Aztec literature was also
essential for Sullivan, for these were works that were meant to
be performed.

Texts that were clearly a part of native oral traditions Sullivan
generally broke into lines reflecting a proper reading. She did
this on the basis of syntactic features, repetitions, parallelisms,
and metaphoric structures. She often read the texts aloud and
made revisions to endow them with a feeling of the orality of
the original.

The post-Conquest historical narratives and explanations
were generally kept in prose form in translation because she
suspected that such materials were not a legitimate part of Classic Aztec literature. They showed little of the structure of traditional narrative with its florid embellishments and bright
metaphors. If such materials did in fact reflect pre-conquest
traditions, they were surely not very important in the hierarchy
of native accomplishments. They reflected simple, functional
language use, and thus the English translation should also reflect this.

The vast majority of Sullivan's translations were from the
encyclopedia of the Aztec world prepared under the direction
of Fray Bernardino de Sahagún, which contained vivid descrip-
tions and explanations, as well as lively narratives and elegant
orations concerning all aspects of Aztec society. The encyclopedia format was not a part of pre-conquest literary tradition,
but was developed for Sahagún by his scribes and assistants in
the process of putting together his *History of All Things of New
Spain.* When translating, Sullivan generally left these descriptive, explanatory, hybrid texts in prose form.

The rhetorical orations, the *Huehuetlatolli*, were one of Sullivan's consuming passions. These were an essential part of the
canon of traditional Aztec literature and represented some of
the most complex and elegant forms of the Nahuatl language.
Had she lived, it was her intention to translate all of the surviving rhetorical orations, for she had spent years assembling
copies of the entire corpus from libraries throughout the world.

The songs include the entire corpus of Classic Aztec poetry contained in the *Cantares Mexicanos* and *Romances* manuscripts, as well as the twenty sacred hymns of the *Primeros Memoriales* manuscript, plus fragments from other manuscripts such as the *Anales de Cuauhtitlan* (see I, 1 and III, 2 and 3). There are numerous distinctions that can be made within this genre and Sullivan had extensive notes on them. Unfortunately she only published a few fragments from this extensive body of Classic Aztec poetics. Her translation of Sahagún's *Primeros Memoriales*, including the "Twenty Songs" contained in the manuscripts, unfortunately still remains in press after ten years.

To the Western eye, prayers and songs are two genres that appear to merge in Aztec literature. They are, however, quite distinct. The prayers, such as the prayer to Tlaloc (see III, 1), have more in common with the rhetorical orations than they do with the songs, the poetics of the Aztec world. Prayers are direct forms of address to the deities of the pre-Columbian pantheon. They are clear, moving, impassioned addresses to the powers of the supernatural, and they illustrate the type of direct relationship that was maintained with the supernatural in ancient Mexico.

Sullivan used a wide range of techniques to elucidate her translations. She always sought to capture the tone, sense, and style of a text in English in the context of Aztec society, and to make the translations clear and readable. Sullivan always maintained that one had to "know the culture to translate the language." When she translated she brought every bit of knowledge she had to bear on the problems of bringing the text out in a way that would be coherent and meaningful to those in the Western world.

Sullivan knew almost everyone in Mexico who worked in the fields of pre-Columbian art, architecture, archaeology, anthropology, linguistics, aesthetics, philology, psychology, and philosophy. Whenever she was having a problem with a particular translation and there was someone she knew who might be able to shed a bit of light on a difficult passage, they could expect a phone call.

In addition to being a superb pre-Columbian scholar, Sullivan was well versed in the early colonial history of Mexico, having a broad knowledge of sixteenth-century Mexican art, literature, architecture, language, and politics. Whether from her weekend home in the Valle de Bravo on the foothills of the Toluca volcano, or while on a trip deep-sea fishing from her favorite spot in Zihuatenejo, Sullivan constantly sought out obscure villages, markets, fiestas, and folk art that could shed light on Mexico's pre-Columbian past. All of this knowledge helped to put her translations in the proper context.

Another element of understanding that was essential for Sullivan was her knowledge of modern Mexico: the rise of nationalism and the role of Mexico's glorified past in the modern discourse of nationhood. Sullivan was one of the few Americans I have known in Mexico who appreciated the irony of glorifying the past in modern political discourse. She knew how much the Aztec world remains today as an essential part of the modern nation.

The style of a text was another essential consideration for her. An elegant rhetorical style in Nahuatl should of course sound like an elegant rhetorical style in English. A prayer requires a high, reverential tone, and the explanation of a metaphor requires a clear exposition (see IV, 1). The narratives presented here constitute dramatic performances, for, as she points out in the introduction to her translation of the *Mexicayotl* (see I, 2), a teller of tales in Nahuatl is an actor and a buffoon.

Once the tone, sense, and style of a translation are considered, the most important part of the work is at hand: the selection of the proper word. There are profound differences between English and Classic Aztec, which make it sometimes extremely difficult to find exact linguistic parallels. Nahuatl is an agglutinative language that composes words by stringing them together. As Benjamin Whorf, one of the founding fathers of anthropological linguistics, noted, Nahuatl has an almost infinite capacity to coin new words, making the selection of the proper terms even more difficult.[1] Sullivan often pored over dictionaries seeking just the right nuance in other dialects of Nahuatl, in other Uto-Aztecan languages, in sixteenth-century Spanish, and in etymologies and philology. In her work Sullivan always employed what she called an etymological method.[2] She believed that by proper semantic and grammatical analysis she could elucidate the proper meaning of each word in its context.

Sullivan constantly refined her translations. Even when galleys came back from the printer she would change as much as she could and note further changes on her own originals. In most cases the changes were not substantial, but rather evolved with her understanding of the nature of the text she was translating. I have made only the changes that were indicated in her own voluminous notes on these translations, despite the fact that there are always places where translators will disagree on the rendering of a particular passage.

Part I

THE AZTEC WORLD

THE SELECTIONS FROM THE TRANSLATIONS OF THELMA
D. Sullivan contained in this section reflect the birth of the Aztec
world, its mythological origins, and its final demise in the Spanish
lust for gold. The first two selections are from among the few
translations that Sullivan made of materials not contained in the
vast Sahaguntine corpus. Although Fray Bernardino de Sahagún
compiled an encyclopedic history of the Aztec world, it was from
a Spanish and European point of view. The passages from the
Anales de Cuauhtitlan and the *Mexicayotl* presented here instead
reflect the labors of the few native historians long after the
conquest to preserve some of their own tradition.

The final selection forms the last chapters of Sahagún's
magnum opus, the *Historia general de las cosas de Nueva España*. It
recounts the *coup de grâce* of the Spanish conquest of the Aztec
empire. Appropriately this is the only translation from Spanish
in this volume.

1

The Ancient Suns of Mexico and Quetzalcoatl

CODEX CHIMALPOPOCA
The *Anales de Cuauhtitlan*

THE CODEX CHIMALPOPOCA is a relatively late document written many years after the conquest.[1] The manuscript is a very curious history laden with copious calendric references and dates. It depicts the divinatory Aztec calendars that contain the dates and lists of rulers responsible for founding and legitimizing the noble line of Cuauhtitlan. Interspersed with this material are bits and pieces of what is a vivid oral tradition. Although the dates and names may well have been read from a painted hieroglyphic manuscript, the sections, such as the story of Quetzalcoatl the priest, are obviously not read, but told in the best tradition of Aztec performers and narrators. Sullivan writes in her introduction to her translation of this material:

> Although it is not known to what extent the art of dramaturgy was developed in pre-Hispanic times, there is abounding evidence that drama existed, apart from their religious festivals in which people assumed the roles of gods. The Myth of Quetzalcoatl from the Codex Chimalpopoca is probably one of the best examples of this.
>
> The devout, humane, and rather naive Quetzalcoatl, who brought riches to his people, the Toltecs, who had taught them all the arts, was being plagued by sorcerers who wanted him

to perform human sacrifices. . . . When [the sorcerers] saw
that he would not submit to them, they decided to circumvent
his piety through trickery and deception. . . . At this point we
can see the drama as it might have been presented.

The dramatic nature of these fragments, within the context
of a seemingly dry historical document, bursts forth as part of
a living tradition, as much more than a reading of a hieroglyphic
script. Although the events appear to follow a linear historical
progression, they often actually seem a confused patchwork of
vague remembrances organized by a linear time frame. For example, the words and battle of Itzpapalotl are narrated twice in
this selection, and the formation of the Suns, or mythical ages,
of ancient Mexico is given in far greater detail in the ten folio
pages that follow the *Anales de Cuauhtitlan* entitled the *Leyenda
de los Soles*.

The material that follows is from the first eight folios of the
Anales de Cuauhtitlan, and although it follows the exact progression of the manuscript I have edited it to conform with
Sullivan's view of the text.[2] The narratives take far more than a
calendric reading or historical account. These passages are in
and of themselves a monument to the artistic endeavors of the
Aztec peoples. The dramatic narratives shine like jewels imbed-
ded in the tedious body of vaguely remembered historical material. It is almost as if one of the elders, asked to recall his
people's long and tedious history, has flashes of recollections
that were once a part of his personal past. These become the
few gems that remain of the once glorious empire, guarded in
his memory.

The Origins of the Peoples of Cuauhtitlan

. . . There you are to shoot the yellow eagle,
the yellow jaguar, the yellow serpent,
the yellow rabbit, the yellow deer.

Shoot your arrows to the south, to the southland,
to the humid southland, to the land of flowers [Tlalocan].

There you are to shoot the red eagle, the red jaguar. . . .

And when you have shot your arrows
place them in the hands of Xiuhtecutli,
the God of Fire, the Old God
the three who are to guard him—
Mixcoatl, Tozpan, and Ihuitl
these are the names of the three hearth stones.

Thus Itzpapalotl instructed the Chichimeca.

And then the Chichimeca came;
the Mixcoa, the Four Hundred Mixcoa led them.
They came out of the nine places where one becomes
    black,
on the nine plains.
And there they fell into the hands of Itzapapalotl;
she ate the Four Hundred Mixcoa, she consumed them.

Only Iztoc Mixcoatl,
who was called the youngest Mixcoatl, ran, he escaped;
he jumped into a barrel cactus.
Itzpapalotl grabbed the barrel cactus.
Mixcoatl leaped out.
Then he shot her with arrows.
He called the Centzonmixcoa that had died.
They came tumbling down and shot her with arrows.
And when she was dead, then they burned her.
And they smeared the ashes on their eyes,
and blackened the sockets of their eyes.

And when this was over,
their packs were made,
in the place called Mazatepec,
they all arrayed themselves.
There began the year calendar by fours. . . .

In the Year 1-Reed,
the Chichimeca left Chicomoztoc.
It is said, it is recounted,
it is their tradition, that the year count,
the day count, the count of twenty-day periods
was the task of Oxomoco and Cipactonal.

Oxomoco was a man and Cipactonal, a woman.
Both of them were old.
And afterwards, old men and old women
were also called by those names. . . .

In the year 13-Rabbit the year count began, there were the Chichimeca
of Texcoco.

In the year 1-Reed Chicontonatiuh became king of Quauhtitlan. In
Quetzaltepec he assumed the rule. . . .

In the year 5-Reed the Chichimeca, the people of Quauhtitlan, arrived
in the land, in Macuexhuacan, Huehuetocan. It is said, it is recounted,
that they came forth from Chicomoztoc, the seven caves. . . .

. . . They had been wandering about shooting their arrows;
they had no houses, they had no land,
they had no woven capes as clothing;
only hides, only Spanish moss did they use to cover
    themselves.
And their children grew up in mesh bags,
in cagelike crates used for carrying things.

They ate the prickly pear, the barrel cactus,
the *tetzihoactli*, and the bitter prickly pear.
They suffered great hardships for 364 years
until they arrived in the city, Quauhtitlan.
In that year it began, it originated
the rule of the Chichimeca,
the people of Quauhtitlan.

It must be told, it must be understood . . .
that while on their way they gave themselves a king.

The Ancient Suns of Mexico

During these years, of the Chichimeca's wandering.
It is said, it is recounted
that it was still the time of darkness.
They say that it was still the time of darkness

because as yet no fame, no glory was theirs;
there was no joyousness.
They wandered from place to place. . . .

In the first age,
according to accounts, according to the recollections
of the ancients for they knew it . . .
the earth, the world,
came into existence, was established. . . .

The age of the 4-Sun . . .
the sign was 4-Wind.

The second age was named, was called,
the age of the 5-Sun. . . .

The third age: the age of the 9-Sun
the year 9-House. . . .

It is recounted, it is said
that four kinds of life were created. . . .

The old men knew that in 1-Rabbit,
in that year the earth and heaven were established,
and they also knew that
when the earth and heaven were etablished
there were four kinds of beings,
four kinds of life were created.
They knew that each one was a Sun.
And they said that he created,
he fashioned their gods from ashes;
they attributed this to Quetzalcoatl. . . .

In the beginning was the first Sun,
4-Water was its sign;
it was called the Sun of Water.
In this Sun all was carried off by water,
the people were transformed
into dragonfly larvae and into fish.

The second Sun was established.
4-Jaguar was its sign;

it was called the Jaguar Sun.
In this Sun it happened that the heavens collapsed,
that the Sun did not move on its course from its zenith.
It began to darken, when all was dark,
then the people were devoured.

And Giants lived in this Sun.
The elders say that their greeting to each other was
"May you not fall,"
because everyone who fell,
fell forevermore.

The third Sun was established.
4-Rain was its sign;
it was called the Sun of Rain.
In this Sun it occurred that it rained fire
and the people were consumed by fire. . . .
It rained stones.
They now say that this was when the stones we now see fell,
and the lava rock boiled up.
And also, it was when the great rocks formed into masses,
and became red.

The fourth Sun:
4-Wind was its sign;
was called the Sun of Wind.
In this Sun all was carried off by the wind,
the people turned into monkeys.
And afterward the monkey men
that lived there dispersed about the forests.

The fifth Sun:
its symbol is 4-Motion.
It was called the Sun of Motion
because it moves, it follows a course.
And say the ancients:
that in this Sun it shall come to pass
that the earth shall move,
that there shall be famine,
and that we all shall perish. . . .

In the year 13-Reed,
they say that the Sun that now exists was created.
At that time the Sun of Movement
arose at dawn, gave its light. . . .
In this fifth Sun the earth shall move,
there shall be famine,
then we shall perish.

In the year 13-Reed Chicontonatiuh died in Macuexhuacan. He reigned sixty-five years in Quauhtitlan.

In the year 1-Flint the Toltecs took a king. They took as their king Mixcoamazatzin, he originated the Toltec rule. In this same year Xiuhneltxin became king of Quauhtitlan in Ximilco. When they were there one year they moved to Quaxoxouhcan. It was in the time of the god Mixcoatl, when he still accompanied them. And it was in the time of Xiuhneltzin that the boundary lines were set down. Afterwards Mixcoatl sent the Chichimeca off; they wandered from village to village, he parceled out, he distributed among them the possessions, the adornments that were his.

In the year 1-Flint the Chichimeca of Quauhtitlan took a king. It was the first time, it was the beginning of the Chichimeca's rule in Quauhtitlan. There in the place called Nequameyocan the first time they took as their king, Huactli.

The Chichimeca

According to the history of the Chichimeca that exists, the ancients said that when the rule of the Chichimeca began, a queen called Itzpapalotl spoke to them, she said to them:

"You are to install Huactli as your king.
Go to Nequameyocan,
establish the House of Cactus, the House of Honey Maguey,
and there you are to put down
the Cactus Mat, the Honey Maguey mat.

"And then you shall go to the East;
there you shall shoot your arrows.

"Also, to the North; there, into the great plain
you shall shoot your arrows.

"Also to the West,[3]
there you shall shoot your arrows.

"Also to the South, to the land of the flowers;
there you shall shoot your arrows.

"And when you have shot your arrows,
when you have captured the gods,
the green, the yellow, the white, the red,
eagle, jaguar, serpent, rabbit, *etc.*
then you shall place Tozpan and Ihuitl and Xiuhnel
in the hands of Xiuhteculti[4] to guard him, *etc.* . . .
When Huactli has fasted the king's fast for nine days,
your captives will be needed, *etc.*"

And the Chichimeca took as their kings those that are named
    here: . . .

And then, there in Nequameyocan they appointed a lord,
a Chichimeca noble, to lead them always.
And they made a heron feather banner
for their chief to carry wherever he went,
wherever he established himself,
so that it would be seen,
so that they would gather there.
It was not to be his seat.

*And after this occurred, in the precise year of 1-Flint, the Chichimeca
went off, they dispersed. They went everywhere, from place to
place. . . .*

*And some returned; they went to Cuextlan. Some went to Acolhuacan.
They wandered from place to place, they roamed from place to place.
It was said that the first ones to go to Huexotzinco were: Tepolnextli,
Tlanquaxoxouhqui, and Xiuhtochtli. These the demon separated in
Quaxoxouhcan; he took them from place to place.*

Quetzalcoatl, the Priest

So ends the account related above. When Xiuhneltzin ruled in Quax-
oxouhcan, the city of Quauhtitlan was established. . . .

In the year 1-House died the king of the Toltecs who founded the rule
whose name was Mixcoatlmazatzin, Huetzin was then made king of
Tollan. . . .

In the year 6-Reed Quetzalcoatl's father died; his name was Totepeuh.
Then Ilhuitimal became king of Tollan. . . .

1-Reed.
According to what is told, to what is said,
in this year Quetzalcoatl was born,
he was called Topiltzin, Tlamacazqui, Ce Acatl,
   Quetzalcoatl,
and they say his mother was called Chimalman.
It was also said that Quetzalcoatl's mother conceived
after having swallowed a jade. . . .

In 9-Reed, in this year,
Quetzalcoatl searched for his father.
He was now able to reason a little,
he was nine years old. He said,
"What was my father like?
Let me see him, let me look at his face!"

Then he was told
"He is dead. He is buried over there [pointing].
Look!"

Quetzalcoatl went there and then dug;
he found his bones.
When he removed the bones
he buried them inside of the palace of the goddess called
   Quilaztli. . . .

In the year 10-House died Huactli.
He had been king of Quauhtitlan. He had ruled for fifty-
   two years.

This king did not know how to plant maize, the food;
his people did not know how to make capes.
They still wore leather clothing;
their food was still birds, snakes, rabbits, and deer.
As yet they had no houses; they still wandered,
they were still roaming from place to place.

In the year 11-Rabbit Xiuhtlacuiloxochitzin became
   queen.
Her grass hut was in Tianquistenco, which is now
   Tepextitenco.
The city, Quauhtitlan, was left to this queen;
it is said that she was the wife of Huactli
and that she was able to talk to the goddess
   Itzpapalotl. . . .

2-Rabbit.
In this year Quetzalcoatl arrived in Tollantzinco.
He remained there four years;
he built his House of Fasting, his turquoise house of
   wood.
From there he passed to Cuextlan;
at a certain place he constructed a stone bridge
and thus crossed the river called Pánuco.
They say it is still there.

5-House.
In this year the Toltecs brought Quetzalcoatl back;
they made him king of Tollan
and he was their priest.
In another place his story has been written. . . .

2-Reed.
Topiltzin, Ce Acatl, Quetzalcoatl built his House of
   Fasting,
his place of penance, his place of prayer.
The houses he built were four in number:
his turquoise house of wood [blue-green, South],
his house of coral [red, East],
his house of conch shells [white, North],
his house of quetzal feathers [green, West],

where he prayed, he did penance, and fasted.
And at the stroke of midnight,
he went down into the water at a place called Atecpan,
   Amochco.
And he pricked himself with maguey thorns on top of
   the hills
of Xicocotl and Huitzxcoc and Tzincoc and
   Nonohualcatepec.
And he made his thorns of jade,
his fir boughs of quetzal feathers.
His offering of fire was of turquoise, jade, and coral [the
   coals].
And his sacrificial offering
was of snakes, birds, and butterflies;
those he slew.

And it is told, it is said, that he sent up prayers,
that he directed his supplications to the center of the
   four heavens,
and invoked Citlalinicue and Citlallatonac,
Tonacacihuatl and Tonacatecutli,
Tecolliquenqui and Eztlaquenqui,
Tlallamanac and Tlallichcatl.
And he cried out, as it was known
to the Place of Duality, to the Place of the Nine Tiers,
which are in the heavens,
and as was known, he invoked,
he prayed to those that dwelled there,
most humbly, most plaintively.

Further, in his time, during his lifetime,
he discovered great riches:
jade, turquoise, gold, silver,
coral, conch shells, quetzal feathers, lovely cotinga
   feathers,
roseate spoonbill feathers, troupial feathers,
trogon feathers, and ayoquan feathers.
And he also discovered cocoa beans of diverse colors,
   and cotton of diverse colors.
And he was a great artist in all of his creations;

in his food and drink,
and pottery painted blue, green, white, yellow, red,
and many other colors.

And when Quetzalcoatl lived
he began, he started, a temple.
He built pillars in the form of snakes
but he did not finish,
he did not built it to the top.

And while he lived,
he did not show himself to people.
He was in an inaccessible place,
in the innermost recesses of the houses;
he was guarded.
His heralds guarded him,
they cloistered him in many places.
And wherever he was cloistered, a group of his heralds
    was there;
in them were jade mats, quetzal feather mats, gold mats.
And they said, they recounted
that he built four Fast Houses.

And they say, they recount that when Quetzalcoatl
    lived,
the sorcerers frequently tried to trick him
in order that he would make offerings of humans,
in order that he would sacrifice humans.
But he never wanted to, he refused,
for he loved his people, the Toltecs, very much.
His offerings were always just serpents, birds,
and butterflies that he sacrificed.

And it is said, it is told,
that because of this he was vexed by the sorcerers,
that they provoked his anger because
they ridiculed him, they scoffed at him;
they said they wanted to afflict Quetzalcoatl
and drive him out,
which came true, which came to pass. . . .

*1-Reed. In this year Quetzalcoatl died and it is said that he went to
the place of the black and the red in order to die. Then one called
Matlaxochitl became king and ruled in Tollan.*

Then is recounted how Quetzalcoatl departed.
When he did not submit to the sorcerers
and make offerings of humans, sacrifice humans,
then the sorcerers,
who were named Tezcatlipoca, Ihuimecatl, Toltecatl,
held a council.
They said:
"It is necessary that he leave this city.
There [pointing] is where we shall live.

"Let us make pulque," they said,
"Let us make him drink it so that we may corrupt him,
and thus he will do penance no more."

"I say," said Tezcatlipoca, "let us show him his body.
How shall he find it?"

They agreed to do this.
Tezcatlipoca went first.
He took a two-sided mirror measuring about six
    inches[5]
and wrapped it up.
When he arrived at the place where Quetzalcoatl was
he told the heralds who guarded him:
"Tell the priest, Telpochtli[6] has come,
he has come to present you with, to show you your
    body."

The heralds entered, they informed Quetzalcoatl.
He said to them:
"What is that, grandfather heralds?
What has he brought for my body?
Look at it, then he shall enter."

He did not want to show it to them.
He said to them: "I alone shall show it to the priest. ·
Tell him."

They went to tell him: "He refuses.
He alone wants to show it to you."

Quetzalcoatl said: "Let him come, grandfathers."
They went to summon Tezcatlipoca.
He entered, he was greeted, and he said,
"My prince, Priest, Ce Acatl, Quetzalcoatl,
I greet you and I come to show you your body."

Quetzalcoatl said: "You have wearied yourself,
    grandfather.[7]
Whence have you come?
Where is my body?
Let me see it."

Tezcatlipoca said to him:
"My prince, priest, I am your vassal.
I have come from the foot of the Nonohualca
    mountains.
Please look at your body."

Then he gave him the mirror.
He said: "Know yourself, regard yourself, my prince.
You shall appear in the mirror."

Then Quetzalcoatl looked at himself.
He became very frightened.
"If my people see me," he said,
"perhaps they will flee!"
This was because his eyelids were very swollen,
his eyes were deeply sunken in their sockets,
his face was lumpy all over.
He was monstrous.

After he had looked into the mirror he said:
"My people shall never see me. I shall remain here."

Then Tezcatlipoca withdrew, he departed.
He and Ihuimecatl deliberated
on whether it was not possible to trick him.
Ihuimecatl said: "Let Coyotlinahual,
the featherwork artist, go to him now."

They advised him that he should go and
  Coyotlinahual,
the featherwork artist, said:
"Very well I shall go, I shall see Quetzalcoatl."

Then he went off.
He said to Quetzalcoatl:
"I say to my prince, 'Won't you go out and let the
  people see you?
Let me array you that they may look at you.' "

Quetzalcoatl said: "Fashion the adornments
so that I may see them, my grandfather."

Then Coyotlinahual, the featherwork artist, fashioned
  it.
First he made Quetzalcoatl's feather headdress,
then he made him his turquoise mosaic mask.[8]
He took the color red and painted his lips red.
He took the color yellow and with it painted bars on
  his face.
Then he gave him serpent's fangs,
and then he fashioned a beard for him of lovely
  cotinga feathers,
and roseate spoonbill feathers,
which covered the bottom of his face.

When he had finished arraying Quetzalcoatl in the
  adornments that were properly his,
he gave him the mirror.
He looked at himself, he admired himself greatly.
It was then that Quetzalcoatl left the place
where he had been cloistered.

And then Coyotlinahual, the featherwork artist,
  departed.
He went to tell Ihuimecatl:
"I have caused Quetzalcoatl to go out.
Go now!"
Ihuimecatl said,
"Very well."

Ihuimecatl made friends with one called Toltecatl.
The two of them went off to do what was to be done.
They arrived at Xonacapacoyan.
They placed themselves next to one of Quetzalcoatl's
    farmers
who guarded Toltecatepec, the Toltec Mountain.
Then they, too, cultivated greens, green tomatoes,
    chiles, snap beans;
in a few days they were grown.
And there were also magueys there
for which they asked Maxtlaton.
In only four days they prepared pulque.
Then they collected it: they found small honey jars[9]
and in these they collected the pulque.

Then they went to Quetzalcoatl's house in Tollan.
They took all their greens, chiles, green tomatoes . . .
and the pulque.
When they arrived they tried to enter
but those guarding Quetzalcoatl refused.
Twice, three times they returned but were not
    admitted.
Then they were asked where they lived.
They replied, they said:
"Tlamacaztepec, the Priest Mountain, Toltecatepec,
    Toltec Mountain."

When Quetzalcoatl heard this, he said:
"Let them enter."
They entered and greeted him.
At last they offered him the greens, the chiles . . .
When he had eaten them, they urged him once again
and offered him the pulque.

He said to them:
"I will not drink it, I am fasting.
Has it not intoxicated people, or killed them?"

They said to him:
"Just take a taste of it with your finger.[10]
It is very strong, it is new pulque."

Quetzalcoatl tasted it with his finger and he liked it.
He said: "Let me drink it, my grandfather."
After he took one drink the sorcerers told him:
"You must drink four." Thus they gave him five.[11]
They said to him: "It, the fifth, is your libation."[12]

After he had drunk,
they served pulque to all of his heralds;
they all drank five.
When they had gotten all of them drunk,
the sorcerers spoke to Quetzalcoatl once more:
"Sing my prince. Here is the song you shall sing."
Then Ihuimecatl sang:

> "Of quetzal feathers, of quetzal feathers is my
>   house,
>   of troupial feathers is my house,
>   of coral is my house.
>   I must leave it, Oh!"

Quetzalcoatl was now gay.
He said: "Bring my sister Quetzalpetlatl! Let us drink
together!"

His heralds went to Nonohualcatepec
where she was doing penance.
They said to her: "My princess, Noble Lady,
Quetzalpetlatl,
observer of the fast, we have come to take you with
us.
The priest Quetzalcoatl is waiting for you;
you are to be beside him."[13]

She said: "Very well. Let us go, grandfather herald."
And when she arrived, she sat down beside
Quetzalcoatl.
Then they served her four drinks of pulque
and one more, her libation, making five.
And then the pliers-of-wine sang to Quetzalcoatl's
sister also.
They sang:

"My sister, where will you dwell?
O, Quetzalpetlatl,
let us drink!
ay ya yya in ye an."

Once they became inebriated
they no longer said: "Let us do penance."
And they no longer went down to the water,
no longer did they prick themselves with maguey
    thorns,
no longer did they do anything.

At dawn, when it was daybreak,
they were downcast, dejected,
their hearts were filled with misery.
Then Quetzalcoatl said: "Oh, wretched am I!"
Then he sang the lament he would compose for the
    time that he would leave.

He sang one song.[14] . . .

He sang a second song:

"Oh, my mother carried me,
the goddess Coacueye
I who am her son
I weep, oh!"

When Quetzalcoatl had sung his songs,
all his heralds were desolate, they wept.
Then they too sang, they lifted their voices in song:

"He gave us riches,
my lord, Quetzalcoatl.
The blood-gushing tree is now sundered.
Let us regard him,
Let us weep."

When Quetzalcoatl's heralds ended their song,
he said to them: "Grandfathers, heralds, enough!
I leave the city, I go.
Bid them to make me a stone chest."

Then quickly they fashioned a stone chest.
When it was fashioned, when it was finished,
they laid Quetzalcoatl in it.
After he had lain there in the stone chest four days, he
    felt ill.
Then he said to his heralds: "It is enough,
    grandfathers, heralds.
Let us go. Put away, hide, the riches,
the wealth we have discovered,
all our property, all our possessions."

This his heralds did.
They hid them in Quetzalcoatl's bathing place,
the place called Atecpan, Amochco.

Then Quetzalcoatl departed.
He stood up, he summoned all his heralds and he
    wept over them.
Then they went off, they went to seek
Tlillan Tlapallan, the place of the black and the red,
Tlatlayan, the place of the burning.
He sought everywhere, he tried every place,
but none satisfied him.
And when he reached the place he had been seeking,
once more he wept, he was desolate.
This was in the year 1-Reed.

They say, they recount,
that when he reached the sea, the edge of the sea,
he halted, he wept.
He took his vestments and arrayed himself
in his feather headdress, and his turquoise mask, *etc.*
And when he was arrayed
then he, by his own hand,
set fire to himself, set himself a blaze.
It is for this reason
the place where Quetzalcoatl was consumed by fire is
    called
Tlatlayan, the place of the burning.

And they say that while he was burning,
his ashes ascended, and there appeared,
they saw, all the birds of precious feathers ascend into
    the heavens;
they saw the roseate spoonbill, the lovely cotinga, the
    trogon,
the ayoquan, the yellow parrot,
the scarlet macaw, the white-bellied parrot,
and all the other birds of precious feathers.

And when his ashes were consumed,
then they saw the heart of the Quetzal bird,
Quetzalcoatl, ascend, thus they knew
that he had gone to the heavens,
that he had entered the heavens.
The ancients said that he was transformed
into the star that appears at dawn.
According to what they say, it appeared
when Quetzalcoatl died; for this reason he is called
Tlahuizcalpantecutli, the lord of the dawn.

They said that when he died,
he was not seen for four days;
they said that when he went to Mictlan, the land of
    the dead.
And in the course of another four days he made
    himself arrows.
On the eighth day the morning star,
they called Quetzalcoatl, appeared.
They say it was then that he ruled.

And they knew when he appeared and under which signs he shot his
arrows, he struck with his arrows, he became vexed with diverse groups
of beings. If he comes out, coincides with 1-Crocodile, he shoots his
arrows at all the old men and women alike. If it is in 1-Jaguar, 1-Deer,
1-Flower, he shoots his arrows at the children. If it is 1-Reed, he shoots
all the rulers alike with his arrows. If it is 1-Death and 1-Rain, he
shoots the rain with his arrows; it will not rain. And if it is 1-Move-
ment, he shoots youths and maidens with his arrows. And if it is 1-
Water, there is drought.

For these diverse reasons
the men and women of old
venerated the man called
Quetzalcoatl all the time that he lived.
He was born in 1-Reed and he also died in 1-Reed.
This is a total of fifty-two years that he lived,
which ends in the year 1-Reed.

2

The Finding and Founding of Mexico-Tenochtitlan

THE MEXICAYOTL

THIS IS WITHOUT DOUBT one of the most important texts that Sullivan translated.[1] It is as important today for Mexico's concept of nationhood and ideology as it was at the time of the conquest. It defines Mexico's national symbol and how it came to be as well as the finding and founding of Mexico-Tenochtitlan: Mexico City.

In the central plaza of present-day Mexico City, the Zócalo, between the National Palace and Mexico's City Hall, stands the statue depicting the finding and founding of Mexico-Tenochtitlan; opposite the newly excavated ruins of the Aztecs' Great Temple, this epitomizes the ideology embodied in this text: a poor and outcast tribe that came to dominate all of Mesoamerica.

The city-state that Cortéz found, the Aztecs' resplendent capital that he and his men so marveled at, was at its peak. As Bernal Díaz del Castillo wrote:

> . . . [we] continued our march toward Ixtapalapa and when we saw so many cities and villages built in the water and other great towns on dry land and that straight and level causeway going towards Mexico we were amazed and said that it was like the enchantments they tell of in the legend of Amadis, on account of the great towers and buildings rising from the water,

and built of masonry. And some of the soldiers even asked whether some of these things were not a dream.

What Sullivan states, almost anecdotally at first, in her original introduction is the key to the way that she viewed this text.[2] She noted:

A young friend of mine recounted to me an experience that he had in North Africa not too long ago that, regardless of all knowledge of what constitutes the "Oral Tradition," truly makes it come alive.

"In a small town in North Africa—I've forgotten where— every evening the square filled with hawkers of one kind or another, fakirs, and without fail, a storyteller who drew a fair crowd evenly divided between children and adults." My friend, though he knew no Arabic, caught the mood of the crowd and apparently the meaning of the storyteller. The latter had something for everyone: for the children, an exciting tale; for the grown-ups, salacious asides.

As he wove his tale the audience would grow more and more rapt and tense. At the highest point of tension, when the plight of the protagonists of the tale became unbearable to contemplate, the storyteller would break off the narration. Those who wished to hear the end had to pay up, and a plate was passed around. Those who did not pay up were few in number, for young and old alike were impatient to hear the end. My friend saw the tension gradually ease in the audience as he brought the hero out of his predicament, and for the same pennies began another hair-raising episode.

No doubt something like this existed in the markets in pre-Hispanic Mexico. The word for storyteller is *tlaquetzqui*, he who holds something back.[3] They could be found at the markets, at the fairs, at private parties, and the best of them at public functions.

They were performers, as are storytellers all over the world, and they dressed the part. We find this description by a noble father to his son, by way of warning:

In this manner you should tie your cape:
you should not tie it so long that you step on it
you should not tie it too short;

you should not tie it poorly
nor should you have your shoulder exposed.

The "shorn head," who is called the "wild warrior,"
who only prizes death,
as well as the teller of tales, the jester, the dancer, and the
  demented,
snatch any kind of cape, no matter how,
and they drag it along,
they step on it,
they go about ridiculously, kicking their legs out.
They pull the cape under the arm and go about with the
  shoulder exposed.
They move their legs about bizarrely,
they walk stiff-legged,
they drag their feet,
they roll from side to side.
And their sandals are outsized,
the sides flap, and the laces are too long and drag.

(F.C. ff. 101v–102r)

The following account of the finding and founding of
Mexico-Tenochtitlan is taken from Tezozomoc's *Crónica Mexicayotl*, the most extensive and the most poetic of all the accounts. Even though written well on in post-conquest times,
the best elements of the pre-Hispanic oral traditions are preserved: the poetry, suspense, drama, conflict, and triumph are
all there.

The great sagas of the emergence of the Aztecs from Aztlan,
equated with Chicomostoc, the mythical place of origin of the
Aztecs and others, their peregrinations and vicissitudes until,
guided by their titulary god, they come upon their promised
land, were told over and over again among the Aztecs.[4] . . .

In this translation, I have attempted to trace the thread of
the story from the break between Huitzlopochtli and his sister,
Malinalxoch; the birth of Copil, Malinalxoch's son; the attempt
and failure of Copil to avenge his mother, telling how Copil's
death is linked to the founding of Tenochtitlan. . . . We can
only assume that [the Aztecs] were the most warlike of Mesoamerican peoples and that they carried human sacrifice to
the extreme. . . . In the simplest and most obvious of analyses

the myth of the Aztecs finding their promised land and founding their city on the place that Copil's heart [was found] . . .
upon which an eagle eating a serpent was sighted . . . set the
tone for the Aztec culture that Cortéz found.

The tense narrative tone of this tale is maintained in Sullivan's
translation to a degree that no other translation can match. She
appreciated the story value not only for the ancient Mexicans,
but for their modern descendants. In this piece she tries to bring
forth some of the basic elements, not only of the finding and
founding of Mexico-Tenochtitlan, but of the modern nation that
she was so much a part of.

In the translation I am offering here, which as far as I know
is the first in English, I have selected and threaded together
only those texts that, in my opinion, narrate the events that
directly led the Aztecs to the finding of their promised land.
I have not, in any way, altered the sequence of events as they
appear in the text. . . . I believe that my translation will clarify
a number of texts that have long puzzled scholars.

This is a tale as it should be told, with all the flourish of Aztec
rhetoric and drama.

The Crónica Mexicayotl

f.67 Here it is told, it is recounted,
how the ancients who were called, who were named,
Teochichimeca, Azteca, Mexitin, Chicomoztoca[5] came,
 arrived,
when they came to seek,
when they came to gain possession of their land here,
in the great city of Mexico Tenochtitlan. . . .

In the middle of the water where the cactus stands,
where the eagle rises up,
where the eagle screeches,
where the eagle spreads his wings,
where the eagle feeds,
where the serpent is torn apart,

where the fish fly,
where the blue waters and the yellow waters join,
where the water blazes up,
where the feathers come to be known,[6]
among the rushes, among the reeds where the battle is
    joined,
where the people from four directions are awaited,
there they arrived, there they settled. . . .

f.73 They called themselves Teochichimeca, Azteca, Mexitin.
They brought along the image of their god,[7]
the idol that they worshipped.
The Aztecs heard him speak and they answered him;
they did not see how it was that he spoke to them. . . .
And after the Azteca, Mexitin sailed here from Aztlan,
they arrived in Culhuacan. . . .

f.76 They went everywhere in Culhuacan,
in far-off Culhuacan, in Tonalichuacan or Tollan.
All of them journeyed far—
the people of Michoacan, kin of the Mexicans,
and the people of Malinalco—
for all of them came.
And when the Aztecs abandoned the people of Michoacan,
the men and women were amusing themselves in the water at
    a place called Pátzcuaro.

f.77 They made off with the men's capes and breechcloths
and they took the women's skirts and *huipiles.*

The men no longer had breechcloths;
they went about with their bottoms bare,
rather, they go about with their bottoms bare, uncovered.
The women gave up their blouses and the men became
    wearers of *huipiles.*[8]
In this manner they abandoned the people of Michoacan.

And the reason Huitzilopochtli went off and abandoned his
    sister, named Malinalxoch, along the way,
that all his fathers abandoned her while she was sleeping,
was because she was cruel,
she was very evil.

She was an eater of people's hearts,
an eater of people's limbs—it was her work—
a bewitcher of people,
an enchanter of people.
She put people to sleep,
she made people eat snakes,
she made people eat scorpions,
she spoke to all the centipedes and spiders
and transformed herself into a sorceress.
She was a very evil woman;
this is why Huitzilopochtli did not like her,
this is why he did not bring his sister, Malinalxoch, with him,
that they abandoned her and all her fathers while they were
    sleeping.

Then the priest, Huitzilopochtli, spoke,
he addressed his fathers, called the "idol-bearers," he said to
    them,
"O my fathers, the work that Malinalxoch does is not my
    work.
When I came forth, when I was sent here,
I was given arrows and a shield,
for battle is my work.
And with my belly, with my head,
I shall confront the cities everywhere.
I shall await the people from the four directions,
I shall join the battle with them,
I shall provide the gods with drink,
I shall provide the gods with food.[9]
Here I shall bring together the diverse peoples,
and not in vain, for I shall conquer them,
that I may see the House of Jade, the House of Gold, the
    House of Quetzal Feathers;
the House of Emeralds, the House of Coral, the House of
    Amethysts;
the sundry feathers—the lovely cotinga feathers, the roseate
    spoonbill feathers, the trogon feathers—
all the precious feathers;
and the cacao of diverse colors,

and the cotton of diverse colors![10]
I shall see all this,
for in truth, it is my work,
it was for this that I was sent here.
And now, O my fathers, ready the provisions. Let us go!
Off there we are going to find it . . . !"

And when the sister of Huitzilopochtli, called Malinalxoch,
whom they had abandoned while sleeping,
whom they had gone off and abandoned,
when Malinalxoch awakened, she wept.
She said to her fathers, "O my fathers, where shall we go?
My brother, Huitzilopochtli, has abandoned us by trickery.
Where has the evil one gone?
Let us seek the land where we are to dwell. . . ."
They saw the mountain called Texcaltepetl;
they established themselves upon it. . . .

f.78 Along the way Malinalxoch became big with child,
and the child of Malinalxoch, a son named Copil, was born.
His father's name was Chimalquauhitl;
he was the king of Malinalco. . . .

The others settled at Coatetepec.
the Mexicans erected their temple, the house of
    Huitzilopochtli . . .
and they laid down Huitzilopochtli's ball court
and constructed his skull rack.
Then they blocked the ravine, the gorge,[11]
and the water collected, it filled up.
This was done at the word of Huitzilopochtli.

Then he said to his fathers, the Mexicans,
"O my fathers, the water has collected.
Plant, sow willows, bald cypresses, reeds, rushes, and water
    lilies!"
And the fish, frogs, *ajolotes*,[12] crayfish, dragonfly larvae,
    ahuihuitlame, ephydrids,[13] and the salamanders multiplied,
and also the *izcahuitli*,[14]
and the birds, ducks, American coots, and the red-
    shouldered and yellow-throated grackles.[15]

And Huitzilopochtli said,
"The *izcahuitli* are my flesh, my blood, my substance."[16]
Then he sang his song,
they all sang and danced;
the song was called Tlaxotecayotl and also Tecuilhuicuicatl;[17]
he composed it there.

Then his fathers, the Centzonhuitznahua,[18] spoke, they said
    to Huitzilopochtli,
"O Priest, the work for which you came shall be done here.
You shall await the people,
you shall meet in battle the people from the four directions,
you shall arouse the cities.
With your belly, with your head,
and your heart, your blood, your substance,
you shall capture them,
that you may see what you promised us—
the many jades, the precious stones, the gold,
the quetzal feathers and sundry precious feathers,
the cacao of diverse colors,
the cotton of diverse colors,
the diverse flowers, the diverse fruits, the diverse riches,
for, in truth, you have founded,
you have become the ruler of your city, here in Coatepec.
Let your fathers, your vassals, the Aztecs, the Mexicans,
    gather here!" the Centzonhuitznahua beseeched him.
Huitzilopochtli became enraged,
"What are you saying?" he said.
"Is it your work?
Are you greater than I?
I know what I must do!"

Then, atop the temple, his house, Huitzilopochtli began to
    array himself.

When he had arrayed himself,
when he had arrayed himself for battle,
he painted himself the color of a child's excrement,[19]
he made circles around his eyes,
and he took up his shield. . . .

f.79 Then he went off;
  he went to destroy, he went to slay his uncles, the
    Centzonhuitznahua.
  On the sacred ball court he devoured his uncles;
  and his mother, she whom he took to be his mother, called
    Coyolxauhcihuatl . . .[20]
  he cut off her head there and devoured her heart,
  Huitzilopochtli devoured it. . . .

  The Mexicans were frightened.
  The Centzonhuitznahua had thought that the city was to be
    there in Coatepec,
  that Mexico was to be there,
  but Huitzilopochtli did not want it so.
  He made a hole in the dam where the water had been,
  and the water broke the dam.
  All the bald cypresses, willows, reeds, rushes, and water
    lilies withered.
  All the fish, frogs, *ajolotes*, ephydrids, and insects,
  and the crayfish and dragonfly larvae that lived in the water
    died . . .
  and all the birds perished.

  Then Huitzilopochtli set out,
  he went off with his fathers, his vassals, the Mexicans. . . .
f.80 They came, they settled behind Chapultepec in a
    pace called Techcatitlan. . . .
  Huitzilopochtli gave orders to the Mexicans . . .
  he said to the idol bearers,
  "O my fathers, wait, for you shall see,
  wait for I know what is to happen.
  Gird yourselves, be courageous.
  Gird yourselves, prepare yourselves.
  We shall not dwell here,
  we shall find it [the place] off there,
  there is where we shall possess it.
  Let us await those who come to destroy us . . . !

  The son of Malinalxoch, the sister of Huitzilopochtli, whose
    name was Copil, spoke, he said to her,

"O my mother, well I know that your brother is off there."
"Yes, your uncle named Huitzilopochtli, is yonder," she said.
"He abandoned me,
he abandoned me while I was sleeping,
he abandoned me by trickery along the way.
Then we settled here in Texcaltepeticpac."[21]
"Very well, O my mother," said Copil.
"I know that I must look for him in the place he has found
    contentment,
in the place he has settled.
I shall destroy him.
I shall devour him,
and I shall destroy, I shall vanquish his fathers
and the vassals that he took with him,
Well I know all the gifts that are marked for him who is to
    see,
who is to behold manifold riches.
And it shall be I.
Mine shall be the knowledge of the sundry jades and gold,
of the quetzal feathers and other feathers,
of cacao of varied colors,
of the cotton of varied colors,
of diverse flowers and diverse fruits.
O my mother be not sad.
I go now to seek out the evil one, my uncle. . . ."

Then he came.
He arrayed himself, he adorned himself, he who was called
    Copil.
He was very evil,
he was a greater sorcerer[22] than his mother, Malinalxoch;
Copil was a very evil man.

He came in the year 1-House, 1285,
and in the place called Zoquitzinco he transformed himself.
Once more he came in and in the place called Atlapulco he
    transformed himself.
He came once again and in the place called Itzapaltemoc he
    transformed himself,

and because Copil transformed himself, because he turned
    himself into a flagstone,[23]
as it is now called, all of us call it Itztapaltetitlan.
And after the transformation of Copil,
f.81 after Copil transformed himself into flagstone,
    once again he returned to his home called Texcaltepeticpac;
    (they now call it Malinalco because Malinalxoch dwelt
        there . . .).

Once more Copil came . . .
and in the place called Tecpantzinco he transformed himself.
But Huitzilopochtli knew him at once,
he recognized his nephew, now grown, called Copil.
Then he said to his fathers,
"O my fathers, array yourselves, adorn yourselves,
my nephew, the evil one, is coming.
I am off.
I shall destroy him, I shall slay him!"

He encountered him at the place called Tepetzinco,
and when he saw him he said,
"Who are you? Where do you come from?"
"It is I." He replied.
Again he spoke to him.
"Where is your home?"
"In Texcaltepeticpac." He answered.
Then Huitzilopochtli said, "Good, are you not he who my
    sister, Malinalxoch, brought into the world?"
"Yes, I am he." Copil said,
"And I shall capture you, I shall destroy you!
Why did you abandon my mother while she was sleeping?
Why did you abandon her by trickery?
I shall slay you!"

"Very well," Huitzilopochtli said, "Come!"
They pursued each other with cunning,
and he captured Copil in Tepetzinco.
When he was dead Huitzilopochtli cut off his head and
    slashed open his chest,
and when he slashed open his chest, he tore out his heart.

Then he placed his head on top of Tepetzintli, which is now
   called Acopilco,
and there the head of Copil died.

And after Huitzilopochtli slew him,
he ran off with Copil's heart.
And the idol-bearer, called Quauhtlequetzqui, came upon
   Huitzilopochtli.
When he encountered him, he said,
"You have wearied yourself, O Priest."
"Come, O Quauhtlequetzqui," he said.
"Here is the heart of the evil one, Copil.
I have slain him.
Run with it into the rushes, into the reeds.
There you shall see the mat of stone
on which Quetzalcoatl rested when he went away,
and his seats, one red and one black.
There you shall halt
and you shall cast away the heart of Copil."

Then Quauhtlequetzqui went off to cast away the heart.
When he came to the place he had described to him,
he saw the mat of stone,
and he halted there and cast away the heart;
it fell among the rushes, in among the reeds. . . .
The place where Quauhcoatl[24] stopped and cast away the
   heart,
we now call Tlalcocomoco. . . .

f.82 Then the Mexicans went to Acuezcomac,
they passed through Huehuetlan, Atlixocan,
Teoculhuacan, Tepetocan, Huitzilac, Culhuacan,
Huixachtla, Cahualtepec, Tetlacuixomac.
They settled in Tlapitzahuayan in the year 2-Rabbit, 1286.

In the year 11-Reed, 1295. . . . The Mexicans passed through
   Zacatla. . . .
The people of Chalco drove them out,
they stoned them.
Once again they went to Chapultepec. . . .

Behind Chapultepec all the Tecpaneca, Azcapotzalca and
    Culhuaca,
the Xochimilca, Cuitlahuaca and Chalca besieged the
    Mexicans. . . .
The Mexicans were besieged in Chapultepec in 2-Reed, 1299.

f.83 Then the Mexicans moved to Acuezcomac. . . .
Then they came, they settled in Mazatlan,
and then all the Mexicans gathered in Tepetocan.
From there they went to Culhuacan[25]
Coxcoxtli was the king of Culhuacan. . . .

Then Huitzilopochtli said to the Mexicans,
"My fathers, say to Coxcoxtli, 'Where shall we live?' "
They addressed Coxcoxtli, they said to him,
"O lord, O king, we are beseeching you.
Where shall we go?
We have known this to be your city.
Have mercy with a small piece of your land on which we may
    live."
Coxcoxtli replied, he said, "Very well."
He summoned his Culhuacan chiefs, he said to them,
"Where shall they live?"
"O lord, O king, let them go there," his chiefs said.
"Let the Mexicans live beside the mountain, here in
    Tizaapan."
Then they took them, they established them in Tizaapan.
They advised Coxcoxtli, the king, they said,
"O lord, O king, we have taken the Mexicans to Tizaapan."
"Good," Coxcoxtli said. "They are monstrous, they are evil.
Perhaps they will end there,
perhaps they will be devoured by the snakes,
for it is the dwelling place of many snakes."

But the Mexicans were overjoyed when they saw the snakes.
They cooked them,
they roasted them over the fire, and they ate them. . . .

f.84 In the year 13-Reed, 1323,
the Mexicans had passed, had spent twenty-five years in
    Tizaapan, Culhuacan.

Then Huitzilopochtli spoke to his fathers, he said to them,
"O my fathers, another person shall appear whose name is
    Yaocihuatl.[26]
She is my grandmother and we shall have her.
And hear this, O my chiefs, we are not to remain here.
We shall find it [the place] off there.
There is where we shall possess it. . . .
And now gird yourselves,
make yourselves ready,
for you have heard that Yaocihuatl, my grandmother, will
    manifest herself there.
I command that you go,
that you ask Achitometl for his child, his daughter.
You are to ask him for his precious child,
for I know how I shall give her to you."

And then the Mexicans went off,
they went to ask Achitometl for his daughter.
The Mexicans spoke to him, they said,
"O my prince, O lord, O king, we your grandfathers, we
    your vassals, and all the Mexicans,
pray that you grant, that you give us, your jewel, your
    quetzal feather,
your daughter, our granddaughter, the princess.
There beside the mountain in Tizaapan she will keep guard."

Achitometl said, "Very well, O Mexicans, you may take her
    with you."
He gave her to the Mexicans.
They went off with the daughter of Achitometl,
they brought her,
they settled her in Tizaapan.

Then Huitzilopochtli spoke . . . he said to them,
"O my fathers, I order you to slay the daughter of Achitometl
    and to flay her.
When you have flayed her you are to dress a priest in her
    skin."
Then they slew the princess and they flayed her,
and after they flayed her, they dressed a priest in her skin.[27]

Huitzilopochtli then said,
"O my chiefs, go and summon Achitometl."
The Mexicans went off, they went to summon him.
They said, "O our lord, my grandson, O lord, O king . . .
your grandfathers, the Mexicans beseech you, they say,
"May he come to see, may he come to greet the goddess.
We invite him."
Achitometl said, "Very well, let us go."
He said to his lords, "Let us go to Tizaapan,
the Mexicans have invited us. . . ."
They took along rubber, *copal*, papers, flowers, and
    tobacco,
and also what is called the "lord's food"[28] to set down in
    offering before the goddess. . . .
And when Achitometl arrived in Tizaapan, the Mexicans said,
    as they received him,
"You have wearied yourself, O my grandson, O lord, O king.
We your grandfathers, we, your vassals, shall cause you to
    become ill.[29]
May you see, may you greet your goddess."
"Very good, O my grandfathers," he said.
He took the rubber, the *copal*, the flowers, the tobacco, and
    the food offering,
and he offered them to her,
he set them down before the false goddess whom they had
    flayed.
Then Achitometl tore off the heads of quail before his
    goddess;
he still did not see the person before whom he was
    decapitating quail.
Then he made an offering of incense and the incense-burner
    blazed up.
When Achitometl saw a man in his daughter's skin
he was horror-struck.
He cried out, he shouted out to his lords and vassals.
He said, "Who are they, eh, O Culhuacans?
Have you not seen?
They have flayed my daughter!
They shall not remain here, the fiends!

We shall slay them, we shall massacre them!
The evil ones shall be annihiliated here!"

They began to fight. . . .
The Culhuacans pursued them, they pursued the Mexicans,
they drove them into the water. . . .
The Culhuacans thought that they had perished in the water,
but they crossed the water on their shields,
they crossed on their arrows and shields.
They bound together the arrows, called *tlacochtli*,
and those called *tlazontectli*,[30]
and, sitting upon them, they crossed the water . . .
f.86 and sitting upon the shields they crossed the water
when the Culhuacans pursued them.
And they came into the rushes, into the reeds at
   Mexicaltzinco. . . .
There they dried their battle gear which had become wet,
their insignia, their shields . . . all their gear.
And their women and children began to weep.
They said, "Where shall we go? Let us remain here in the
   reeds. . . !"
And then the old Mexicans, Quauhtlequetzqui, or
   Quauhcoatl, and also the one called Axolohua went off,
they went into the rushes, into the reeds
at the place that is now called Toltzalan, Acatzalan;[31]
the two of them went to look for the place where they were
   to settle.
And when they came upon it,
they saw many wondrous things in the reeds.
This was the reason Huitzilopochtli had given his orders to
   the idol-bearers, his fathers,
Quauhtlequetzqui, or Quauhcoatl, and Axolohua, the priest.
For he had sent them off,
he had told them all that there was in the rushes, in the
   reeds,
that there he, Huitzilopochtli, was to stand,
that there he was to keep guard.
He told them with his own lips,
thus he sent off the Mexicans.

f.87 And then they saw the white bald cypresses, the white
      willows,
   and the white reeds, and the white rushes;
   and also the white frogs, the white fish, and the white snakes
      that lived there in the water.[32]
   And they saw the springs that joined;
   the first spring that faced east was called Tleatl and
      Atlatlayan,
   the second spring that faced north was called Matlalatl and
      also Tozpalatl.[33]
   And when they saw this the old men wept.
   They said, "Perhaps it is to be here!
   We have seen what the priest, Huitzilopochtli, described to
      us
   when he sent us off.
   He said, 'In the rushes, in the reeds, you shall see many
      things!'
   And now we have seen them, we have beheld them.
   It has come true, his words when he sent us off have become
      true!"
   Then they said,
   "O Mexicans, let us go, for we have beheld them.
   Let us await the word of the priest;
   he knows it shall be done."
   Then they came, they sojourned in Temazcaltitlan.
   And during the night he saw him,
   Huitzilopochtli appeared to the idol-bearer, called
   Quauhtlequetzqui, or Quauhcoatl.
   He said to him, "O Quauhcoatl, you have seen all there is in
      among the reeds, in among the rushes,
   you have beheld it.
   But hear this:
   There is something that you still have not seen.
   Go, go and look at the cactus,
   And on it, standing on it, you shall see an eagle.
   It is eating, it is warming itself in the sun,
   and your hearts will rejoice,
   for it is the heart of Copil that you cast away
   where you halted in Tlalcocomoco.

There it fell, where you looked, at the edge of the spring,
among the rushes, among the reeds.
And from Copil's heart sprouted what is now called
   tenochtli.[34]
There we shall be, we shall keep guard,
we shall await, we shall meet diverse peoples in battle.
With our bellies, with our heads,
with our arrows, with our shields,
we shall confront all who surround us
we shall vanquish them all,
we shall make them captives,
and thus our city shall be established.
Mexico Tenochtitlan:
where the eagle screeches,
where he spreads his wings,
where the eagle feeds,
where the fish fly,
and where the serpent is torn apart.
Mexico Tenochtitlan!
And many things shall come to pass."

Then Quauhcoatl said to him; "Very well, O priest, your
   heart has granted it.
Let all the old men, your fathers, hear."
Then Quauhcoatl gathered the Mexicans together,
he had them hear the words of Huitzilopochtli;
the Mexicans listened.
And then, once more, they went in among the rushes, in
   among the reeds, to the edge of the spring.
And when they came out into the reeds,
there at the edge of the spring, was the *tenochtli*,
and they saw an eagle on the *tenochtli*, perched on it,
   standing on it.
It was eating something, it was feeding,
it was pecking at what it was eating.[35]
And when the eagle saw the Mexicans, he bowed his head
   low.
[They had only seen him from afar.]
Its nest, its pallet, was of every kind of precious feather—

of lovely cotinga feathers, roseate spoonbill feathers, quetzal
   feathers.
And they also saw strewn about the heads of sundry birds,
the heads of precious birds strung together,
and some birds' feet and bones.
And the god called out to them, he said to them,
"O Mexicans, it shall be there!"
(But the Mexicans did not see who spoke.)
It is for this reason that they call it Tenochtitlan.
And the Mexicans wept, they said,
"O happy, O blessed are we!
We have beheld the city that shall be ours!
Let us go, now, let us rest. . . ."
f.88 This is in the year 2-House, 1325.

And then Quauhtlequetzqui, or Quauhcoatl, said to the
   Mexicans:[36]
"O my nobles, let us make a mound of earth,[37]
let us build a small mound,
our altar of earth where we found the eagle.
Perhaps occasionally the priest, our god, Huitzilopochtli,
will come to rest there."
Then the Mexicans said to him:
"Very well, let us do this."

They erected the mound and their altar by the edge of the
   spring, where the cactus was.
And it was because Huitzilopochtli had foretold this,
he had ordered Quauhtlequetzqui, or Quauhcoatl,
the Mexicans were to carry out his orders.

3

◧⊏⌐⌐⌐⌐⌐⌐⌐⌐⌐⌐◨

The Conquest of Mexico: The Words of the Conquered

FRAY BERNARDINO DE SAHAGÚN'S
History of all Things of New Spain (The Florentine Codex):
The Final Chapters of the Conquest

THE FOLLOWING SELECTIONS are the last two chapters of the twelfth and final book—"The Book of the Mexican Conquest"—of Sahagún's encyclopedia of the wonders of New Spain. These two chapters epitomize the loss of the Aztec world to the Spanish conquest and the ultimate clash of values between the new and old worlds.

The surrender of the Mexicans, in their soiled cloaks—no self-respecting noble would ever have been seen in the Aztec world in a soiled cape—was a symbol of ridicule and humiliation. The Mexicans were commanded by Cortéz, through his Nahuatl interpreter, Marina, the hated Malinche, to produce one thing: *gold*. The Nahuatl version of this text clearly states: "The Spaniards sought gold. They had no interest in precious jades, quetzal feathers or turquoise" (F.C. XII 491v). This was incomprehensible to the Aztec nobles. Feathers and jades were far better indicators of an Aztec's wealth than gold. The contrast between the Spanish[1] and Aztec texts clearly shows that well into the sixteenth century most Spanish readers still could not comprehend the fundamental differences in values[2] between these two disparate cultures.

The final words of the chief justice of the Ancient Mexicans, Ahuelitoctzin, are an attempt to explain to Cortéz how the empire functioned to produce the vast wealth the Spanish found there. Perhaps they were even a veiled attempt to persuade Cortéz to leave them their empire, which could produce the wealth for him that it did for Motecuzoma. Unfortunately, blinded by their lust for gold, the Spaniards probably never understood what they were being told.

Although this is one of the few pieces of prose contained in this anthology translated from Spanish,[3] it is the voice of the conquered as it was meant to be heard by the conquerors. This is a version that, perhaps, was hoped would be heard in the courts of Spain.

How the Tlaltelolcans with the Mexicans and Their Lords Surrendered to the Spaniards

Reaching the shore, Cuauhtemóctzin, the Lord of México, and all who accompanied him landed near the house where the captain was waiting. The Spaniards standing on the bank took Cuauhtémoc by the hand in a friendly manner and led him to Capitán Don Hernando Cortéz on the rooftop.

When Cuauhtémoc came before him, the captain embraced him and gave many indications of his love for him. The Spaniards looked on jubilantly, and then, elated that the conflict had come to an end, they fired all their guns and cannons.

While this was taking place, two canoes filled with Mexicans went off. The Mexicans made their way into the house of a *principal* named Coyohuehuetzin where there were some Tlaxcalan Indians and there was a fight. Several warriors were killed, and the Mexicans fled, hiding themselves.

Capitán Don Hernando Cortéz then ordered it proclaimed that all the besieged were free to go to their homes. The Mexicans came out in bands, carrying their weapons, and wherever they came upon Indian allies of the Spaniards, they killed them. This incensed the Spaniards greatly.

On the heels of the departing Mexicans, some of the Tlaltelolcans left their homes, thinking that even they would be killed if they remained. Those whose houses were on the water went off in canoes, or waded or swam, carrying their children and possessions on their backs. Many fled by night, others by day.

Posting themselves along the roads, the Spaniards and their Indian allies robbed all who passed, seizing the gold they carried and searching through their clothing and possessions. Nothing else was taken, just the gold, and beautiful young women. In order to escape, some of the women disguised themselves, smearing mud on their faces and dressing in rags. The Spaniards also seized the strong young men and boys for slaves, to whom they gave the name *tlamacazque*, servants, branding many on their faces.

The Mexicans surrendered and the fighting ceased in the year counted as 3-Houses[4] and by the count of the days under the sign called *Ce Coatl*, 1-Serpent.

The same day that Cuauhtemóctzin surrendered, he and all the *principales* were taken to Acachinanco where Don Hernando Cortéz had his quarters. The following day a great number of Spaniards entered Tlaltelolco marching in combat order. They all covered their noses because of the stench of the dead yet to be buried and along with them they brought Cuauhtemóctzin, the *principales* Coanacotzin and Tetlepanquetzatzin, and the other *principales* who were guarding the treasure.

They proceeded directly to Acachinanco, where the Mexicans had fortified themselves during the battle, and entering the house of Coyohuehuetzin, they went up to the roof, where they seated themselves. A canopy was placed there for Capitán Don Hernando Cortéz and he took his seat beneath it. Marina, the Indian woman who served as interpreter, placed herself next to him.

On the other side was Cuauhtemóctzin, the lord of México, wearing a cape called *quetzalichpetztli*, the cape of quetzal feathers. Next to him was Coanacotzin, the lord of Texcoco, wearing a cape of maguey fiber called a *xoxochiteyo*. Next were Tetlepanquetzatzin, the lord of Tlacopan, in a cape that was shoddy and soiled; Ahuelitoctzin, chief justice; and last the *principal* called Yopicatl Popocatzin. Across from them were several other Mexican *principales:* Tlacutzin; Petlauhtzin; Motelchiuhtzin, the high commander of Mexico; Coatzin, the high priest; and Tlazolyauhtl, the treasurer.

Remarks Directed by the Capitán Don Hernando Cortéz to the Lords of México, Texcoco, and Tlacopan, After His Victory, Demanding the Gold That Had Been Lost when the Spaniards Fled México

When the lords of México, Texcoco and Tlacopan, and their *principales* were gathered together before Don Hernando Cortéz, he told Marina to ask them where the gold was that had been left in México. Thereupon the Mexicans emptied a canoe filled with treasures they had hidden and set them all before the captain and the Spaniards who had accompanied him.

"Is there no more gold than this in México?" the captain asked, when he saw what was there. "Bring all of it, every bit of it!"

A *principal* named Tlacutzin said to Marina, "Tell Our Lord and God that the first time he entered the royal palace he saw all of the gold that there was. We sealed those rooms with bricks and we do not know what was done with the gold. We thought that they had carried all of it off. We have no more than what is here now."

"It is true that we took all of it," the captain replied, "but it was seized from us when we were crossing the Toltec canal. All of this must be produced at once!"

"Tell the lord captain," the *cihuacoatl*, Tlacutzin, said to Marina, "that we Mexicans do not fight on the water in canoes, that we are not versed in that kind of fighting. Only the Tlaltelolcans fight on water. It was they who intercepted our lords the Spanish and we think that it was they alone who took the gold."

"What are you saying?" said Cuauhtemóctzin to the *cihuacoatl*. "Although the Tlaltelolcans did take the gold, they were caught and returned it all. It was amassed in Texopan, and this is all of it, there is no more!"

"Our captain says this is not all of it," said Marina.

"Perhaps it was stolen by one of the commoners," replied the *cihuacoatl*. "A search shall be made and the gold brought to the captain."

"The lord captain says that you are to find two hundred pieces of gold of this size," Marina said, indicating with her hands a size about as big as the paten of a chalice.

Once again the *cihuacoatl* spoke: "Perhaps some of the women have the gold hidden under their skirts," he said. "A search shall be made and the gold brought to the captain."

Then another of the *principales*, Ahuelitoctzin, the chief justice, spoke: "Tell the lord captain that when Motecuzoma lived, the manner in which conquests were effected was such that the Mexican, Texcocan, Tlacopan, and Chinamoa warriors marched on the city or province that they wished to conquer and after conquering it, they returned to their cities and their homes. Later, the rulers of the conquered cities gave their tributes of gold, feathers, and precious stones to Motecuzoma, and all the gold came into his possession."

Part II

LIFE AND DEATH
IN ANCIENT MEXICO

The Orations of the Elders

THE TWO SELECTIONS CONTAINED IN THIS SECTION
are, for the most part, taken from Book VI of the Florentine Codex,
"The Book of Rhetoric, Moral Philosophy and Theology," part of
Fray Bernardino de Sahagún's encyclopedia of the Aztec world.
Sahagún not only preserved gems of Classic Aztec literature, he
also trained the sons of the Aztec nobility to read and write
Nahuatl as well as Latin, Spanish, and Greek. These young men

brought us much of what we now know of the Aztec world and were probably responsible for many of the histories that have come down to us today.

The first selection is a compilation of texts translated by Sullivan from a wide range of publications and strung together like a necklace for a view of life and death in the Aztec world. The second selection consists of Sullivan's translations of the words of the elders, the *Huehuetlatolli*, concerning pregnancy and childbirth. These texts constitute the most powerful statement extant on the role of women in Aztec society.

1

A Necklace of Jades

THE HUEHUETLATOLLI
Words of the Ancients; Words of Wisdom

The huehuetlatolli, *"the words of the elders, the words of the ancients," were the words of the mothers, the fathers, the rulers, the
elders, the wise men, and the ancients. They embodied the wisdom
passed down by tradition through the ages. They were, as was said,
the words of wisdom that were composed:*

> . . . at a time, in a place, which no one now can reckon,
> which no one now can recall,
> by those who sowed the seeds of the ancestral
>   grandfathers, of the ancestral grandmothers;
> those who came first, those who arrived first, who came
>   sweeping the way . . .
> were wise men.
> They were called "possessors of the books" . . .
> But the wise men soon departed . . .
> They took with them the writing, the books, the
>   paintings,
> they took with them the learning,
> they took with them all the books of song [and] the flutes.
>
> (F.C., x, 190R)

*The knowledge the wise men of tradition left behind was precious. These
words were jewels: precious jades, turquoises, and quetzal feathers. For
it was said that when such words were spoken there was:*

> . . . a sowing, there was a scattering.
> This was said of a royal orator,
> who gives good council to the people.
> After he spoke,
> after the oration had been delivered,
> They understood its truth,
> and they told him:
> The people have been enriched,
> they have become wealthy,
> there has been a sowing, a scattering of jades.
>
> (F.C., vi, 205v)

The huehuetlatolli *were formal rhetorical orations. They were known to the elders, the trained orators. These people generally were of the nobility, trained for years in the* calmecac, *formal schools for the sons and daughters of the nobility:*

> where (like gold, like jade), the sons of nobles are cast, are
>   perforated . . .
> From there come our lords, the lords, the rulers,
> those who watch over the city.
>
> (F.C., vi, 213v)

Formal rhetorical orations were a part of many events in life, for they imparted the wisdom of the ancestors in such situations. Before the merchants left on their long and arduous missions the elders would address them:

> And they [the elders] delivered their words, their
>   utterances . . .
> only accompanied by food and drink;
> it was then that the words of wisdom came
>   forth.
>
> (F.C., ix, 26v)

These words were not always kind: They warned, they admonished, and they cautioned:

. . . they admonished the merchant,
they proffered words
words full of sticks and stones,
the words of the elders, the *huehuetlatolli.*
They heaped reprimands upon him that were icy water,
  stinging nettles,
painful words that were burning, a smoking stick.
They lashed out at him thus, so that his life would be
  longer.

(F.C., ix, 33v)

*Such words of wisdom were part of an ancient tradition that kept the
fabric of society together. It was said that they were:*

. . . (the words) which the men, the women of old left you,
  handed down to you,
which are carefully folded away, stored away, in your entrails,
  in your throat.

(F.C., vi, 161r–v)

*These precious words guided people. They taught them and were woven
into their very being: their throats, their entrails. These words were
the wisdom of generations of ancestors; they embodied the precepts by
which people were expected to live.*

Death

*Life in the Aztec world was full of suffering. It was harsh. Death was
looked upon as a relief. For one who died an ordinary death, one destined
for* Tlalocan, *the underworld, a world of moisture and plenty, death
was not a terrifying thought. There was a fascination with death. Death
was a sentient being. Even in modern Mexico the Day of the Dead is
one of the most festive celebrations. Death comes to take one away,
death seeks men out, death goes his own way. In the Aztec world the
dead were bid farewell in this way:*

O my son, you have known hardship, you have endured
  suffering;

Our lord has shown you favor.
In truth the abode of us all is not here on earth.
Only for a moment, for an instant, do we warm ourselves (in
   the sun) . . .
And now the Lord of the Region of the Dead takes you, . . .
you have gone to the dwelling place of the dead,
the place of the unfleshed,
the place where the journey ends,
a place without a smoke-hole, a place without a vent.
Never again shall you return,
never again shall you make your way back . . .

(F.C., III, 24R)

*For those who died a glorious death—those who met their end according
to the precepts of society in carrying out an arduous task—their blood,
their hearts, their deaths fed the Sun and kept it moving in the cosmos,
maintaining and sustaining society on the earth. The warriors who
died in battle or became sacrificial victims, the women who died in the
battle of childbirth with a captive still in their wombs, and the merchants
lost along the way in their battle to carry out the missions of empire
were those who nourished the earth with their blood and went to live
with the Sun. The ruler, for example, would exhort his subjects to the
glory of the battlefield in the following manner:*

. . . the mother of the Sun, the father of the Sun, are born,
   come into being,
it is the Tecateccatl, the Tlacochcalcatl, the high military
   commanders
who provide food, who provide drink,
for the Sun and the Lord of the Earth.

(F.C., VI, 58v)

*Women who died in childbirth were warriors just as were men who
died on the battlefield. They too, in death, accompanied the Sun in its
glory. They were the warrior women.*

O my little one, my daughter, beloved mistress,
you have wearied yourself, manfully you have fought.

By your labors you have won Our Lord's noble death,
   glorious death
truly, now, you have toiled for it, well you have merited it;
the good, the fine, the loving death was your recompense,
   your reward . . .
Farewell my daughter, my little one!
Go to them, join them:
let them take you, let them receive you.
Be with them, amusing, shouting the praises of our mother
   and father, the Sun,
accompany them wherever they go in their rejoicing. . . .

O, our mistress, may you think of us,
may you remember us in our deprivation!
We who were a part of it,
we who were imprisoned in it here on the earth.
Truly, we are twisted by the heat, and by cold icy winds,
wizened, trembling, streaked with dirt and mud,
our entrails are filled only with misery;
we are helpless!
May you think of us, my precious daughter, Quauhcihuatl,
   divine woman.

                              (F.C., vi, 142v)

The merchants who perished carrying out their arduous missions criss-crossing the empire, both for economic gain, and the glory of empire, and sometimes as spies, were granted a glorious death too. The Marco Polos of the Aztec empire were assured of their place in the Sun. They were exhorted by the elders as follows:

Take up . . . the staff, the carrying frame.
May it be that somehow you shall perish in the desert, on
   the planes,
at the foot of a tree, at the base of the crag,
that your bones be scattered, your hair strewn about. . . .
For us who are merchants, it is our true battle.

                              (F.C., ix, 34r)

*The merchants were not just warriors in a metaphorical sense carrying
out the mission of the empire, they were soldiers, for example:*

> The merchants of Tlatelolco were also called captains and
>   soldiers,
> distinguished in merchant dress . . .
> who lay siege and make war on provinces and towns. . . .
> These merchants were like knights already and had
> special insignia for their great deeds.
>
> > (F.C., IX, 20R)

And like the warriors they accompanied the Sun.

> . . . the merchants did not truly die;
> they went to heaven,
> they accompanied the Sun on its course.
> Like those who died in battle,
> they say they accompanied the Sun,
> they went to heaven.
>
> > (F.C., IX, 22R)

Life

There were great markets throughout the empire as there are today:

> They also had fairs every twenty days—
> the number of days in a month— . . .
> and even today this type of great fair is held in
>   Tulantzinco,
> although in the cities and villages daily they sell all the
>   necessaries in the market.
> However, when this great *tianquiz* was held,
> there were many people from different provinces.
> Fairs were not held in all cities,
> but only in Tula, Tulantzinco, Teotihuacan,
> Cuauhnahuac, Tultitlan, Cholula,

and five or six other cities or places.

(Ixtlixochitl, vol. I, 283)

In the markets all manner of goods were sold. The markets offered the bounty of the empire, as great as the abundances provided by the near mythical ancestors the Toltecs had once boasted:

THE BOUNTY OF THE TOLTECS

They enjoyed great bounty;
there was an abundance of food, of the sustenances of life.

They say that the squash was so huge
that some measured six feet around
and that the ears of corn were as long as grinding stone
   mullers;
they could only be clasped with both arms.

(P.M., 171R)

There were sellers of all manners of goods in the great markets. The tortilla, a flat corn bread that may resemble in appearance slightly the Spanish omelet called a tortilla, was, and still is, the staff of life through-out Mesoamerica. The tortilla sellers were described as follows:

She who sells . . . tortillas,
sells thick ones and thin ones.
Some are round, some long, some rolled up and round.
Some are filled with cooked or uncooked bean paste and
   are fluffy,
and some are filled with chile or meat.
There are folded-over tortillas,
those that are covered with chile
and rolled up between the hands,
those that are rolled and covered with *chilmole*,
and yellow ones and white ones.

She also sells large, thin tortillas and large, thick ones;
tortillas made with eggs;

those in which the dough is made with honey,
which are shaped like gloves;
small Toluca bread [tortillas];[1]
tortillas cooked in the coals;
tortillas made of amaranth seeds and ground squash seeds
and of green corn and of prickly pears.
Some of these are cooked, others toasted,
some are cold, others hot.

                                              (F.C., x, 50R)

Tamales were another source of sustenance for the people of Meso-
america. They are described as follows:

They also ate many kinds of tamales,
like pellets they are white and roundish,
though not completely round or exactly square,
and on top they are twisted up, they are mixed with beans.
Other tamales are white but not as fine as the
   aforementioned
and somewhat tougher.
Another kind were red and are twisted shut on top;
they turn red because after the dough is made they keep
   them in the sun
or over the fire for two days, mixing it,
and thus it becomes red.
Another type is simple, not very white
but middling in color.

                                              (F.C., x, 50v)

The People and Their Ruler

The people in the Aztec world sustained the ruler, but he was also their
slave. As was said:

A bale of people, a cargo of people
you have taken upon you and loaded on your back.

This phrase was said of someone who had been installed
as king and ruler. He was told:
"You have taken upon you and loaded on your back,
a bale of people, a cargo of people.
You shall become fatigued, you shall become weary because
   of the people.
You have loaded on your back, you have taken upon you a
   great burden.
What shall be the will of our Lord tomorrow or the day
   after? . . .

(F.C., VI, 213R)

The power of the ruler was recognized to come from the people, not the
nobility.

Where have I seen that one dines on nobility?
They are the sustenances of life . . .
are what walk, what move, what rejoice, what laugh. . . .
In all truth it is said, they are the lords,
they are the rulers, they are what conquer

(F.C., VI, 72v)

Captives and sacrificial victims were also essential, not only meta-
phorically, but for the empire to influence the conquered. It was said:

. . . by means of them [the sacrificial victims], Moctezuma
   was nourished,
by means of them his destiny was fortified[2]
by means of them he was given new life[3]
by means of them he was reprieved [from death],
because of them he became a youth once more so that he
   might live a long life. . . .

(F.C., IV, 28R)

Upon his election the ruler was counseled with the wisdom of the
ancients, the Huehuetlatolli. *He was told:*

You are the substitute, the surrogate of Tloque Nahuaque,
   the lord of near and far.

You are the seat [the throne from which he rules], you are
   his flute [the mouth through which he speaks],
he speaks within you,
he makes you his lips, his jaws, his ears. . . .
He also makes you his fangs, his claws,
for you are his wild beast, you are his eater of people,
   you are his judge.

(F.C., VI, 42R)

The ruler, surrogate of Tezcatlipoca and Xiuhtecutli, was likewise told:

   . . . the flute of the lord;
   from within you he speaks.
   He has made you his lips, his mouth, his ears.

(F.C. VI, 42v)

They addressed Tezcatlipoca:

It is said that [the rulers] will make pronouncements for
   you . . .
and that they shall make pronouncements for your sire,
the mother of the gods, the father of the gods,
Huehueteotl [the Old God] who sits in the hearth, in the
   turquoise enclosure,
Xiuhtecutli, who bathes people, who cleanses people,
who metes out, who accords, the destruction, the
   glorification of commoners, the people.

(F.C., VI, 34R)

Tezcatlipoca was a capricious deity:

He thinks as he pleases,
does as he pleases;
he mocks us.
As he wishes, so he wills.
He puts us in the palm of his hand, he rolls us about;
like pebbles we spin and bounce.

He flings us this way and that,
we make him laugh; he laughs at us.

(F.C., VI, 43R)

Although the deity was capricious and arbitrary, the ruler was counseled by the elders to care for his people in this way:

Receive, speak to those who come in anguish,
who come to receive what is fated to them. . . .
Take, reach for, arrive at the truth,
for it is said, and it is true,
that you are the substitute, the surrogate, of the Lord of All,
    the Supreme Lord,
you are his drum, you are his flute, from within you he
    speaks.

(F.C., VI, 42R)

The ruler was expected to give good counsel to his subjects, to his vassals, to the other nobles, to his own family. He addressed his daughter in this way:

Pay heed to, apply yourself to, the work of women, to the
    spindle, the batten.
Watch carefully how your noblewomen, your ladies, our
    ladies, the noblewomen,
who are artisans, who are craftswomen,
dye [the thread], how they apply the dyes [to the thread],
how the heddles are set, how the heddle lashes are fixed. . . .
It is not your destiny, it is not your fate, to offer [for sale] in
    people's doorways,
greens, firewood, strings of chiles, slabs of rock salt,
for you are a noblewoman.
[Thus] see to the spindle, the batten. . . .

(F.C., VI, 77v–78R)

The ruler also had to deal with merchants, who easily became bold and arrogant because of their riches and importance:

And when they become proud and haughty
and were corrupted by the favors and honors of [their] riches,

the king was saddened and began to hate them.
He sought false or trumped-up reasons to oppress and kill
   them
although they were guiltless, out of hatred for their pride and
   arrogance,
and he distributed their wealth to the old soldiers of his court
called *cuauhchichictin,* Otomí, and *yautachcahuan,*
and thus maintained their pomp and ostentation.

(F.C., IX, 27R)

*For all this the ruler was considered a deity. He too won the battle of
empire in death and by this was destined to accompany the Sun:*

The ancients said that a ruler who died became a god.
They said, "He has become a god,"
which meant that he had died.
And thus the people were deluded
so that those who were rulers would be obeyed.
All who died were worshipped as gods:
some became images of the Sun,
others images of the Moon, etc.
[meaning other heavenly bodies and natural phenomena].

(F.C., X, 143R)

2

❏❐❐❐❐❐❐❐❐❐❐❐❏

O Precious Necklace, O Quetzal Feather

PREGNANCY AND CHILDBIRTH[1]

THESE TEXTS comprise one of the finest examples of sustained women's rhetoric that has come down to us from ancient Mexico. The texts encompass the essence of women in Aztec society and must be read from this point of view. Although these concepts may not be consonant with modern feminist views on the role of women, the Aztec notions of the battle of childbirth and the warrior status of women afforded them an ideological position and a status on par with men, who in a militaristic society represented the pinnacle of achievement as victorious soldiers or sacrificial victims. Sullivan brings out the elegance and refinement of the texts. The translation is done from a woman's point of view, and it is one of the few pieces we have of Aztec society told from this perspective. From Sullivan's original introduction:

> In the militaristic theocracy of the Aztecs the glories of battle were not limited to men alone. Every woman brought to bed with child was looked upon as a warrior going to battle, and like the warrior who achieved glory, whether he was captor or captive, so it was with a woman. If she waged her battle successfully and brought her child into the world, her glory was the glory of motherhood, the prize of her battle the child. If not, if she succumbed in her battle with the child still captive

in her womb, hers was the noble death of the warrior and she, like he, went to heaven, to the house of the sun.

For her first great battle, the preparation of the young woman begins as soon as she has conceived. . . . The announcement (that a woman is with child) is made at a feast before a gathering of both families, an occasion both joyful and solemn. It is joyful because she has in her womb "a precious stone, a quetzal feather," the seed of the ancestors sprouting anew, the promise of the continuation of the line. It is solemn because birth is a mysterious thing, dark as the womb itself, and fraught with danger. At this time she receives from the elders her first instructions on caring for herself and her unborn child.

When she is in her seventh or eighth month of pregnancy the families again gather at a feast to discuss the hiring of a midwife. The critical time has arrived. Now she needs the special ministrations of a *toltecatl, amantecatl, itlanhuatil in totecuyo*, "an artist, a craftswoman, one who receives her powers from Our Lord." An expert versed in what we still call the magic medicine.

Here the curtain goes up on our texts, the only texts in Nahuatl literature that deal with the beliefs and practices concerning pregnancy and childbirth. Starting with the hiring of the midwife and her acceptance of the case, they include rules laid down by the midwife for the pregnant woman to follow during her final months of pregnancy in order that she fight her battle to a successful conclusion—some of it is sound advice, some of it is pure superstition, and some of it is an artful brew of the two: the preparturition treatments given by the midwife in the form of massages, baths, and manipulation of the womb; the details of the delivery in normal as well as difficult cases; the operation performed by the midwife to remove a dead child and save the mother's life; and finally the account of a woman permitted, by decision of her family, to perish with the dead child in the womb in order to go to greater glories, to become one of the *Cihuapipiltin*, or Deified Women. Not the least, there is woven into the narrative the poetry of the women's orations.

Taken together, however, these texts offer something more than just an interesting collection of pre-Cortezian medical data. They also contain the essence of the Nahuatl concept of woman. As symbolized in the pregnant woman going into the battle of childbirth, in the midwife whose powers come from the deity, in the *temazcalli*, or bathhouse, the domain of the mother goddess who exercises her powers over the sick and pregnant, and best of all in the *Mocihuaquetzqui*, the woman who has died with the child in the womb, parts of whose body have the power to make young warriors invincible in battle and help sorcerer-thieves cast spells over their victims, and who is invoked to intercede with the deity on behalf of the living, the Nahuatl woman emerges as a figure of considerable force.

Students of Nahuatl culture, as well as anthropologists and social psychologists, will find a wealth of material in these texts.[2]

In the Modern Aztec world of the Sierra de Puebla, women are the makers of tortillas, the sustenance of mankind and the supernaturals of the ancient underworld, *talocan*. It is women's work that sustains life on the earth and in the holy earth. It is the Aztec woman who can still be seen "feeding" the ancestors, tossing a bit of a tortilla, perhaps unconsciously, into the home fire under her griddle. Women remain the keepers of traditions and ancient lore that has never been conquered. These translations must be read with the knowledge that many things which they contain are as true today as they were five hundred years ago.

Hiring the Midwife[3]

An elderly and honored kinswoman of the married couple addresses the midwife:

Here you are seated
here Tloque Nahuaque, has placed you
O beloved lady, our mistress, esteemed lady.
And behold, here are the old men and women, your elders.

Ah, you learn, you hear,
that the child, the little one, this girl,

wedded to him, your servant has conceived.
Your elders place her before you.

Ah, in truth now, the heart of our lord wishes to be merciful!
The Lord of the Earth would let fall from his hand
a precious necklace, a quetzal feather;
into the womb of this poor creature,
the child, the girl, wedded to this poor boy,
our lord wishes to put, wishes to place, a life.

And thus, you hear, he is leaving her, he is placing her,
in your hands, in the cradle of your lap, upon your back.
Ah, behold! Here are the old men and old women, the sires
    of the families,
who brought forth their issue like the head its hairs, the
    fingers their nails;
and also the mothers and fathers.
They give their child to you now.

Now it is time that you put her into our lord's House of
    Flowers;[4]
there the Mother, the Grandmother, the Goddess Yohualticitl[5]
strengthens people.

Let her take a vapor bath, let her be shown the bathhouse,
for it is now three or four months since conception.
How do you regard this?
Let us not be the cause of disorder;
perhaps she is not to be kneaded yet.

These few words are all that you hear, all that reaches your
    ears,
O beloved lady, our mistress, esteemed lady.
Oh that in your heart and body you were not pained by
    them, oh, that you were not vexed by them!

Who is there to address you?
Who shall put forth the words, the utterances,
intone them truly,
arrange and speak in an orderly manner
what you are listening to, what you are hearing?

They are not being hidden from you, they are not being
    concealed from you,
the men and women of old, spouters of progeny
like the head its hair, the fingers their nails, the maguey its
    thorns, the prickly pear its prickles
the grandfathers and grandmothers who departed
casting behind them, leaving behind them, the girl, the
    young woman,
and him, your servant, your Eagle, your Jaguar.[6]
By chance now, in their absence, their backs turned,
they give a thought to things here?
They have gone
they have gone to lie in the final abode of all,
a place without a chimney, a place without a vent;
now they repose beside, close to, Our Mother and Father
    Mictlantecutli.[7]

Would that it had been their time!
Would that it had been in their presence!
Ah, they would have wept, they would have been moved
by what we dream by what we see as in a dream,
the marvel, the wonder!
that inside their offshoot, their issue,
our lord wishes to put a life.
Ah, it would have been they who addressed you!

But in their absence, their backs turned, we do childish,
    puerile things:
stuttering and stammering, we utter the words, the phrases
    here,
crudely and in a jumble, we intone them, we arrange them.

With these words, with these phrases, oh, we entreat you!
May you be merciful to the child, the little one, the girl,
may you perform your office, your functions.
For you, the midwives, are our lord's artists and
    craftswomen,
you are empowered by him.

This is all you hear, all that reaches your ears.
May you toil, may you labor,
may you work in concert with our lord, may you aid him!

*The midwife, by whose ministrations children are born, who adjusts
the womb, who delivers women, speaks. She says:*

Here you are,
here our lord, the Lord of the Earth, has placed you,
you, the old men and women,
begetters of these precious necklaces, of these quetzal
    feathers,
spouters of progeny like the maguey its thorns, the
    prickly pear its prickles,
like hair, nails, eyebrows.

And behold, you are here,
here you are present, you our elders,[8]
for you are the great mothers and fathers
our lord ordained as divine;
you are Oxomoco and Cipactonal.[9]

I hear, I grasp, your words, your utterances,
and your weeping, your sorrow.
It is because of her, your precious necklace, your quetzal
    feather,
the young woman who is your middle daughter,
perhaps your eldest daughter, perhaps your youngest
    daughter
that you weep and are sorrowful;
it is because of her that you are anguished.
Ah, in truth now, you call, you cry out to,
you invoke the Midwife, Mother of the Gods, Our Mother,
    Yohualticitl,
who has in her care, in her hands, in her trust,
the House of Flowers on earth, the bathhouse.
There the Grandmother, Yohualticitl, uses her skill,
she puts people in order, she strengthens them.
In her hands, in her lap, upon her back,
you place your precious necklace, your quetzal feather,

and what adorns her,
what our lord, Tloque Nahuaque, has bestowed upon her,
what he has put in her womb.

These few words are all I have to say.
Oh, hapless wretched woman that I am!
Who am I that you should choose me,
whose eyes do not see, whose ears do not hear,
who does nothing well for our lord?
I know nothing, I understand nothing!

There have been, there have existed, there have excelled,
artisans of our lord possessed of eyes, possessed of ears.
They were entrusted with the knowledge;
the lord, our god, looked into their eyes,
he blew his breath upon them,
they were empowered by him.
And now there are those who are as they, who do as
    they,
his workers, also.
This that I am told here, that I hear,
is their knowledge, is their profession.
In truth now, how have you settled on me?
Perhaps it comes from the lips of our lord Tloque
    Nahuaque,
the great lord, invisible as the night, impalpable as the
    wind.
Perhaps he sets me there,
perhaps there shall be my ruin, my destruction.
Perhaps our lord has become weary;
perhaps, in something, I have become wearisome.

And though it be said that I am a midwife,
by chance shall I, with my hands, create, fashion, the
    precious necklace, the quetzal feather?
Is the lot willed for us the precious necklace, the quetzal
    feather,
our lord puts into the womb of your precious necklace,
    your quetzal feather?

And though I be skilled at my craft,
am I, perhaps, to put myself behind the shield, the
    buckler,
of my daughter, my little one, present here,
on whose account you are anguished?

Perhaps our lord shall be careless though I have done my
    work,
though it be done and I am overweening in it.
Perhaps I shall place the child sideways,
perhaps I shall set it on its side,
or perhaps I shall shatter it![10]
Oh, hapless, wretched woman that I am,
perhaps our lord shall devise my end!

Oh, my children, our lords, beloved lords, my
    grandchildren,
perhaps it is not of your human contriving; you merely
    cry out.
Perhaps it comes from the lips of the Lord of the Earth.

So let the command of our lord be fulfilled, be done,
and let your words be answered.
Let us put all of our strength into it,
let us toil for this gift that our lord sends, that he drops
    from his hand,
with which he adorns the young woman, the little dove,
    our little one.

And what are we to say now?
By chance, shall we say that Tloque Nahuaque has
    favored us?
Rather, that now he wishes to favor us,
for it is the mysterious, the obscure that we speak about.
Hence, what are we to say?
Let us now put our trust in him by virtue of whom one
    lives;
let us await what is being determined,
or what, perhaps has been determined Above, in the
    Region of the Dead, and in the Region of Darkness.

What is it that has been determined for us?
What has been fated for us?
What has been meted out to us?
By chance is it true?
By chance Tloque Nahuaque shall make the day dawn,
    the Sun to shine?
By chance are we to look upon the head, the countenance
    of him
who, like a precious necklace, a quetzal feather,
our lord wishes to let fall from his hand?
Or, by chance, wee as he is, shall he be destroyed?
Shall he destroy the little one, perhaps?
Or, by chance shall the little creature carry off my
    daughter, the precious dove?
O, my children, our lords, I am wearying you!
Let us work in concert with Tloque Nahuaque!
Let our lord's House of Flowers be warmed, be heated,
let my daughter enter the Mother of All, the
    Grandmother, Yohualticitl.

The kinswomen of the pregnant woman, the old women, speak. They say to her:[11]

May you do your work, O beloved lady, honored mother, our
    mistress;
may you work in concert with the goddess, Quilaztli.[12]
And may you put the child, the girl, into our lord's House of
    Flowers, the bathhouse,
where the Grandmother, the Grandmother of the Bathhouse,
    Yohualticitl, dwells,
where she watches over it.

Then the midwife herself kindles the fire, heats the bathhouse, and puts the girl into it. There she kneads the pregnant woman's stomach; she rights the child, she sets it straight, she changes its position, she manipulates it, she places it correctly.

If the midwife is a bit unwell, some alternate kindles the fire, heats the bathhouse, and when the pregnant woman leaves the bath it is then that the midwife massages her. She kneads the pregnant woman's stom-

ach often; sometimes the pregnant woman is not in the bathhouse, nor does she bathe. This is called "massaging her dry."

In the bathhouse the midwife sometimes orders them not to beat the pregnant woman's back with force;[13] nor that the bath be too hot, for the midwife says the child will adhere, it will be stuck fast. Neither shall they beat her, nor shall her stomach become too hot, as the child will die of the heat, it will fill up with heat.

The midwife also orders the pregnant woman not to heat herself unduly nor heat her back, either with sun or with fire, as her child will adhere, also.

And she also orders, she instructs the pregnant woman not to sleep during the day, as the eyelids of the child will be swollen when it is born.

The midwife leaves her many instructions, she watches over her, she regulates her life during the time she is with child.

She tells the pregnant woman not to chew gum, for when the child is born its lips will be enlarged, it will do nothing but open and close its mouth. Because of this, it is said, its lips will be enlarged, it will be thick-lipped. As a consequence it will not be able to suckle and it will die.

She tells her that it is not good to look at things that anger people, that frighten people, that upset people, it will do the same to the child.

Also, what the pregnant woman desires, she is to be given at once, it is not to be delayed, for her child will suffer if she is not given what she desires at once.

The midwife also tells her, she orders her, not to look at the color red, as the child will be born sideways.

The midwife also tells the pregnant woman that she must not neglect to eat, as the child will go hungry. And she tells the pregnant woman not to eat earth, not to eat chalk, as the child will be born unhealthy, deranged, perhaps sickly, perhaps deformed, for what the mother drinks, what the mother eats, is incorporated into the child, it takes it from her.

The midwife also instructs the pregnant woman that when the child is still not large, in the first, the second, the third months, she and her husband should lie with each other occasionally so that the child will become robust; if not, it will come into the world sickly, it will not be strong.

And the midwife instructs the pregnant woman and her mothers that when she nears her term, when her stomach is now big, she and her husband are not to take their pleasure with each other even occasionally, she is not to enjoy copulation at all because the child will not be born clean, it will come out covered with filth as if it had been washed in thick corn gruel, and from this it will be apparent that they never stopped, they continued copulating all during the time she was with child, as if there were little shame in it then. Furthermore at the time of the pregnant woman's childbed, the delivery will become arduous. She will be in great suffering a long time—two or three days—and then, when she is giving birth, she will scream with pain. She might suffer two days, perhaps, as the semen will be like liquid amber; that was not the time for her to have received, to have taken in the semen. In order that she give birth, the midwife will have to cut her, or someone will have to shake her, will have to hold her up in her arms. And also she will have to dismember the child so that it is reduced to bits inside her when she is giving birth. Some children die in the mothers' wombs because they adhere somewhere, or else are lying sideways. Also, because of this, the women often die when they give birth. They say the semen adheres to her loins, meaning her womb, that it spreads over the child's sack and, as a result, the child cannot be born, it cannot come into the world, and it dies there. Because of this, the mother also dies and is called a "woman warrior." For the child no longer absorbs the semen; it becomes like an oozing sore, it adheres to the healthy flesh of the woman.

(Something remarkable must also be told here. When the child adheres to the mother's womb, if the child has died, the midwife inserts an obsidian knife into the woman's womb. There she cuts up the child and removes it piece by piece. By this means the mother is helped.)

The midwife orders that the pregnant woman is not to weep, that she is not to be made unhappy, that she is not to be upset, as the child will become ill as a result.

The midwife orders that she eat well, that she drink well, that everything she eats be good, that it be hot and savory, particularly at the time they say, "the child is washing its feet," when the mother has her period so that the child does not dry up, so that it does not become disordered.

The midwife orders the pregnant woman not to attempt to do too much, not to overexert herself, not to lift anything heavy, not to run. Neither is anyone to frighten her nor startle her now, for they say that

*then the mother will miscarry, they say the child will be born
prematurely.*

*These few things related here are instructions for the pregnant
woman.*

The midwife speaks:

O my children, beloved lords, our lords!
Here you are.
Are you children? Are you babies?
We who address each other are old women.
You understand that for all women our death is in our
    wombs.
By chance does the child, the girl, know this yet?
Do not neglect the child;
have great concern for her now.
Now let your eyes, your labors, be exercised,
lest we meet with something,
lest something befall us at the time of the child's birth.

Behold, here I am, I who am called a midwife!
In truth I am just a simple midwife.
By chance do I have a remedy for death?
By chance shall I snatch someone from it when something
    happens?
By chance is the remedy for death in my hands?
Do I carry it around with me?
One is only aided, one is only helped by our lord,
and we merely fan away the flies.
By chance are we to say,
"Let it be thus, let the child be born without mishap?"

By chance shall we presume,
and shall we assume the mercy of Tloque Nahuaque?
However it is, so shall it be.
In truth now let us pray.
Let us put our trust in our lord.
What does he will?
Perhaps something is our due, our reward?
Perhaps, also nothing?

Only weeping, only tears are wanted now.
May you consider this, O our lords, O my grandchildren,
  beloved lords!

The Lying-in

*When the time has come for the woman's confinement, they summon
the midwife, the accoucheuse, the woman in whose hands is the delivery.
With respect to the offspring of the wealthy and prosperous, about four
or five days before they are to give birth, the midwives take their places
beside them. They take care of them, they wait with them for the time
to arrive for the moment they will feel pain. . . .*

*And when the woman now feels pain, when she is soon to give birth,
the midwife quickly gives her a vapor bath. Then she has her drink a
potion of an herb called* cihuapahtli, *which is an impellant and ex-
pellant. If the woman's labor is causing her great suffering, she has
her drink a potion of about two small pieces of an opossum's tail. Finally
she expels it completely, with this she gives birth easily. . . .*

If the woman has drunk potions of cihuapahtli *and opossum, and
if her womb does not react, the midwife and the old women become
alarmed. They weep, they are sorrowful. The midwife says:*

> O my child, what does our lord will?
> What is to befall us?
> Let us await the word of Tloque Nahuaque,
> that he snatch nothing from us!

*Then the midwife begins. She holds her up, she shakes her, she beats
her on the back with her feet, saying to her:*

> My daughter the battle is yours.
> What are we to do for you?
> Here are your mothers,
> yours alone is the task.

> Take up the buckler, my daughter, my little one.
> You are Quauhcihuatl; work with her!
> This means, put forth all your strength,
> emulate Quauhcihuatl, Cihuacoatl, Quilaztli. . . .

And when the child was born, the midwife cried out, she gave the war
cry that signified that the woman had fought her battle well, that she
had been a valiant warrior, that she had taken a captive, that she had
captured a child.

Then the midwife spoke to it. If it is a male child she said:

> You have come into the world, my little one, my beloved
>   boy, my beloved youth.

> (If it is a girl she said: "My beloved girl, my little one, noble
>   lady.")

You have wearied yourself, you have fatigued yourself
Your father, the lord, Tloque Nahuaque, Creator of People,
    Maker of People has sent you.
You have arrived on earth
where your relatives, your kin, suffer hardships, endure
    affliction,
where it is hot, it is cold, it is windy.
It is a place of thirst, it is a place of hunger,
a place without pleasure, a place without joy,
a place of suffering, a place of fatigue, a place of torment.

O my little one, perhaps, for a brief time, you shall shine
    as the sun!
By chance are you our reward, our recompense?
By chance shall you look into the faces, on the heads,
of your grandfathers, your grandmothers, your kinsmen,
    those of your line?
And by chance shall they look into your face, upon your
    head?

And how have you been arrayed, how have you been
    adorned?
How has your father, your mother, Ometecutli, Omecihuatl
    arrayed you?
What have they bestowed upon you?
How have you come?
With what have you come arrayed?

By chance something is our reward?
By chance something is our recompense?
By chance our lord, Tloque Nahuaque, shall count you as
   something?
By chance he shall reward you as something?
Or perhaps there is no merit, there is no favor.
Perhaps you were born a blighted ear of corn.
Perhaps dirt, filth, is your lot, your destiny.
Perhaps you shall steal from other people's bowls, from
   other people's vessels.
With what are you arrayed, with what are you clothed in
   Yohuayan [darkness]?

You have wearied yourself, you have fatigued yourself, my
   little one,
my beloved child, precious necklace, quetzal feather,
   precious one.
You have arrived.
You may rest, you may repose.

Here are your grandfathers, your grandmothers who have
   been awaiting you.
Here, into their hands, you have come.
Do not sigh, do not sorrow.
What is to be done? You have arrived, you have come!
Ah, in truth, you shall suffer torment, you shall endure
   affliction!

O my little one, my beloved child, you have wearied
   yourself, you have fatigued yourself.
May Tloque Nahuaque, your mother, your father, the
   Maker, adorn you, provide for you!
And we who are parents, shall we, perhaps, regard
   ourselves as worthy of you?
Perhaps wee as you are the Maker shall summon you, shall
   call to you.
Perhaps you shall merely pass before our eyes.
Perhaps we have had only a brief glimpse of you.
Let us await the word of our lord, my beloved child.

Cutting the Umbilical Cord

Then the midwife cuts the child's umbilical cord, she removes the umbilical cord. And she takes what is called the afterbirth, which had covered the baby, which had enveloped him. She buried this in a corner [of the house]. The child's umbilical cord is kept. It is set out to dry. Later [the warriors] take it with them to battle.

(The midwife addresses the infant boy.)

My beloved child, my precious one,
here are the precepts, the principles
your father, your mother, Yohualtecutli, Yohualticitl, have
    laid down.
From your body, the middle of your body, I remove, I cut
    the umbilical cord.

Know this, understand this:
Your home is not here.
You are the Eagle, you are the Jaguar,
you are the precious scarlet bird,
you are the precious golden bird of Tloque Nahuaque;
you are his serpent, you are his bird.
Only your nest is here.
Here you only break out of your shell,
here you only arrive, you only alight,
here you only come into the world.
Here like a plant, you sprout, you burst into bloom, you
    blossom.
Here like a fragment struck from a stone, chipped from a
    stone, you are born.
Here you only have your cradle, your blanket, your pillow
    where you lay your head.
This is only the place of arrival.

Where you belong is elsewhere:
You are pledged, you are promised, you are sent to the
    field of battle.
War is your destiny, your calling.
You shall provide drink,

you shall provide food,
you shall provide nourishment for the Sun, for the Lord of
the Earth.
Your true home, your domain, your patrimony is the House
of the Sun in heaven
where you shall shout the praises of, where you shall
amuse, the Everlastingly Resplendent One.

Perhaps you shall merit, perhaps you shall earn,
death by the obsidian knife in battle,
death by the obsidian knife in sacrifice.

This cord is removed from your body,
that comes from the middle of your body,
That I take from you,
is the property, the possession of the Lord of the Earth, of
the Sun.
And when war stirs, when war breaks out,
it shall be put into the hands of the Eagles, the Jaguars, the
valiant warriors.
They shall give it to your mother, your father, the Sun, the
Lord of the Earth.
They shall bury it in the middle, in the center, of the
battlefield,
and with it you shall be pledged, you shall be promised to
the Sun, to the Lord of the Earth.

With this you shall make yourself an offering,
with this your name shall be inscribed,
your name shall be set down, in the middle, in the center
of the battlefield,
so that you are not forgotten,
so that your name, your glory are not lost.
This precious object taken from your body
shall be counted as your offering of maguey thorns,
tobacco, reeds, pine branches.
It shall be your act of penance, it shall stand as your vow.

And now let us be hopeful.
Perhaps you shall merit,
perhaps you shall be worthy of some reward.

Work, my precious child!
May Tloque Nahuaque mold you, provide for you;
may he adorn you.

*If the child is a girl, when the midwife cuts the umbilical cord, she says
to her:*

My beloved daughter, my little girl, you have wearied
    yourself, you have fatigued yourself.
Our lord, Tloque Nahuaque, has sent you here.
You have come to a place of hardship, a place of affliction,
    a place of tribulation.
A place that is cold, a place that is windy.

Listen now:
From your body, from the middle of your body, I remove,
    I cut the umbilical cord.
Your father, your mother, Yohualtecutli, Yohualticitl, have
    ordered, have ordained
that you shall be the heart of the house.
You shall go nowhere,
you shall not be a wanderer.
You shall be the covering of ashes that banks the fire,
you shall be the three stones on which the cooking pot
    rests.
Here our lord buries you, inters you,
and you shall become worn, you shall become weary.
You are to prepare drink, you are to grind corn,
you are to toil, you are to sweat, beside the ashes, beside
    the hearth.

*Then the midwife buries the girl's umbilical cord next to the hearth. It
is said that this signifies that a woman goes nowhere, that her place is
in the house, in the home; that it is not proper for her to go anywhere.
And it means that it is her duty to prepare meals: that she is to prepare
drink, that she is to prepare food, that she is to grind corn, that she is
to spin, that she is to weave.*

The Washing of the Newborn Child

When the midwife had finished, when she had cut the child's umbilical cord, then she bathed it [the child], she washed it. All the while she spoke to it. If it was a boy she said:

Go to your mother, Chalchiuhtlicue!
May she take you.
May she cleanse you.
May she purify you.
May she carry away, many she remove, the filth you received
   from your mother, your father.
May she cleanse your heart;
may she make it good, may she make it pure.
May she bestow upon you a good life, a pure life.

Then the midwife addresses the goddess, Chalchiuhtlicue, the water. She says:

O goddess, our lady, Chalchiuhtlicue, Chalchiuhtlatonac,
   the creature has arrived.
Our father, our mother, Ometecutli, Omecihuatl, who are
   in Omeyocan, in the ninth heaven,
have sent him here.
What was given him in Yohuayan?
What does he bring with him?
In what does he come arrayed?
In what does he come swaddled?
Does he come free of imperfection, perhaps?
What evil, what taint of his mother, of his father does he
   have?
What blackness, what filth, what corruption of his mother,
   of his father does the child possess?

He is in your hands now.
Take him, cleanse him, purify him,
for it is you who know what must be done.
He has been left in your hands.
Remove from him the blackness, the filth, the corruption
   of his mother, of his father.

Does he come free of imperfection, perhaps?
Let the evil, the corruption with which he comes be
    carried off by the water;
let it be destroyed.
Let his heart, his life, be made good, be made pure, be
    made clean,
that he may live his life on earth peacefully, tranquilly.
Let the water carry off the dirt, the filth, deposited on him;
let the water carry it off, let it be destroyed.
Now, O goddess, our lady, Chalchiuhcihuatl,
    Chalchiuhtlicue,
Chalchiuhtlatonac, mother of the gods, sister of the gods,
he is in your hands,
the creature has been left in your hands,
and you were given the gift, the power, in Yohuayan to
    cleanse, to purify people.
Now he shall come before you.
O, our lady, may your heart be bountiful!

*Here is another prayer that the midwife says, that she addresses to the
goddess Chalchiuhtlicue. She says to her:*

O, our lady, Chalchiuhtlicue, Chalchiuhtlatonac, the creature
    has arrived!
May you receive him.

*The midwife takes the water; she blows her breath on it. Then she has
the child taste it and puts some on his head and chest. [As she does
this] she speaks to the child. She says:*

Oh my precious one, my beloved boy (or she says, "my
    beloved girl")
go to your mother, your father Chalchiuhtlicue,
    Chalchiuhtlatonac.
Let her take you.
It is she who will bear you in her arms,
it is she who will carry you on her back in this world.

Then she washes the child, saying to it:

Enter descend into the blue water, the yellow water.
May Tloque Nahuaque cleanse you, purify you.
May he carry away the filth deposited on you, smeared on
   you, in Yohuayan.
Let the evil, the taint, of your mother, your father,
and the dirt, the dung, of your mother, your father, be gone!

*After she has finished washing the child, she wraps it up. As she does
so, she speaks to it. She says:*

O precious necklace, O quetzal feather,
O jade, O armlet, O turquoise!
In Omeyocan, the ninth heaven, you were created;
your father, your mother, Ometecutli, Omecihuatl,
   fashioned you, created you.
You have come into the world, a place of suffering, a place
   of affliction,
a place of searing heat, bitter cold, harsh winds.
It is a place of hardship, a place of thirst, a place of hunger.
It is a place of cold, a place of tears.
Indeed, it is not an agreeable place;
it is a place of weeping, a place of sorrow, a place where
   one suffers affliction.
Here your task shall be weeping, tears, sorrow, fatigue.
O my precious one, my beloved boy (or "my beloved girl"),
   you have arrived.
Rest now, repose on this earth.
May our lord, Tloque Nahuaque, mold you, provide for
   you.

The Midwife Addresses the Newly Delivered Woman

O my daughter, O valiant woman, you worked, you
   toiled.
You soared like an eagle, you sprang like a jaguar,
you put all your strength behind the shield, behind the
   buckler;
you endured.

You went forth into battle, you emulated our mother,
  Cihuacoatl Quilaztli,
and now our lord has seated you on the Eagle Mat, the
  Jaguar Mat.
You have spent yourself, O my daughter,
now be tranquil.
What does our lord, Tloque Nahuaque will?
Shall he bestow his favors upon each of you separately, in
  separate places?
Perhaps you shall go off, and leave the child that has
  arrived.
Perhaps, as small as he is, the creator will summon him,
  will call out to him,
or perhaps, he shall come to take you.
Do not be boastful [of the child].
Do not consider yourself worthy of it.
Call out humbly to our lord, Tloque Nahuaque. . . .

The Warrior Woman

*If after a day and a night the woman does not give birth, then once
again she is put in the bathhouse. There once more a vain attempt is
made, the midwife adjusts the womb. If the efforts are hopeless, if the
child is not born, then they shut the woman in a room; only the midwife
is by her side. Who knows how the midwife prays. She calls upon them
all, she prays to Cihuacoatl, Quilaztli, then she cries out to Yohualticitl,
and who knows to which others she cries out.*

*And the midwife who is expert, adept, skilled at her craft, if she has
seen that the child has died, if it no longer moves, and if the woman
is still in great pain, she then inserts her hand into the woman's vagina,
she introduces the obsidian knife. She cuts the child up, and piece by
piece she removes the child's body.*

*If the parents cannot face having the midwife do this, then the woman
is shut securely in the room.[14] And if she should die in childbirth, if
she is called, she is given the name, she becomes a Mocihuaquetzqui,
a Warrior Woman.[15]*

After her death, they bathe her, they soap her, and they dress her. . . . They carry her off, take her to be buried,[16] her husband bears her on his back. Her hair is loose, it covers her.

The midwives and old women gather.
They accompany her carrying shields, shouting war cries,
    beating their mouths with their hands and shouting.
Shouting huzzahs to her, they are like the warriors
    following along.

She is taken to be buried at twilight, before the images of the goddesses,[17] the Cihuapipiltin, the Celestial Noblewomen. Having arrived there, they bury her, they lay her in the earth. For four nights her husband and others who assist him guard her so that no one steals her body. . . .

The Telpopochtin,[18] whose occupation is war, fight them, do battle with them, they seek to capture the woman's body. This is not a sham, they do not play a child's game, they fight each other in earnest.

. . . They say that they [the young warriors] keep nightly vigils over it [the body], they regard it as something magical. If along the way they force the midwives to surrender the body of the Mocihuaquetzque, right there, in front of everyone, they cut off her finger. . . .

. . . When they go off to war they put the hair or the finger inside the shield so that they will be brave, so that they will be valiant, so that no one will be able to face them in battle. . . . They say that the hair and the finger of the Mocihuaquetzque have great powers; they say that they benumb the feet of their foes.

The thieves who are called the sorcerer-thieves[19] also covet the body of the Mocihuaquetzque. . . . They carry it [the arm] with them when they rob, with it they mesmerize the householders.

Although they weep and grieve for the Mocihuaquetzqui because she has died in childbirth, when she is dead they say that she has become a warrior woman, and for this reason, the parents and husband are also joyful. They say she is not going to Mictlan,[20] that she is going to heaven, the House of the Sun.

According to legend, according to lore, the valiant warriors, the Eagle and Jaguar warriors who die in battle go to the House of the Sun and dwell in the East where the Sun rises. When the Sun is about to rise, just before daybreak, they adorn themselves, they don their array and they go out to receive the Sun when he comes up. They bring him out, they come out shouting huzzahs to him. They carry him to the middle of the heavens, to the zenith.

. . . It is said that the women who die in battle, the women who die in childbirth, dwell in the region of the setting Sun, in the West. Thus, the ancients, who created the traditions, named the West Cihuatlampa, the region of the women, because there the women dwell.

And when the Sun has risen, when it is moving on its course, the warriors who died in battle, the valiant warriors accompany him shouting huzzahs and amuse him. When the Sun is well on his way, then the women adorn themselves, they don their array, they take their shields and weapons. They arise, they ascend, they go out to receive the Sun at the zenith. There from the hands of the Eagle and Jaguar warriors who died in battle they take the Sun. There in the hands of the women the Eagle and Jaguar warriors leave the Sun, and then they scatter. Everywhere (in the heavens) they sip nectar, they sip the nectar of the myriad flowers.

Now the women start out with the Sun; they carry him, they bring him down. With quetzal feather crosspieces for a seat they convey him; he journeys borne in a litter of quetzal feathers. While bearing him they also go along shouting huzzahs, amusing him, amusing him with skirmishes. They leave him at the place called "where the sun goes in." It is said that they leave him in the hands of the Micteca, which means the people of the Region of the Dead, the inhabitants of the Region of the Dead. . . .

The ancients said that when it is nightfall here, it is dawn, it is daybreak in the Region of the Dead. And when the women leave the Sun in the hands of the people of the Region of the Dead, they too scatter, they go off, they descend to earth. They come to take, they come to look for spindles, battens, baskets—they come to look for all the womanly implements.

In this way the demon of the night, the demon of the winds,[21] practiced deception: many times he would appear, he would show himself to people in the form of a Mocihuaquetzqui. He would call to, he would appear to her husband[22] and he would demand, he would ask for skirts, blouses, and all the womanly implements.

Invocation of the Warrior Woman

. . . The woman who dies with a child in her womb, who is called Mocihuaquetzqui, at the moment she died was deified, they say. When she was still lying there, when her body was still reposing there, the midwife invoked her, prayed to her, supplicated her, entreated her. She said to her:

O, Chamotzin,[23] my little child,
O, Quauhcihuatl, O little one, little dove, O my daughter!
You have labored, you have toiled,
your labors have come to rest;
you have worked with your mother, the goddess
    Quauhcihuatl, Quilaztli.
You took up, you raised aloft, you wielded the shield, the
    buckler,
that your mother, the goddess Cihuacoatl, Quilaztli, placed
    in your hand.

Awake! Arise! Stand up!
It is now day, it is now dawn.
The scarlet glow of daybreak has risen, the dawn has
    come up;
the flame-tinged curassow and the flame-tinged swallow
    are singing now,
so sing the sundry flame-tinged roseate spoonbills.
Arise! Stand up! Array yourself!
Be off, betake yourself to the good place, the fine place,
the House of your mother and father the Sun!
Let his sisters, the divine celestial women, take you to
    him,
they who always and forever know joy and happiness,
    gladness and delight,
next to, beside, our mother and father the Sun,
amusing him, shouting his praises!

O my little one, my daughter, beloved mistress,
you have wearied yourself, manfully you have fought.
By your labors you have won Our Lord's noble death,
    glorious death

truly, now, you have toiled for it, well you have merited it;
the good, the fine, the loving death was your recompense,
    your reward.
By chance have you died in vain?
Perhaps you have died, it has been your penance.
Who is granted what you have merited?
Eternally you shall live and know joy and gladness
next to, beside, our mistress, the divine woman.

Farewell my daughter, my little one!
Go to them, join them:
let them take you, let them receive you.
Be with them, amusing, shouting the praises of our
    mother and father, the Sun,
accompany them wherever they go in their rejoicing.

O my little one, my daughter, my mistress,
you have gone off leaving us behind,
you have gone off kicking us away, we the old men and
    women,
and you have departed flinging aside your mother and
    father.
But was it you who willed it?
You were summoned, you were called!
And what now!
In your absence, with your back turned, we shall perish!
What now?
A pauperous old age filled with misery,
and we shall end our days beside others' walls, in the
    corners of others' houses!

O, our mistress, may you think of us,
may you remember us in our deprivation!
It is as if we were beholding it,
as if we were imprisoned in it here on the earth.
Verily, we are twisted by the heat, and by cold icy winds,
wizened, trembling, streaked with dirt and mud,
our entrails are filled only with misery;
we are helpless!

May you think of us, my precious daughter, Quauhcihuatl,
  divine woman.

For you have gone on to be happy;
in the good place, the fine place where you now dwell,
and beside, next to Our Lord, you now live.
You behold him now with human eyes,
you invoke him now with human voice.
May you pray to him for us, may you invoke him for us!
With all this we commend ourselves to you.
It is finished.

Part III

PRAYERS AND SONGS
OF THE GODS

THE SONGS OF THE AZTECS WERE SOME OF THE MOST
fully developed and enigmatic pieces that have come down to us.
The songs were the highest form of aesthetic achievement, as well
as the most archaic and difficult to translate, for they sought to
maximize meaning through metaphor. Most of the translations
of these pieces that we have in English, with the notable
exceptions of the work of Brinton and Bierhorst and a handful of
others, are in fact taken from translations to Spanish.

The first of the three selections presented is a prayer, perhaps
one of the most moving in the entire Sahaguntine corpus, which
has more in common with the *Huehuetlatolli* than with the songs.
The second piece consists of five short examples of Classic Aztec
poetry, the so-called flowersongs. The third is taken from the
corpus of twenty hymns, called by Brinton the "Rig Veda
Americanus," found in the *Primeros Memoriales* of Sahagún.

1

⟨▨▨▨▨▨▨▨▨▨⟩

A Prayer to Tlaloc

THE PRAYER TO TLALOC is a special literary genre, different from the formal orations of the Aztec elders, in that it is addressed directly to the deity. The best possible introduction to this piece is, as Sullivan observed, Sahagún's own heading for the text.

The prayer they delivered with great feeling when they invoked Tlaloc to whom they attributed the rain. They said he ruled over Tlalocan, which they regarded as a sort of Garden of Eden, where other gods, called Tlaloque, also dwelled, and a goddess, their sister, called Chicomecoatl, who is similar to Ceres. The fire priests made this supplication when there was drought and they asked for rain. It is a remarkable prayer, and in it are revealed many of the false notions that existed in the past.

This prayer is truly a jewel of Classic Aztec literature. As Sullivan writes:

A moving and eloquent plea for the survival of man and beast, and the vegetation upon which both depend, this prayer sharply etches the physical anguish that man, animal, and the earth suffer as a result of drought and famine, and, in addition, a deeper anguish regarding the fate of the world, a fear the people lived with daily and which motivated much of their thinking: whether, as predicted in ancient times, the cataclysm that was to eventually destroy the world was now imminent. This impassioned and mellisonant appeal to the god of rain takes us into the mind of the believer, bringing to life for us

Tlaloc, the Tlaloque, Chicomecoatl, the various hereafters, and numerous other Nahuatl concepts, with an immediacy few other texts have.

This prayer, together with thirty-nine other lofty and lyrical prayers and orations delivered on a diversity of religious, political, and social occasions, combines to make Book VI of the Florentine Codex a magnificent anthology of Nahuatl prose and poetry, one of the best—if not the best—sources for the study of the language (and the most difficult), and an inexhaustible mine of information of Nahuatl beliefs and customs. More than any other of the eleven other books of this great codex, it brings us closest to the living spirit of the Nahuatl people.

By Sahagún's own testimony at the end of the book, we know that he gathered the material in 1547, twenty-six years after the conquest, when the old culture was still very much alive in those who had been born into it. As for the authenticity of the texts, the final word on this was said by Sahagún four hundred years ago: *What is written in this book is not possible for a human mind to invent, nor is there a man living capable of inventing the kind of language contained in it.*

This piece addresses directly the anguish and deprivation that results from drought, pleading with the Lord of the Earth, Tlaloc, for his favor, the precious moisture that he alone controls, an essential ingredient for sustaining life. The prayer is a supplication.[1]

O, Tlaloc!

O Lord, Our Lord, O Provider, O Lord of Verdure
Lord of Tlalocan[2], Lord of the Sweet-Scented Marigold,[3] Lord of Copal![4]
The gods, Our Lords, the Providers
the Lords of Rubber,[5] the Lords of the Sweet-Scented
    Marigold, the Lords of Copal,
have sealed themselves in a coffer, they have locked
    themselves in a box.
They have hidden the jade and turquoise and precious jewels
    of life,[6]

they have carried off their sister, Chicomecoatl,[7] the fruits of
   the earth,
and the Crimson Goddess, the chile.

Oh, the fruits of the earth lie panting;
the sister of the gods, the sustenances of life,
feebly drags herself along,
she is covered with dust, she is covered with cobwebs,
she is utterly worn and weary.

And behold the people, the subjects[8] are perishing!
Their eyelids are puffy, their mouths as dry as straw,
their bones are desiccated, and they are twisted and gaunt,
their lips are thin, their necks pale and scrawny.

And the children, the little ones—
those who barely walk, those who crawl
those still on the ground making little piles of earth and
   broken bits of pottery
and the infants lashed to their boards and slats[9]
all of them are hollow-eyed.

Everyone knows anguish and affliction,
everyone is gazing upon torment;
no one has been overlooked.

All living things are suffering.
The troupial and roseate spoonbill[10] drag themselves along,
they topple over and lie prostrate on their backs,
weakly opening and closing their beaks.
And the animals: the dogs[11] of the Lord of All and the
   Everywhere are reeling;
they take refuge among us, vainly they lick the earth.
Man and beast alike are crazed for the want of water,
they die for the want of water,
they are perishing, they are wasting away, they are vanishing!

The breast of our mother and father, Lord of the Earth is dry;
no longer can she nourish, no longer can she feed,
no longer can she suckle what sprouts, what comes forth,
what is the very life, of the people, their food and their
   sustenance.

Oh, the sustenances of life are no more, they have vanished;
the gods, the providers, have carried them off,
they have hidden them away in Tlalocan;
they have sealed in a coffer, they have locked in a box,
their verdure and freshness—
the cuphea and fleabane, the purslane and fig-marigold—[12]
all that grows and puts forth,
all that bears and yields,
all that sprouts and bursts into bloom
all vegetation that issues from you
and is your flesh, your generation and renewal.

It is the jade, the armlet, the turquoise—
the most precious, the only precious thing there is;
it is the sustenance, the substance, the life of the world,
whereby those who are alive, live
and talk and rejoice and laugh.

Oh, the fruits of the earth, the green and growing things
    have gone,
they have hidden themselves away!

O Lord, Our Lord, Lord of Tlalocan, O Provider!
What does your heart will?
By chance have you let this fall from your hand?
Is it to be thus? Is this all? Is this the end?
Are the people, the multitude, to die out, to vanish from the
    earth?
Is the city to be left empty and desolate?
Is this all? Is it to be thus?
Was it so ordained Above and in the Region of the Dead?
Was it so decreed for us? Was it so determined?

But all the little ones suffer—
Those who barely walk, those who crawl, those on the
    ground still,
the infants lashed to their boards and slats,
who are sensible of nothing—
give them, at least something to eat,
at least provide them with something,
for as yet they do not reason.

If we have vexed the Above and the Region of the Dead
If our foulness and corruption rose up,
If it wafted up to the Above, to the heavens,
then, perhaps this is all; perhaps, this is the end.
Perhaps, at this very moment darkness shall come
and all shall perish, all shall disappear from the earth.
What can we say? What is the use? To whom can we appeal?
It has been ordained.

At least let the common people have fullness and abundance;
let them not know total dissolution.
Their hearts and bodies are in torment,
day and night their hearts burn, their hearts are on fire!
A monstrous serpent is within them
slavering and panting and shrieking;
It is terrifying how it burns, how it shrieks, how it howls!

Perhaps now is coming true, now is coming to pass,
what men and women of old knew, what they handed down:
that the heavens over us shall sunder,
that the demons of the air shall descend
and shall come to destroy the earth and devour the people,
that darkness shall prevail, that nothing be left on the earth.
Our grandmothers and our grandfathers knew it,
they handed it down, it was their tradition
that it would come to pass, that it would come to be.[13]

And now to the ends of the earth, to the outmost bounds of
   the earth,
the land is devastated.
It is all over now, it is the end;
the earth's seeds have withered,
like old men and women they have shriveled,
and nothing has food, no one shall give food and drink to
   another.

O, Our Lord, let it not go on like this,
Let there be fullness and abundance for all!

Or, let pestilence seize the people in its grip,
Let the Lord of the Region of the Dead do his work, take up
   his duties.

Then, perhaps, Chicomecoatl and Centeotl[14] shall sustain
  them, shall succor them a little;
perhaps, into their mouths she shall put a drop of corn gruel,
  a scrap of food,
as provisions for their journey.[15]

Or let the Sun, the Eagle Ascendant, the Precious Child, the
  Valiant One,
the Brave Warrior, the Everlasting Resplendent One,[16] do his
  work.

Then the people, and the Eagle and Jaguar Knights shall
  rejoice,
for in the middle, in the center of the battlefield they shall be
  charred,
and their hair shall scatter, their bones whiten, their skulls
  split open.
And they shall know the House of the Sun,
where the sun is amused, where his praises are sung,
where the nectar of sundry sweet and fragrant flowers is
  sipped,
where the Eagle and Jaguar Knights,
the brave and valiant who die in battle, are glorified.[17]

And the little child, the tot,
still a chick, still a mite, not sensible to anything,
as jade, as turquoise, he shall go to heaven, the House of the
  Sun;
a perfect jade, a perfect turquoise, a smooth and lustrous
  turquoise,
is the heart he shall offer the sun.

And your sister, Chicomecoatl, shall sustain him,
the sister of the gods, the Providers, shall enter his belly,
and thus he shall be provided for his journey;
she shall lift him to that far-off place.
For she alone is our flesh and bones,
she alone is our staff and support,
she alone is our strength and fortitude;
she is man's entire recompense.

O Lord, Our Lord,
the people, the subjects—the led, the guided, the gov-
    erned—[18]
now behold, now feel, now are filled to bursting
with searing pain of affliction.
Their flesh and bones are stricken by want and privation,
they are worn, spent and in torment;
indeed, the pain reaches to the heart of them.
Not only once, or merely twice
do they behold, do they suffer death!
And the animals, also.

O Lord, O King,
Lord of Verdure, Lord of Rubber, Lord of the Sweet-Scented
    Marigold!
May it be your will,
may you, at least, cast a sidelong glance at the people.
They are going, they are perishing, they are vanishing, they
    are breaking and crumbling,
they are disappearing from the earth,
the suckling infants are wizened and dying,
the little ones that crawl are wasting away!

May it be your will, O, Our Lord,
may you grant that the gods, the Providers,
the Lords of the Sweet-Scented Marigold and the Lords of
    Copal do their work,
that they see their tasks on earth.
May bounty and good fortune be unleashed,
may the sweet-scented marigold rattles shake,
may the rattleboards of the mist clatter,[19]
may the gods don their rubber sandals!
Oh with a sprinkle, with a few drops of dew,
may you succor, may you aid, Tlaltecutli, Lord of the Earth,
who feeds and nourishes man!
And may you comfort the anguished fruits of the earth,
beloved child, sister of the gods,
who feebly drags herself through the rows,
who is wilting and withering in the rows!

Let the people be blessed with fullness and abundance,
let them behold, let them enjoy, the jade and the turquoise—
    the precious vegetation,
the flesh of Our Lords, the Providers, the Gods of Rain,
who bring, who shower down, the riches that are theirs
    alone.
And let the plants and animals be blessed with fullness and
    abundance,
let the troupial and roseate spoonbill sing,
let them flutter their wings, let them sip the sweet nectar.

Oh, let not the Gods of Rain loose their wrath and
    indignation,
for the people are enfeebled
and they shall frighten them, they shall strike terror into
    them.
Let them not lash themselves into a fury,
but let them only take, let them only strike the one who is
    theirs,
who was born, who came into the world, marked for
    Tlalocan,
who is their property, their possession.
Let them not deceive the people
that inhabit the forests and open plains,
that dwell in the wild, untilled fields.

Neither let them do this:
let them not blight the trees, the magueys, the prickly pears,
    and all that grows,
for they are the root of the life of the people,
the sustenance of the poor and hapless,
those living in misery and want, the destitute,
who have nothing to eat in the morning, nothing in the
    evening,
who go about empty, their stomachs rumbling.

O Lord, Beloved Lord, O Provider!
May it be in your heart to grant, to give, to bring comfort to
    the earth
and all that lives on it and all that grows on it.

And you who inhabit the four corners of the universe,
you Lords of Verdure, you the Providers,
you the Lords of the Mountain Heights, you the Lords of the
  Cavernous Depths.

I call out, I cry out to you:
come, bring yourselves here,
comfort the people, slake the thirst of the earth;
the earth and the animals, the leaves and the stalks
are watching and waiting and crying out.
O Gods, Our Lord, make haste!

2

The Songs of Ancient Mexico

THIS IS THE ONLY selection of Aztec poetry that Sullivan published in her lifetime. The earliest draft of these translations appeared in *Mexico This Month* in 1963 and, though the article contained but a few short selections, each one was a gem. As she wrote in her original introduction to these pieces:

Mexico's great heritage is not only manifest in its archaeological treasures. There are also hundreds—thousands perhaps—of folios in Nahuatl containing poems, songs, and chronicles that are equally overwhelming in their creative vigor and complexity. They were preserved, after the conquest, by Indians who had learned them by rote and later adapted the Latin alphabet they had acquired from the Spanish friars to their own language. This literature is another kind of monument, a more intimate one, for it takes us into the hearts and minds of the people.

The Nahuatl term for poetry was, itself, a metaphor. They called it "Flower and Song." They believed that it was a gift bestowed on them by the gods and that in it the divine and earthly were fused. Like a flower, it is of the earth—material, finite, visible. Like a song, it is of the air—impalpable, omnipresent, invisible—and therefore touched with divinity, for one of the names of the Supreme God was *Yohualli Ehecatl*, the Night and Wind, meaning invisible and impalpable. The poet, they believed, possesses a "deified heart." He receives his inspiration from God, he is favored by God with a glimpse of the truth that he reflects in the imperfect mirror of his earthbound symbols—his words. His poem is the merest approximation of truth, but as one Nahua poet remarks: "Is it, perhaps, the only truth there is on earth?"

In each of these poems there is at least one thought, one lament, that will stir the reader, though the symbolism may be obscure. Man, looking outward at the universe and inward at himself, has, since the beginning of time, asked the same questions, felt the same fears, brooded over the same doubts, and even arrived at the same answers. Only his symbols differ. And his symbols are not pure invention, the contrivance of an ingenious mind; like the food that nourishes him, they grow out of the soil on which he lives. To understand the symbols of a people is to understand its civilization. But for one man to understand another, he has only to hear his cry.

Although there were but five pieces published in this short selection of poems that Sullivan translated, in each one signs of the Aztec world leap out and the cry of the conquered is heard through her translation. These few fragments are monuments, as durable as stone, to the humanity of the Aztecs, and perhaps more indicative of the nature of their civilization than the sacrificial altars where their still-beating human hearts were offered to the Sun.

Five Poems

I

Where will I go?
Where will I go?
To the road, to the road
That leads to God.
Are you waiting for us in the Place of the Unfleshed?
Is it within the heavens?
Or is the Place of the Unfleshed only here on earth?

We vanish,
We vanish,
Into his house;
No one abides on earth.
Does someone ask,

"Where are our friends?"
Rejoice!

II

Be indomitable, O my heart!
Love only the sunflower;
It is the flower of the Giver-of-Life!
What can my heart do?
Have we come, have we sojourned here on earth in
    vain?

As the flowers wither, I shall go.
Will there be nothing of my glory ever?
Will there be nothing of my fame on earth?
At most songs, at most flowers.
What can my heart do?
Have we come, have we sojourned on earth in vain?

III

Our Lord,
Ever-present, Ever-close,
Thinks as he pleases,
Does as he pleases,
He mocks us.
As he wishes, so he wills.
He has us in the middle of his hand
And rolls us about,
Like pebbles we spin and bounce,
He flings us every which way.
We offer him diversion,
He laughs at us.

IV

Can it be true that one lives on earth?
Not forever on earth; only a little while here.

Be it jade, it shatters.
Be it gold, it breaks.
Be it a quetzal feather, it tears apart.
Not forever on earth; only a little while here.

V

The gold and black butterfly is sipping the nectar,
The flower bursts into bloom.
Ah, my friends, it is my heart!
I send down a shower of white frangipani.

3

◻⧅⧅⧅⧅⧅⧅⧅⧅◻

The Songs of the Gods: Ten Prayers of the Primeros Memoriales

THE SONGS OF THE GODS are beyond doubt the most ambiguous, enigmatic, esoteric, and difficult of all surviving texts in the Aztec language. They represent the most sophisticated forms of Classic Aztec poetics to survive the conquest. Almost every major translator of Nahuatl from Arthur J. O. Anderson and Daniel G. Brinton to Eduard Seler and Thelma Sullivan has attempted a rendition of these texts. Volumes of different versions of these texts have been produced by scholars, each with distinct variations and at times with vastly different interpretations. Careful study of this genre of Classic Aztec literature reveals that there is perhaps no one final correct version.

The songs in fact were a special genre that sought to maximize meaning through metaphor and were intentionally packed with double entendres, multiple metaphors, and complex meanings. For her version of these beautiful but perplexing pieces, Sullivan relied most heavily on the work of Eduard Seler, her mentor Father Garibay, Anderson and Dibble, and Daniel G. Brinton. She worked on these particular translations right up to the time of her death and unfortunately never completed them.[1]

Sahagún left two different versions of these twenty songs. In the earlier version, found in the *Primeros Memoriales* manuscript, which was an early draft of his encyclopedia, he had a separate column with notes clarifying the obscure meanings of these songs. In many cases the notes themselves are as perplexing as the songs. In his final draft of this work, now known as the Florentine Codex, Sahagún added a separate Spanish text, but he left out the notes to these pieces and made no attempt whatsoever to provide even a rough Spanish gloss of them. The friar probably considered them too complex, or perhaps dangerous, given the disposition of the Holy Office of the Inquisition, to even attempt a translation.

The true nature of these texts was perhaps best expounded by Sahagún himself. He wrote in the introduction to the pieces in the Florentine Codex:

> It is a very ancient custom for our adversary, the devil, to seek out hiding places where he can engage in his affairs, in accordance with the Holy Gospel that stated, "He who does evil abhors the light." Thus our enemy has planted a forest, a thicket, dense with brambles from which to conduct his affairs and in which he can hide, like the wild beasts and venomous serpents, so as not to be discovered. This forest or thorny thicket, is the darkness of the songs he contrived to have composed in this land to be utilized in his services and for his divine worship and as psalms in his praise both inside the temples as well as in other places. They are so artfully devised that they can say whatever they wish and proclaim whatever he orders, being understood only by those to whom he addresses them. It is a well-known fact that the cave, the forest, and the thicket where today this accursed adversary conceals himself, are the songs and psalms he had had composed and which are sung to him without their contents being understood, save by those who are native speakers of and thoroughly familiar with this language. Thus assuredly everything he so desires is sung, be it of war or peace, his own private praise or contumely of the Christian, without others being able to understand. (T.D.S. trans.)

Although Sahagún saw the Satanic hand behind these songs where today we would scoff at such a notion, they do remain devilishly difficult pieces for the translator. His reluctance to even attempt a translation of them in the Florentine Codex is understandable given his healthy respect for the Inquisition, which had already made considerable trouble for him in his work.[2]

In his prologue to the *Psalmodia Cristiana*, which was the only work that he saw published in his lifetime, Sahagún steadfastly maintained that the ancient songs contained idolatry and were the tools of "others," the Satanic forces opposing the Christian faith, for as he stated:

> . . . yet they continue to sing the ancient songs in their homes, their patios, their tecpas, palaces. This gives one deep suspicions as to the sincerity of their Christian faith, because in these ancient songs they chant idolatrous things in a style so obscure that there is no one except they themselves who could possibly understand the meaning. There are songs used to persuade the people in ways "the others" would wish, to war, or in other affairs that bring no good. They are specifically composed by "our enemy" to those ends, and yet the people do not wish to abandon these ancient songs.
>
> In order to resolve this problem, in this year 1583 we have the songs printed in this volume, the *Psalmodia Cristiana en lengua Mexicana.* This is so that all the ancient songs will cease to be sung, and that severe penalties may be exacted from those who continue to sing the ancient songs. (T.J.K. trans.)

The friar understood full well that the multiple levels of metaphor and meaning concealed in such songs were inextricably bound to the ancient beliefs of the Mexican peoples.

Fray Bernardino de Sahagún's *Primeros Memoriales:* Of the Songs That Were Given Voice in Honor of the Gods Both Within Their Temples and Beyond Them[3]

The Song of Huitzilopochtli

1 Huitzilopochtli is the warrior.
No one is my like.
Not in vain did I take the yellow parrot feather vestment, yya, ayya, yya, yyo, huia.
Because of me the sun shown, yyaya, yya yyo.

2 Terror!
Now the Mixtec, the Pichahuaztec, have one foot.
He took from them, ovayyeo, ayyayye

3 O, the walls of Tlaxotlan!
Feathers were given out.
He goes along churning up the earth.
He declares war, ayya yyo,
my god who is called tepanquizque.

4 The Tlaxotec is fearful.
The dust, the dust whirls.
The Tlaxotec
The dust, the dust whirls.

5 The Amanteca are our enemies.
Join with me!
The enemy is gathered in his house.
Join with me!

6 The Pipiteca are our enemies.
Join with me!
The enemy is gathered in his house.
Join with me!

This song is to Huitzilopochtli, "left of the hummingbird," the titular deity of the Aztecs, "the warrior who went off," who was called by the name reserved for both him and Tezcatlipoca, "the sorcerer," and "the one who had no equal." The yellow parrot feather cape was a special offering for Huitzilopochtli, which perhaps represented the sun.

The Mixtecs, "cloud people," and the Pichahuaztecs, "the ones frozen stiff," may have lost feet to Huitzilopochtli in battle, or rather may have had the one-footed deity. The meaning and the reading is intentionally obscure. Huitzilopochtli is sometimes depicted as having one foot like Tezcatlipoca.

Tlaxotlan was a district within the city of Tenochtitlan as well as one of the possible places the Aztecs passed through in their migrations. It was an essential stop during the procession of the festival of Huitzilopochtli, Panquetzaliztli. This is perhaps the same song performed on such an occasion. Chalk, as indicated in the gloss provided by Sahagún, and feathers were given to sacrificial victims, who were often captured warriors, the booty of battle. Battle churned the earth and drove up the dust as a metaphor for war. Tepanquizque was an epithet for one of several deities involved in the creation of man in the Fourth Sun. Fray Alonso de Molina's sixteenth-century dictionary of Classic Aztec glossed the term as "actor" or "imitator," and the great German translator Eduard Seler interprets it as "one who makes war," which fits the context and gloss, yet both these possibilities may be correct.

The Tlaxoteca are fearful and the battle is fought, as implied by the whirling dust metaphor. The Tlaxocayotl was a song sung in honor of Huitzilopochtli at the festival known as Panquetzaliztli.

The Amanteca are the people of Amantlan, and likewise the Pipiteca are people of Pipitlan, both possible sites of historical and/or mythical battles.

The Song of Yaotl, "The Enemy" of Huitznahuac

1 Ahuiya! My valiant warrior of the House of Spears.
Covered with feathers is the man who maligns me;
for I know I am Tetzahuitl.
Ahuiya! I know ya I am Yaotl.
of whom it was spoken, "My valiant warrior of the House of Spears?"
They revile my noble house.

2 Huia! The Warrior, the Tocuiltecatl,
wears the eagle feather vestment with thorns in diverse places.

3 Huiya! Telpochtli of Oholopan
covered with feathers is my captive.
I am afraid, I am afraid.
Covered with feathers is my captive.

4 Huiya! Telpochtli of Huitznahuac
covered with feathers is my captive.

I am afraid, I am afraid.
Covered with feathers is my captive.

5 Huiya! Telpochtli of Itzcotlan
covered with feathers is my captive.
I am afraid, I am afraid.
Covered with feathers is my captive.

6 The priest of the temple of Huitznahuac,
his sign descends.
The day has dawned, the day has dawned.
His sign descends.

7 The priest of the temple of Tocuillan,
his sign descends.
The day has dawned, the day has dawned.
His sign descends.

There were no glosses provided by Sahagún with this song in the *Primeros Memoriales*. The following is Sullivan's interpretation:

The song of Yaotl, "the enemy," one of the epithets of Tezcatlipoca, the sorcerer deity, from Huitznahuac, "the place near the thorns," "the south," which was also a district lineage in Tenochtitlan. This is another song filled with the polyvalent ambiguities that load this genre with meaning. The valiant warrior here is a master warrior who has taken captives and paid them as sacrificial tribute to the gods. The Warrior from the House of Spears is equivalent to the "Enemy of the North" and represents Tezcatlipoca; he is, thus, the Necoc Yaotl, "Enemy on Both Sides." The "prodigy" or "marvel," Tetzahuitl, was an epithet for both Huitzilopochtli and Tezcatlipoca. In this case there may be reference to both deities.

The Tocuiltecatl is a high military officer who would wear such a robe, but perhaps without the thorns. It was also a man from Tocuillan, a temple mentioned in the last verse. The term for thorns here is a possible archaism.

Telpochtli is another of the epithets for Tezcatlipoca meaning "young man" and implying all the virility of a young warrior. It may have also implied "pure" or "virgin" young man, as it does in some modern dialects. *Oholopan is the location of a temple with which there was possibly a military rank associated as there is with the temples mentioned in the two following stanzas. In these three stanzas the derivation of the term for fright is by implication from the gloss for the fifth stanza of the previous piece.*

In the sixth stanza the term for priest is an archaism. The sign that descends is clearly the day sign or sun sign of the day, which in modern dialects is said to descend from the time the sun rises. In a way the "face" or "luck" of the day begins to diminish from the dawn. Aztec reverses the value we place on the up/down, high/low, ascend/descend metaphors; speakers of Modern Aztec dialects will lower their voices in prayer, descend to the day, and look for hope from below in the earth. In these two final stanzas the descent of the day sign has no negative implication.

The Song of Tlalloc

1 Ahuiya! Mexico had the god on loan.
Paper flags stood at the four sides.
At last this was his place of weeping.

2 Ahuiya! I have been fashioned.
My idol is stained with blood.
The festival day is already long.
I bring water to the temple courtyard.

3 Ahuiya! My master, Nahualpilli, the Sorcerer Prince
truly you have brought forth your own sustenance.
That which is the offering of the first fruits, only offends you.

4 Ahuiya! But they offend me.
They do not please me
my fathers, my shorn-head priests, my ocelot-serpent priests.

5 Ahuiya! From Tlalocan, the House of Turquoise,
your fathers, Acatonal came forth, seeped forth.

6 Ahuiya! Go forth, gather in Poyauhtlan.
With the mist rattle water is brought from Tlalocan.

7 Ao! My older brother is Tocuecuexi
I shall go,
it is his time of weeping.

8 Ahuiya! Send me to the unknown beyond.
His words were lowered.
I said to Tetzauhpilli "I shall go."
It is his time of weeping.

9 Ahuiya! For four years it befell us.
Not in my time was the occurrence in your account.
The place where all go, the place of quetzal feathers, the
place shared by all,
is the property of the nourisher of people.

10 Ahuiya! Go settle in Poyauhtlan.
With mist rattles water is brought to Tlalocan.

The spelling of Tlaloc with the double el is taken by Sullivan as
further support for her etymological interpretation of the meaning of Tlaloc as "He Who is Made of Earth." The notion of
having the god on loan is more complex than our notion of a
simple loan; it is rather, as Molina says, "to take something and
return it in kind." Metaphorically it expresses the ephemerality
of the actual object; the deity; its image; its life-giving moisture,
which is constantly exchanged between earth and sky. It could
be that Tlaloc has been borrowed as the rain and is returned in
kind with tears and/or the blood of sacrificial victims. Thanks is
given for brief rains with sacrificial blood returned for the deity.
Paper flags were put out for sacrificial victims on the four sides
of the earth; the verb here is probably archaic. "The place of
weeping" is fixed in both time and space with an intentional double entendre. Weeping can also imply humility or devotion rather
than simply sadness. Ritual weeping in political speeches is common among the Huichol and is commonly seen in supplications
in Maya-speaking regions and among speakers of Modern Aztec dialects. It was considered propitious for babies sacrificed
for Tlaloc to be weeping profusely at the moment of sacrifice.

The staining of the idol with blood and the day-long festival
were a part of the Tlaloc ceremonies of Eztlaqualiztli. Here the
deity appears to speak directly.

Tequihuia is not only a rank of warrior, but also someone who is a master of whatever trade or labor she does. Here it appears that the "Sorcerer Prince" is an epithet applied to Tlaloc, rather than Tezcatlipoca, more commonly known as the sorcerer. The Huastecs worshipped the Sorcerer Prince. The practice of offering the first fruits of the harvest to Tlaloc continues today in the Sierra de Puebla.

The offering of first fruits can be small and thus offensive. The "Shorn-Head Ones" can also be called the "Head Takers." They were the old priests. The ocelot serpents appear in the text and the old ocelot priests in the gloss. These are two names for the old priests who participated in Tlaloc ceremonies. This is another example of the parallelism that is ubiquitous in Classic Aztec poetics.

"From Tlalocan the house of verdure" would be another reading of the first line of this fifth stanza. Green, blue, and the terms for precious stones merge here. In this case the double meaning or perhaps even triple meaning is intentional. Both the verb and its subject are problematic, but by analogy with the previous stanza should read "my fathers seep forth" or "emerge" on the basis of the gloss. There are several historical figures named Acatonal, "Reed Day Sign"; which, if any, this may refer to is unclear.

Olmos indicated in his work that the second verb of the sixth stanza is "to gather together," which is what was done on Poyauhtlan, a sacred and mystical mountain, as well as one of the temples in the center of Mexico City. The name of both the temple and the mountain were probably borrowed from another language and Nahuatlized with a suffix.

In the Legend of the Suns the gods demand the daughter of Tozcuecuexi for sacrifice for the lords of Tlalocan. By all accounts the gods then granted life-sustaining relief, rains. Here the weeping may be the onset of the rains.

Literally the "unknown beyond" is the "place of how." Reference here is confusing. Teztauhpilli was the murdered son of the poet-king Nezhualcoyotl, but it is uncertain that this reference is to the historical person.

The four years referred to here may be the famine of 1450, and although the verb is problematic, "it befell us" or "it was brought upon us" appears a correct reading. Ximohmuayan, "the place where all go" is one of the names of Mictlan, "the place of the dead." The verb here expresses mutuality, or something shared in common.

The gloss for this final stanza interprets the verb as "to go," but it is problematic.

THE SONG OF THE MOTHER OF THE GODS

1 Ahuiya! The yellow flower has burst into bloom.
She who is our mother, Lady of divine thigh skin, facial paint
came forth from Tamoanchan.
Avaya yyao, yya, yyeo, ayye, ayy, ayyaa.

2 The yellow flower has opened.
She who is our mother, Lady of divine thigh skin, facial paint
came forth from Tamoanchan.
Avaya yyao, yya, yyeo, ayye, ayy, ayyaa.

3 Ahuiya! The white flower bursts into bloom.
She who is our mother, lady of sacred thigh skin, facial paint
came forth from Tamoanchan.
Avvaye, ovayya, yyao, ya, yyeo, aye aye, ayya ayyaa.

4 Ahuiya! The white flower has opened
She who is our mother, lady of sacred thigh skin, facial paint
came forth from Tamoanchan.
Ovvaye, ovayya, yyao, ya, yyeo, aye aye, ayya ayyaa.

5 Ahuiya! The goddess is atop the barrel cactus.
It is our mother, Itzpapalotl.
Avayya, avayye, yyao, yya, yyeo, ayyaa.

6 O, you saw her on the nine plains.
On deer hearts was our mother Tlaltecutli fed.
Ayao, ayyao, ayyaa.

7 O, she was with new chalk.
She was covered with new feathers.
In all directions she loosed arrows.

8 O, she was transformed into a deer on the plains
Xiuhnel and Mimich had mercy on you.

"Mother of the Gods," Teteo Inan, is but one of the names
of the mother goddess.

Sullivan relies partially on Eduard Seler, and partially on ethnographic and etymological analysis for her translation of "divine thigh skin facial paint," pointing out that the mask of the
mother goddesses in the Ochpaniztli ceremonies is yellow, is
made from the thigh skin of a sacrificial victim, and that the
term demonstrated the same type of consonant assimilation in
its name as the "mother goddess" term. The verb for "she came
forth" is problematic in that it is a reflexive form of an intransitive. Sullivan maintains that it only appears reflexive due to
common metathesis of the honorific particle on-. Tamoanchan
was called by most of the sixteenth-century chroniclers the
"earthly paradise" and home of the gods. Etymologically it appears likely that the term is not of Nahua origin. It may come
from Huastec.

On the basis of etymology and the gloss, Sullivan translates
oyomoxocha in the text, glossed as noxochiuh, as "to open,"
based on the root for flower.

Sullivan points out in the fifth stanza that the identification
of teocontli, or teocomitl, as barrel cactus is descriptive and
perhaps not specific. Itzapapalotl, "obsidian butterfly," was the
goddess of the Chichimeca and the barrel cactus plays an important part in her conflict with Mimixcoa in the Anales de
Cuautitlan (see I, 1).

The verb in the first line of the sixth stanza, though highly
inflected for metric, appears to derive from the verb "to see."
The nine plains may be read as on the nine plains or among
the nine plains. It also implies "battlefield," based on both tex-
tual and ethnographic information. Tlaltecutli, "the Earth
Lord/Lady," is in this case the earth goddess.

Reed is a synonym for arrow and is translated as such, but
also implies the day name and propitious places around the
Valley of Mexico. Chalk and feathers were for sacrificial victims.

Xiuhnel, "True Turquoise," and Mimich, "Arrow Fish," are
two Chichimec brothers in the Legend of the Suns. There is a

possibility that there is a lost myth here, as the relation of the brothers to Itzpapalotl is quite different from that found in the Legend of the Suns.

THE SONG OF CHIMALPANECATL AND TLALTECAHUA, THE MOTHERWOMB

1 On her shield the virgin grows large.
At the call to battle he was brought into the world.
On her shield the virgin grows large.
At the call to battle he was brought into the world.

2 On Coatepetl among the hills,
the *tequihuia* [war master] painted his face, took up his shield.
No one went against him.
The earth shook when he painted his face,
and took up the shield.

Chimalpanecatl literally means the person from Chimalpan, the place on the shield. There was a place known by this name north of Mexico City, but in this context it appears to refer to the birth of Huitzilopochtli, who was born with shield. This may also refer to the pregnant woman's role as a warrior in childbirth (see II, 2). Tlaltecahua is "the Lady/Lord of the people of," or "Ladies/Lords of under the earth." This obviously refers to the mother goddess as the earth mother. Nanotl is the abstractive of mother, which would be motherhood, but the word is also used as womb. In this case both meanings are correct.

Sullivan takes issue with both Eduard Seler's and Father Garibay's readings of Chipuchica as "by means of the maiden, or virgin," and sees this verse and the following as a summary of the myth of the birth of Huitzilopochtli. The Tequihuia is both the master and warrior. In this context it is perhaps best left untranslated if, as Sullivan maintains, it refers to Huitzilopochtli.

THE SONG OF IXCOZAUHQUI

1 Huiya! Oh, my fathers in Tzonmolco.
  I shall offend you in Tetemocan.
  I shall offend you.

2 In Mecatlan, my lords, the beat of the yucca reverberates.
  In Chicueyocan, the sorcerer descended from the House of
    Sorcery.

3 In Tzonmolco we began to sing.
  In Tzonmolco we began to sing.
  Why have you not appeared?
  Why have you not appeared?

4 In Tzonmolco let them offer up people.
  The Sun has shone.
  The Sun has shone.
  Let them offer up people.

5 Huiya! In Tzonmolco the Xoxol song is ending.
  With little difficulty the Lord becomes rich.
  Your beneficence is awesome.

6 Huiya! Little Lady, speak to the gods.
  Lady of the house of mists,
  in the entryway speak to the gods.

Ixcozauhqui, "Yellow Face," is one of the names of Xiuhtecutli, "God of Fire." Tzonmolco, "Flying Hair," was the temple of the god of fire. Tetemocan was also possibly the name of a temple.

Mecatlan, "Place of the Ropes," "among the ropes," or "place where ropes were spun," is the temple where priests were taught to play the shell trumpets. It is also the place where rope is spun and today such places reverberate with the sound of spinning, like the yucca seed rattles that are shaken to imitate the thunder that anticipates the rain. Chicueoyan is "the place of eight," and Seler suspected it was synonymous with Mecatlan as well as being a place of sorcery.

The verb for "appear" or "come forth" presents the problem again of a reflexive intransitive.

There is little agreement on the etymology of "Xoxol song." Sullivan shows both Garibay and Seler to be lacking an accurate etymology, while hesitantly proposing xolotl, a yellow parrot feather, as the term; nevertheless in her final draft she left Xoxol without translation. The second line of the fifth stanza is more problematic. Sullivan offers two alternative readings but shows little confidence in either, preferring the reading of the Lord being enriched on the basis of metaphors.

Sullivan notes that the indefinite personal object prefix often refers to the gods in the Huehuetlatolli, and she translated it as such here.

THE SONG OF MIMIXCOA

1 From the seven caves he set forth.
Zani aveponej.
Zani, zani teyomi.

2 From among the Tzihuactli he set forth.
Zani aveponej.
Zani, zani teyomi.

3 I descend, I descend.
With my tzihuac arrow I descend.

4 I descend, I descend,
I descend with my huacal.

5 With my hands I catch it, with my hands I catch it, yvaya.
With my hands I catch it, with my hands I catch it, ia ayo.
And with my hand it is caught.

The Mimixcoa are cloud serpent deities of the Chichimeca associated with the north and hunting, which is the theme of this song. Chicomoztoc, the place of seven caves, is the point of origin for many Mesoamerican peoples. The second and third lines in the gloss are said to be Chichimec words. Though Anderson and Dibble as well as others translate parts of this supposedly unintelligible section, Sullivan leaves it.

Tzihuactli is a spiny desert plant and also a metaphor for the arid regions that the Chichimeca came from.

"I descend" also implies "to be born"; in a way this is similar to the birth of Huitzilopochtli with a Tzihuactli spine arrow.

A *huacal* is a net or mesh basket or crate often carried on the back with a tumpline attached to the head. The term also refers to a hunter's net in modern usage.

The gloss for the fifth stanza states that "these are hunter's words; with them the Chichimeca went off to hunt; they are Chichimec words." The words of this stanza do in fact have the simple repetitive sound of modern hunter's chants.

THE SONG OF XOCHIPILLI

1 Above the ball court
the quetzalcocoxtli sings.
Centeotl answers.

2 Now our friends sing.
Now throughout the night, the quetzalcocoxtli,
the red Centeotl sings.

3 The Lord of the bells,
the possessor of the thigh skin facial paint shall hear my
     song.
Cipactonal shall hear my song atilili, ouayya.

4 Ayao, ayao, ayao, ayao.
I take leave of the Tlamacazque of Tlalocan.
Ayao, ayao, ayao.

5 Aayao, ayao, ayao.
I take leave of the Tlamacazque of Tlalocan
Ay, ayyao, ayyao.

6 I Centeotl arrived at the place where the roads join.
Where shall I go?
Which road shall I follow?

7 Ayyao, aya, ayao.
Tlalocan Tlamacazque,

O, gods of rain!
Ayyao, aya, aya.

Xochipilli, "The Flower Prince," is the god of dance and games such as the ball game; patolli; a parchisi type of game; and others. Gordon Wasson has also identified this deity as a patron of narcotic and trance-inducing plants. Xochipilli is a solar fertility deity especially associated with the corn goddess, Centeotl. The quetzalcocoxtli is a black pheasant-like bird, possibly a precious curassow, and is closely associated with Centeotl.

The reading of "friends" here can be both singular with an emphatic particle aya or plural as Sullivan has rendered it. Both Seler and Garibay interpret Tlao as Tlahuitl, "the red corn deity," yet Sullivan points out some serious problems with that interpretation, although she can offer no alternative except to propose that it might be an interjection.

Sullivan points out that Seler's interpretation of "Lord of bells" as "Lord of the evening" is probably in error. Her translation is more in accord with Anderson and Garibay. The "possessor of the thigh skin facial paint" here is a clear reference to the mother goddess as Centeotl-Itztlacoliuhqui, who wears the mexayacatl, thigh skin mask, in the festival of Ochpaniztli. Cipactonal, "the one with the crocodile day sign," was one of the original creator deities and together with Oxomoco began the practice of casting grains of corn to divine the future. This practice may have given rise to the divinatory practices of the day count or vice versa.

Seler interprets this section to be the request by a sorcerer for rain, but Sullivan differs with this on both etymological and ethnological grounds, considering it more probable that the maize deity is taking leave of the underworld.

The point where roads join is considered inauspicious.

Upon leaving Tlalocan the corn deity must consult the bringers of sustenance, for without moisture corn will not grow.

The final stanza is a plea for rain and life.

The Song of Xochiquetzal

1 From the place of watery mists,
I Xochiquetzal come
from Tamoanchan.

2 You weep Piltzintecutli of Tlamacazecan.
You are seeking Xochiquetzal.
To the place of blighted corn, to the above, I shall go.

Xochiquetzal, "flower quetzal," Tlahuica goddess of weaving
and games, is the female counterpart of Xochipilli. She was also
closely associated with sexuality. Sullivan does not agree with
Seler, Brinton, Garibay, or Anderson in interpreting Tlacya Mo-
tencalihuan and details her criticism of all previous interpretations. On the early draft she interpreted this phrase in a way
similar to Anderson, but omits that in the later copy, indicating
only that she feels it to be a place of mythic origins.

Piltzintecutli, "Lord Child" or "Lord of Princes," is a solar
fertility deity belonging to the Xochipilli-Macuilxochitl group.
Tlamacazetla as it is reads is a "person from Tlamacazecan, the
place of the Lord of the providers"; yet in another song this is
glossed as "I am a Tlamacazqui, Tlaloc's helper."

The Song of Animitl

The song of Animitl is a Chichimec song and it is impossible
to make it understandable in our Nahuatl tongue.

This is what the gloss says and Sullivan left the final version
of this song untranslated. In the earlier draft for translation into
Spanish she did translate a few lines and noted that they made
little sense and that possibly this was the result of Nahuatl
speakers being asked to set something down in a foreign language. Her opinion appears to be that native speakers forced
the words to make them sound like Nahuatl without understanding them.

Part IV

WORDS OF JADE: PROVERBS, METAPHORS, AND CONUNDRUMS

THESE PROVERBS, METAPHORS, AND CONUNDRUMS embody many of the basic principles of Aztec culture, the ways in which they viewed the world around them. The two collections presented here are very different, though both were brought together to elucidate the complex language of the *Huehuetlatolli*. Sahagún's collection of proverbs, conundrums, and metaphors is almost an appendix to the elegant and refined materials found in book VI, the "Book of Rhetoric, Moral Philosophy, and Theology" of the Florentine Codex. The metaphors of Fray Andres de Olmos, the great sixteenth-century grammarian, are given as a prelude to his examples of the *Huehuetlatolli* and are more a manual of metaphor. In both cases these are the rough jade pebbles that were "polished and perforated" by Aztec orators and transformed into precious jewels. These are the precious jades that were scattered by royal orators and sown among the people.

1

Nahuatl Proverbs, Conundrums, and Metaphors, Collected by Sahagún[1]

To give prudence to the simple,
to the young knowledge and discretion;
That the wise man may hear, and increase in learning,
and the man of understanding may attain unto wise counsels;
To understand a proverb and a figure,
the words of the wise and their dark sayings.

(OLD TESTAMENT, BOOK OF PROVERBS, I: 4–7)

THELMA SULLIVAN's original introduction:

When I started studying Nahuatl with Dr. Garibay, a little over two and a half years ago, I began not merely the study of a fascinating language, but also what has proved to be an intellectual adventure. The translation I offer here of the Nahuatl proverbs, conundrums, and metaphors collected by Sahagún is part of the fruit of this adventure, and it is with the profoundest joy and profoundest humility that I dedicate it to Angel María Garibay K. in commemoration of his fifty years of distinguished scholarship.

Dr. Garibay has done many things in the field of the humanities, not only in Nahuatl literature, but also in Greek and Latin, Hebrew and Aramaic. However, there is one thing that he has not done, and it is this one thing that has made his work outstanding. He has never taken the "human" out of the humanities. Dr. Garibay is not a "scholar's scholar"; he is all the world's scholar, and the knowledge that he has garnered in his lifetime he freely shares with all who are interested. He abhors "deluxe editions" and fights against them, preferring to see his own work published in less-expensive editions or in paperback so that it may be accessible. His books—alas, much of his work is still unpublished—are a delight for any reader, as well as a mine of information for investigators, no little achievement in a field considered reserved for "eggheads."

His accomplishments as a scholar, however, are only the manifestation of what he is as a man. Dr. Garibay has never traveled far from Mexico City, but through his reading and meditation he has ranged over all the world and into the hearts and minds of people everywhere. Because he understands the universal paradox of man being the same everywhere and at all times, and different everywhere at all times, he has been able to give us translations from the Nahuatl (not to mention his recent translations of Greek plays) that make us feel the impact of a living culture. A true *tlamatini*—wise man—he is in the words of the Nahuas, "a light, a torch, a great torch that does not smoke; he shines his light on the world." To work with such a man is truly an adventure, and it has enriched my life forever.

Book VI of Sahagún's monumental *Historia de las Cosas de Nueva España* is the most beautiful of the twelve books that comprise the work. It is a book of *Huehuetlatolli*, or Orations of the Elders, containing forty prayers, exhortations, and orations, and ends with a collections of proverbs, conundrums, and metaphors. Being *Huehuetlatolli* of the nobles, it is the finest example we have of Nahuatl rhetoric and literary style, which, in complexity of thought as well as beauty of expression, rivals any of the great literature that man has produced. Did Sahagún pattern his book after the Book of Proverbs of the Bible, a series of exhortations with a collection of proverbs at the end? We shall never know.

One of Sahagún's aims in preparing his great work was to facilitate the learning of the Nahuatl language by his fellow missionaries, and doubtless it was to this end that he appended to Book VI the proverbs, conundrums, and metaphors he had gathered in the course of his investigation into the pre-conquest life of the Mexicans. From their somewhat crude style and the conversational tone of the texts, it is apparent that they were jotted down verbatim, possibly for his own use at first. They are like an album of photographs, each proverb, conundrum, or metaphor a picture of some aspect of the life of the Nahuas, and since these are word pictures, we not only see something of their life but also something of their thoughts and feelings.

Like all proverbs, the proverbs of the Nahuas are the wisdom and the truths they distilled from their experiences and observations into simple, crystallized, and witty statements. As strange and curious as their world may seem to us, for nearly every Nahuatl proverb we have a similar one of our own. And the Nahuatl conundrums that belong to the world of children are like conundrums everywhere—charming, simple, and concerned with everyday things.

The metaphors, however, are what bring us into direct and intimate contact with the mentality of the Nahuas, for what are metaphors but the images in words of the concepts, beliefs, traditions, and experiences of a people? Since in Nahuatl philosophy and religion the all-pervading concept was that of duality—a supreme dual god and duality in all things—it is not surprising that Nahuatl metaphors generally consist of two words or phrases that combine to form a single idea. Sometimes there are redundancies, sometimes parallelisms, and sometimes disassociated words that in combination have a meaning totally unrelated to the individual meanings of the words. These vivid and imaginative embellishments of the Nahuatl language, together with the proverbs, which themselves are metaphorical expressions, are whorly swatches clipped from the rich brocade of the Nahuatl language and literature. They are just a sample of the treasure over which Angel María Garibay has for so long held his torch.

Some Proverbs That They Said and Still Say

1. *Moxoxolotitlani: A page is sent.*
   This is said about someone who is sent with a message and fails to return with an answer, or else does not go where he was sent. It is said for this reason. They say that when

Quetzalcoatl was the king of Tollan, two women were bathing in his pool. When he saw them he sent some messengers to see who they were. And the messengers just stayed there watching the women bathing and did not take him the information. Then Quetzalcoatl sent another of his pages to see who the bathers were and the same thing happened; he did not return with an answer either. From that time on they began, they started saying: *A page is sent.*

2. **Tomachizoa:** *Our know-it-all.*
This is said of someone who claims to know everything about whatever is said and done.

3. **Nonouian:** *Here, there, and everywhere.*
This is said about a person who enters where he should not enter, sticks his hand where he should not stick his hand, and quickly takes part in whatever others are doing.

4. **Oc nachicomatl, oc mochicomatl, oc ichicomatl:** *Still half a net for me, still half a net for you, still half a net for him.*
This is said when a drunkard assaulted someone who then died. At the time the drunkard killed the other person he was still only in half a net because he did not know that he had killed someone.[2] He had not fallen into the net for having killed someone, therefore was confident that he might get out; he was not all the way into the net and consequently might get out. For this reason they say: *Still half a net for me.*

5. **Ixpetz:** *Polished eye.*
This is said of a person who is very astute in the manner of finding, of discovering, what is necessary, or who quickly sees what is difficult in an enigma.

6. **Tacapitz ueli in tlalticpac:** *One can dig a little in this world.*
This is said when one time we are able to put away a little something, and another time we are in need. Sometimes one can, sometimes one cannot.

7. **Xoxocotioa (i)n tlalticpac:** *To bear fruit in this world.*
This is said of a high functionary who is dismissed, dis-

charged, due to something that is his fault. It is precisely like fruit that has ripened and then falls to the ground.[3]

8. *Ayac xictli in tlalticpac: No one on earth is an umbilical cord.*[4]
We should not sneer at anyone; meaning, we should not disdain anyone even though he appears to warrant disdain, as he might be a wise man, or learned, or able.

9. *Cuicuitlauilli in tlalticpac: By nibbling away in this world.*
This is said when we persist in something, when we take great pains with it and know it well even though it may be difficult, such as carpentry, sculpting in stone, and other arts; or perhaps some kind of knowledge, such as singing, grammar, etc. If one is very persistent, it is said: *By nibbling away in this world.*

10. *Tlatolli itlaqual: A word is his meal.*
This is said about the person who is wounded by any little thing and immediately starts quarreling with people. When lightly reprimanded he replies angrily and he squabbles with the other, or whenever anything is said he starts arguing and shouting.

11. *Tlani xiquipilhuilax: Underneath he drags a bag.*
This is said about someone who outwardly seems like placid water, who has a kind face and appears to be compassionate and good. But he may really be despicable—belligerent, a scandalmonger, and evil-hearted. Outwardly he speaks nicely to people but inwardly he speaks nastily.

12. *Ye onquiza naoalli: anoce onquiz in naoalli: There the sorcerer is now passing there;* or, *The sorcerer passed there.*
This is said when some people, by toiling hard, earn their livelihood and lay by something. Some people, however, are just shiftless; they dedicate themselves to diversion and accumulate nothing, and when others acquire things by working hard, they say: *the sorcerer passed there.*
This can also be said about studying something. Some just fritter away their time, but if others learn well what they are studying, if they learn quickly, then they say: *the sorcerer passed there.* They say that when one says this, *sorcerer*[5] means the devil.

13. **Ixquauitl, uel ixquauh:** *Brazen-faced, truly a face of wood.*
    This is said about the person who is not bashful or timid with others. He rushes ahead of illustrious people.

14. **Tenquauitl:** *Wooden lips.*
    This is said about someone whose words are firm. He cannot be refuted, no one can override him in words.

15. **Pipilpan timalti:** *A reveler in childishness.*
    This is said of a grown person who still clings to childish things; someone who is already a young man and takes delight in digging holes with pieces of stone or painting himself up, or a young woman who still carries around her dolls and makes mud tortillas. That is, the glory in childishness.

16. **Ninotocuiuitla, timotocuiuitla:** *I pull up my shoots, you pull up your shoots.*
    This is said when I love someone who perhaps hurts me in some way. I quarrel with him and humiliate him. If there is something that he had done secretly, I reveal it in public, thus shaming him and throwing it in his face. When this occurs, they say: *I pull up my shoots.*[6]

17. **Oppa icuitl quiqua:** *He eats his excrement over again.*
    This is said if someone gives something to another, such as food or a cape. Then he asks for it back, he takes it away for him.

18. **Aonmati iixco, icpac:** *He has no idea of what is on his face and on top of his head.*
    This is said of someone who is not careful of his person. He is unkempt and his face is filthy. He never uses any soap on himself, nor does he wash his face.

19. **Aommomatoca:** *He does not put a hand to himself.*
    This is the same as, *He has no idea what is on his face and on top of his head.*

20. **Aoompa:** *Scatterbrain.*
    This is said of a person who does not have his wits about him. He is sent somewhere but goes elsewhere, and what he is supposed to get he does not get.

21. ***Niquauhtlamelooa, tiquauhtlamelaoa:*** *I am a fruitless tree, you are a fruitless tree.*
    This is said when I study something but cannot learn it. It is exactly as if I were a fruit tree that bears no fruit. For this reason it is said: *I am a fruitless tree,* or, *I was a fruitless tree,* meaning, I have learned nothing, I have nothing to show for my efforts.

22. ***Mazol:*** *hand-dipper.*
    This is said about a person who swiftly snatches things belonging to others, such as bracelets or paper adornments, or some other object that is safeguarded elsewhere. He swiftly takes it from the basket or place where valuables are kept.

23. ***Notzotzon, motzotzon, anzo cuix no cuel notzotzon nouauhtzon:*** *My hair, your hair; or, Is my hair my amaranth?*
    This is said when I do someone a favor, or else, teach him something. In consideration of my help he should love me, but instead repays me with abuse and disdain. Therefore it is said: *My hair;* or, *My hair also, your hair also.*[7]

24. ***Nitlacocoloa, titlacocoloa:*** *I twist something, you twist something.*
    This is said when I do not speak plainly. For instance, I am asked a question that I should answer clearly, but instead I muddle my words; in some instances I am ambiguous, concealing one thing and stating another with clarity. Or else I speak falsely about someone.

25. ***Campa mixco:*** *With what face do you look at me?*
    This is said when someone hates me and makes an accusation against me, for which I might be harmed or persecuted in some city. However, absolutely nothing can be done; I cannot be harmed or persecuted for this. For this reason I say to the person who hates me: *With what face do you look at me?*

26. ***Can noyacauh, can moyacauh:*** *My very nose, your very nose.*
    This is said when someone has done me harm and I would do him harm also, but he runs from me. No matter where

he has gone, when he turns up I shall torment him. Therefore, one says: *My very nose.*[8]

27. **Toltlanitz:** *Our shin.*
    This is said about the person who speaks of his prowess.
    "I am a captain," he says to someone. "I have captured
    prisoners and am experienced in war." And perhaps he is
    not a captain. Or he is and he has a scar somewhere on his
    body which he shows to people, saying, "These are the
    wounds I received in combat." This is when one says: *Our
    shin.* And we also say: *I boast falsely, you boast falsely.*[9]

28. **Centzon, uel acic:** *He succeeded in achieving four hundred.*[10]
    This is said about someone who knows a great many things,
    such as painting on paper, or such crafts as forging metal,
    carpentry, and goldsmithery. He knows all these things
    well. For this reason it is said: *He succeeded in achieving four
    hundred.*

29. **Uel nomiuh, uel momiuh:** *Strictly my bone, strictly your bone.*
    This is said when I hold fast to something that belongs to
    me, my own possession that I acquired by hard work and
    toil and that I did not take or steal. It meant the same in the
    past when someone took a captive in battle, and then came
    a second that he seized by the hand or foot, and then a
    third and a fourth that he also seized by hand or foot. With
    this the captor said to the novice assisting him: *Strictly my
    bone.* And if someone else came along and seized one of the
    captives by the hand or foot, they said: *It is not his bone!*[11]

30. **Icnopilotl ommomelauh:** *He marched straight into poverty.*
    This is said when I manage to accumulate something after
    a long time and someone comes along and steals it, or else
    I throw it away on the road and it falls into someone else's
    hands.

31. **Tetitech noneoa:** *I dash myself against a rock.*
    This is said when I ask a ruler or some other illustrious
    person to do me some favor, and as a result he becomes
    angry. I provoke his wrath, and perhaps he berates me. It
    is as if I beat myself, I dash myself against a rock.

32. *No tlapapalochiuhtiuh: Like a moth into the flames.*
This is said about someone who is always quarreling with others. When he bullies people and squabbles with them, he fumes and rages, but then he, in turn, is bullied and put to shame. It is as if he has fallen into the fire; flames are shooting from him and he thinks the fire has consumed the other, while it is he who has fallen into the fire, and he soon dies there. So it is with people who are always quarreling with others; they may fall into the hands of the other and perhaps be killed.

33. *Ixnex: Ash-faced.*[12]
This is said about someone who has done or committed something, an iniquity or thievery. He thinks no one knows about it, but his disgrace is already widely known, it has been bruited about. Therefore they say about this person: *Ash-faced.*

34. *Icniuhmoyactli: Friend-dispeller.*
This is said of a person who is belligerent, who cannot look at anyone without fighting with him. If there is a gathering and he sits down among the people there, they just draw away from him, they leave him quickly, as they are afraid that he may fight with somebody. For this reason they say: *Friend-dispeller.*

35. *Onen oncatca: It was in vain.*
This is said when I desire something with all my heart that cannot be done. For example, if I am studying, I cannot learn anything. Therefore one says: *It was in vain.* Or conversely, *it was not in vain.*[13]

36. *Ompa onquiza'n tlalticpac: The world spills out.*[14]
This is said when we are very poor, when hardly anything comes our way, such as mantles or food, by which it is evident that someone is poor and in great want. One's rags are very old and torn, barely covering one. They are worn thin, falling apart, and one's body is spilling out. As a result, it began to be said: *Now the world spills out;* or, *Now the world is spilling out.*

37. *Micicinoa: He brags about himself.*
This is said about the person who brags about himself, such
as about his riches or knowledge, saying: "I have become
wealthy; there are my goods and possessions!" Or else "I
am learned," etc.

38. *Cuix ixquich quitta in huitziltzin: Can a hummingbird see that
much?*
This is said when we share a tortilla or some food divided
into tiny pieces. If someone says "What you have given me
is so small," he then adds "*Can a hummingbird see that much?*"
For a hummingbird has a very thin beak, and when it sips
nectar even from a very tiny flower he sips very little of it.

39. *Tlatoluilax: Word-dragger.*
This is said about a person who is slow in speaking and
who does not reply volubly when spoken to.

40. *Tencuicuitzca: Swallow's beak.*
This is said about a person who talks a great deal, who is
full of words.

41. *Cuix tleuh yetinami in coyotl: Does a coyote carry his fire
around with him?*
This is said when we are ravenous and bolt down something
that is not fully cooked. Like a coyote biting into a green
ear of corn, a person who is starving bolts down tortillas
or meat even though they may not be cooked through. And
if someone is going to cook the food, or would like to hu-
miliate the other, then the hungry one says: *Does a coyote
carry his fire around with him?*

42. *Cuix no nennipatzactzintli: Am I good for nothing, am I a
withered ear of corn?*
This is said if a captain, who is not very well off, gives a
banquet or serves a meal to another. I want to do the same.
I want to give a banquet or serve a meal to someone. For
this reason, one says: *Am I a withered ear of corn?* Or, *Am I
good for nothing, am I a withered ear of corn?*

43. *Ipal nonixpatlaoa: Because of him my face becomes wide.*
This is said when someone's child—a boy or a girl—or else

someone's pupil, was well taught, well brought up, and is commended for his good upbringing. Consequently, the child's parent or teacher is also being commended. Therefore, they say with regard to the child: *Because of him my face becomes wide.* Or, *I make someone's face wide, you make someone's face wide.*

44. ***Tequitl nitotolpixqui: cuix niquinchopini, mochopinque:*** *My job is watching over the turkey hens. Did I peck at them? They pecked at each other!*
    This refers to the turkey hens when they peck at each other and pluck out each other's feathers. The keeper of the turkey hens does not provoke this; they start fighting by themselves and peck at each other. Accordingly, this is also said about the common people when they brawl with each other, when they come to blows over their lands or houses or for some other reason. It is not the authorities who fight with them, but they, of their own accord, join the issue and fight with each other.

45. ***Quennel, tla nel toconilhuitl in quennel: amo zan no quioalitoz: quennel:*** *What can be done? If we just say, "What can be done?" the other person will only say, "What can be done?"*
    This is said when I have been divested of something, or I lose something that does not turn up anywhere. I become excited and say, *"What can be done?"* But if we just say, *"What can be done?"* the other person will only say, *"What can be done?"*

46. ***Ma quimichpil oconatlic:*** *Possibly a mouse drank it.*
    This is said when we are fighting for something and give up, such as, when players, competing in a game of throwing wooden balls, simply give up and lose the game. This is when they say: *Possibly the mouse drank it.*

47. ***Cuix nixilotl nechititzayanaz:*** *Am I an ear of corn that they can scrape the kernels off my belly?*
    This is said when someone was in trouble. He had committed a robbery or adultery, or he seduced someone, or did something that was wrong, and then said to me, "Don't say anything to anyone about what you have seen." I then

reply to him: *Am I an ear of corn that they can scrape the kernels off my belly?*[15]

48. **Icnococotzin:** *Poor little dove.*
This is said about someone who is poor. He has scarcely anything, only a few things to call his own.

49. **Oc nocetonal, oc mocetonal:** *One more day for me, one more day for you.*
This is said when a wild beast was about to devour me, or a poisonous snake was going to bite me and I leaped over him and fled, or a bull was going to eat me, but I ran away and escaped danger. If I had not done all these things, I would have died, or might have lived only a few days. For this reason one says: *One more day for me, one more day for you.*

50. **Quen uel ximimatia in teteocuitlamichi:** *What happened to you, fish of gold? Be careful!*
This is said when someone had lived a life of propriety until a certain time and then something came over him. Perhaps he took a lover, or he struck someone who took sick or died and he was put in jail. Then one says: *What happened to you, fish of gold? Be careful!*

51. **Tla alaui, tlapetzcaui in tlalticpac:** *Things slip, things slide, in this world.*
This is the same as the above. Perhaps until now, someone's way of life was good and then he goes astray. It is exactly as if he had slipped in the mud.[16]

52. **Ayemo qualtlatlatztza:** *He has not yet set his head.*
This is said about someone who does not devote himself to one thing exclusively, who does not stick to anything. Perhaps he studies singing; he does not master it. Then he wants to learn Latin and he does not master it either. Then he studies Spanish and he does not learn this either. About a person who does this, they say: *He has not yet set his head.*

53. **Ayac matlacpa teca:** *No one beseeches another ten times.*
This is said when someone who holds a post and serves in some capacity likes to be coaxed and cajoled. "Oh, if I could

only relinquish my post!" he says, thinking that by doing so he will be loved and esteemed. But when he is removed he becomes downcast. He leaves his post and someone else is put in his place. The person who now offers to do the work, does it better, does it with greater care. This is when it is said: *No one beseeches another ten times.*

54. ***Tepal nitzpiloti:*** *With someone's help I became a vulture.*
This is said when I have nothing to eat and through the offices of a friend I eat a little of his food. Should someone ask me if I have eaten, I reply: *With someone's help I was "vulturing."*

55. ***In oalquiza tonatiuh amo totonqui: quin iquac iye(l)iz ye-tiuh ye totonqui:*** *The sun is not hot when it has just risen: after it has been traveling its course awhile, then it becomes hot.*
This is said about a person who has just married, as he is still very poor when he starts out on life. However after a little time has gone by he is consoled, as he may now have laid by something.

56. ***Can machpa tiuitze:*** *Where have we come from?*
This is said when someone hurts us deeply or wants to do us harm and he is not our enemy but our friend. Hence one retorts: *Where have we come from?*[17]

57. ***Quen tehito:*** *It's the way people are regarded.*
This is said when someone is greatly admired, honored, and esteemed. When someone says, "Why do they make so much of him?" the other then replies: *It's the way people are regarded.*

58. ***Ye iuhqui itoch:*** *Such is his rabbit.*
This is said about people when they get drunk. One weeps copiously, another fights with people and shouts at them. And so, when a drunkard shouts at people or starts weeping, they say: *Such is the rabbit,* because in the past pulque was consecrated to rabbits, whom the ancients worshipped as gods.[18]

This is also said of someone who is extremely belligerent, or of someone who is very kind and loves everyone. Though he is not a drinker, they say: *Such is his rabbit*, which means such is his nature.

59. *Ixtimal: A glorious face.*
This is said about a person who, outwardly, makes a good appearance but does nothing well, executes nothing well. He can do absolutely nothing. This is especially said of women who appear to embroider and spin well but in reality can do nothing well; they just deceive people. For this reason they say: *A glorious face.*

60. *Cuix tecoco in ixcuelli: auh ye no mitoa. Azo noxayac in pinaoa: in nocuitlaxcol cuix no pinaoa: Does a black look hurt? One also says, Is my face mortified, are my innards also mortified?*
This is said when I am very hungry, when I am ravenous, and others are eating. I ask them to give me a little something to eat but they will not give me anything. They become angry and look at me askance. However, because I am starving, I quickly sit down with them and eat, or I snatch some tortillas. This is when one says: *Does a black look hurt?* For looking askance at someone does him no harm; only starvation kills a person and causes death.

61. *Campa xonpati: Where can one be healed?*
This is said when someone quarrels with me and stings me with his words. I then seek out one of my friends, I go to see him so that he can console me, but he upbraids me and also hurts my feelings. He does the same thing to me; I fall right into his mouth. This is when one says: *Where can one be healed?*

62. *Noyollo yitzaya, moyollo yitzaya, etc.: My heart turns white, your heart turns white, etc.*
This is said when we long for something that we like very much. For example when I am either very hungry or thirsty, or when I desire something agreeable. When I see it my heart rejoices. Then one says: *My heart turns white.*

63. **Patlichilpitica:** *It is loosely tied.*
    This is said when someone makes an accusation against me,
    saying many things to bring me harm, and treats me with
    disdain. I am unable to reply but, nevertheless, I deliberate
    about it so that I may defend myself. If anyone should say
    "Why don't you defend yourself?" I reply, saying: *"It is
    loosely tied.* And even if it were tightly tied, he has trumped
    it up; he does not know how I shall take revenge for such
    deceit."

64. **Ayatle iueliyaca:** *His nose has lost its power.*
    This is said when certain tidings are untrue, when they are
    imparted wildly and cannot be proven anywhere. For in-
    stance if someone says, "They say the emperor is dead,"
    this is not true. So one says: *His nose has lost its power.* But
    if it were true, then one would say: *His nose is certainly
    powerful!*

65. **Tlacocualli in monequi:** *Moderation is proper.*
    We should not dress in rags, nor should we overdress. In
    the matter of clothing we should dress with moderation.

66. **Tlacaitleoa**[19] *Everyone goes off.*
    This is said at harvesttime when everyone goes off to gather
    the harvest. It can also be said when everyone goes to the
    fields at the time of tilling.

67. **Quin nicoyutl: ma ica niquitta:** *When I am a coyote I shall see
    it.*
    This is said when someone claims to have done something.
    For example, he says: "I went to Castile," or, "I went to
    Guatemala." Or, he says: "I was mayor." But this is not
    true, he is just lying. For this reason, they say: *When I am
    a coyote, I shall see that he went to Castile, or Guatemala, or that
    at some time he was a mayor!*

68. **Ma Chapultepec ninaalti:** *Oh, that I may bathe in Chapultepec!*
    This is said when I fall ill, when I am stricken by a grave
    illness, or when I have a burdensome duty to perform, and

I long to be well, or for the task to be completed. If I am a little better or my work is done, then I say: *Oh, that I might bathe in Chapultepec!*[20]

69. ***Aicnopilpan nemitiliztli:*** *It is no life among the poor.*
This is said of a king who enters the house of a commoner. They say: *Among the poor is no life for this king.* This means that he should not enter a poor man's house, that it is only proper for him to enter the house of a king.

This is also said of some ungrateful person who is given some object or some food and he thinks little of it, he disdains it. He wants something expensive, a turkey. Hence they say: *It is no life among the poor.*

70. ***Telchitl, anozo, atelchitl:*** *So much the better, or, So much the worse.*
This is said when no sooner do we send someone for something than we receive it. Or when someone is supposed to go for something but does not get it, and comes back saying, "What was it I was supposed to get?" Or else, somewhere he stumbles and falls. Hence, they say: *So much the worse.*

71. ***Omotlatziuiz eoac:*** *Your laziness turned out well.*
This is said when we send someone to call another, but he does not want to go, and a short while later we receive the very person he was to have called, or he meets him just outside the door, or else the person is just coming along. Therefore he is told: *Your laziness turned out well.*

72. ***Muchi oquicac in nacel:*** *Every one of my nits has heard it!*
This is said when a person tells another something and he repeats it many times, he says the same things over and over again.

73. ***Muchin quimomolchioa in tapayaxin nicaci:*** *He makes a stew of all the chameleons he catches.*[21]
This is said when someone is given a task to do that is not difficult, but he regards it as difficult; or he receives an

insignificant order that he considers dangerous and is upset. For this reason one replies: *He makes a stew, etc.*

75. *Nictlatilpatlaoa: I make a smudge.*
This is said when we do something in a way that it should not be done, or say something rude and thus spoil or make a botch of something. It derives from the painters.[22] When they are painting, sometimes they do it poorly, sometimes they make a smudge.

75. *Iuh quito atecocolpil, aye nel to xoxomacayan: So said the little water snail: Truly, the hour of our being crushed is never.*
This is said when someone committed a crime and was punished, or went away somewhere and was killed. For this reason, they say: *So said the little water snail: Truly, the hour of our being crushed is never.*

76. *Can paxo'n naoalli: The sorcerer bit into it.*[23]
This is said when I sell something that is expensive, that has a price of five pesos, for example, and I charge only one peso for it. Or perhaps I put a low price on something small; I do not make anything, I make no profit from it. For this reason one says: *The sorcerer bit into it.*

77. *Ompa ce zotl ommopilo: He hung himself with a piece of rug.*
This is said when I make an accusation against someone because of some trifling thing and he retaliates with something serious that puts me in difficulties; or when something, such as a cape or a cup is slightly ripped or cracked, and when I want to repair it, it rips or cracks more. Then one says: *He hung himself with a piece of rug.*

78. *Canin mach coyonacazco: Where, perhaps, in a coyote's ear?*
This is said when someone derides and openly criticizes another, but what he says does not reveal much, it discloses very little. Hence, one replies to the derider: *Where, perhaps, in a coyote's ear?*
This is also said about a person who is sent to fetch something or to call someone, and is told a second and a third

time but simply does not comprehend. So they say to him:
Where, perhaps, in a coyote's ear?

79. *Ye oyauh in itlatolhoaz: His talker has run down.*
    This is said about someone who is very forceful when he
    makes accusations against others and argues with great ve-
    hemence, but when he finds that he can do nothing to the
    people he accuses, little by little he quiets down.
      This is also said about someone who is overweening, who
    arrogantly tosses his head up and down, and who has no
    regard for anything. Thus, he is reprimanded many times
    over and little by little becomes subdued. He is exactly like
    a colt that is gradually tamed. Therefore, they say: *His talker
    has run down.*

80. *Zan ixquich motlacatili: This is all that was born.*
    This is said when we say something that is brief, not long
    and drawn out, and it is quickly concluded. When it is over
    we say: *This is all that was born.*

81. *Aca icuitlaxcoltzin quitlatalmachica: Someone who arranges
    his intestines artistically.*
    This is said of an artisan, such as a feather artist, who does
    his work beautifully and designs it well, so that it goes, so
    that it is sold quickly.[24]

82. *Occepa iuhcan yez, occepa iuh tlamaniz, in iquin, in canin:
    Once again it shall be, once again it shall exist, sometime, some-
    where.*
    What happened long ago and no longer happens, will hap-
    pen another time. What existed long ago, will exist again.
    Those who are living now, will live anew, will exist once
    more.

83. *Ma amo ixiloyocan taci: ma amo imiyaoayocan taci: You
    never ripen into an ear of corn, you never sprout corn tassels.*
    This proverb is understood in two ways; the first is good,
    the other is not. It is favorable when someone is illustrious,
    rich, and possessed of wealth and abundance, or rules a

kingdom here on earth. They say: *He has ripened into an ear of corn, he has sprouted corn tassels.* He is esteemed and praised. They said that this kind of person achieved this on his own merit.[25]

Some Conundrums That They Tell and Try to Guess

1. What is a little blue-green jar filled with popcorn? Someone is sure to guess our riddle; it is the sky.

2. What is it that drags its intestines as it ambles along the foothills of the mountain? Someone is sure to guess our riddle; it is a sewing needle.

3. What is a two-toned drum of jade ringed with flesh? Someone is sure to guess our riddle; it is an earplug.

4. What is a warrior's hair-dress[26] that knows the way to the region of the dead? Someone is sure to guess our riddle; it is a jug for drawing water from the well.

5. What are ten thin slabs of stone that one is always hauling around? Someone is sure to guess our riddle; they are our nails.

6. What is it that is seized in a black stone forest and dies on a white stone slab? Someone is sure to guess our riddle; it is a louse that we take from our head, put on our nail and then kill.

7. What is a hollow straw that makes songs? It is a sackbut.[27]

8. What is a little darky who writes with a piece of lead? A snail.

9. What is it that points its finger at the sky? A maguey thorn.

10. What are four hundred furrows in search of lice? A comb.

11. What is it that is bending over us all over the world? Corn tassels.

12. What is a frightful old lady that gnaws into the earth? A mole.

13. What is a tiny silver speck tied with a black thread? A nit.

14. What is a little mirror in the middle of fir trees? Our eyes.

15. What is a mountainside that has a spring of water in it? Our nose.

16. What is it that grinds with a stone, strips of leather are all over it, and it is surrounded with flesh? The mouth.

17. What is it that has a face of flesh in front and a little clay bell on the back of its neck? The finger.

18. What is it that has a face of flesh and a neck of bone? It is the same, the finger.

19. What are they that go pushing along wrinkled faces? The knees.

20. What is an old woman with straw hair standing before the door of the house? The granary.[28]

21. What is long, hard, and red, and bites people without any trouble? An ant.

22. What is a "You jump and I will jump?" It is a rubber drumstick.

23. What is a "I go this way, you go that, and over there we shall meet"? A breechcloth.

24. What is a little white stone holding up quetzal feathers? An onion.

25. What is a white-haired pulque jar holding up quetzal feathers? It is the same, an onion.

26. What is it that we enter in three places and leave by only one? Our shirt.

27. What is a screeching locust lying down and scratching its ribs. A bone scraper.[29]

28. What is it that has ribs outside and is standing upright on the road? A carrying frame for loads.[30]

29. What is it that you quickly take from its hole and cast on the ground stiff? It is the mucus from the nose.

30. What is it that goes into a tree and its tongue is hanging out? An axe.

31. What is it that knocks its bib head against the edge of the roof? A ladder.

32. What is it that has a shirt stuck to it? The green tomato.[31]

33. What is it that comes out and now you have your stone? Excrement.

34. What is a cardinal going first and a crow following behind? Something burning.

35. What are upended stones standing in the doorway? Columns.

36. What is it that in one day becomes big with child? A spindle.

37. What is it always standing by the hearth curving upward? A dog's tail.

38. What is it that is filled with round shields inside? A chile, as its seeds are in the form of shields.

39. What is it that goes along the foothills on the mountain patting out tortillas with its hands? A butterfly.

40. What is a black stone standing on its head, cocking its ear toward the region of the dead? The darkling beetle.

41. What is a red stone that goes jumping along? A flea.

42. What is on round stones and is singing? The pot for cooking corn with lime.

43. What is on the road biting people? The stones we stumble over.

44. What is a little multicolored jug sitting in the road? A dog's excrement.

45. What is it that has rounded hips above and when it shakes it cries out? A round rattle.[32]

46. What is in the dancing place getting potbellied and kicking its legs? The spindle.[33]

Some Figures of Speech, Called Metaphors

Difficult Phrases Accompanied by Their Explanations and Interpretations

1. *Tictetezoa in chalchihuitl, ticoaoazoa in quetzalli*
   You scratch the jade, you tear apart the quetzal feather.
   This is said about someone who mutilates something precious, who dishonors something worthy of great honor. For example those who receive the Holy Sacrament without showing it the proper reverence—without bowing, without weeping, etc.—or a commoner who dishonors a noblewoman. They are told: *You have scratched the jade, you have torn apart the quetzal feather.*[34]

2. *Canin mach itzontlan, iqualtla(n) nitlapachoa*
   Where have I walked over the hair, the head of our lord?
   This means: Have I offended Our Lord in some way that he has brought misfortune upon me?

3. *Motzontlan, moquatlan nitlapachoa*
   I put something over your hair, over your head.
   This means: When I admonish you like this, I am protecting your honor and good name, so that you shall not be degraded and that no adversity shall befall you. (I protect your honor and good name. **CGN: 345.** *Ed.*)

4. *Ca nauh, ca notlacual*
   It is my food and drink.
   This means: These are my lands, these are my tools; these are my means of livelihood. (This is my property, this is my sustenance. **CGN: 345.** *Ed.*)

5. *Natzauh, nomecaxicol*
   My heron feather headdress,[35] my jacket of ropes.
   This means: When the city gives me a responsibility I become a slave. If I hurt the city in some way, if I endanger it, I shall be put in jail.

6. *Matzauh, momecaxicol otitlalilioc*
You have been dressed in your heron feather headdress, in your jacket of ropes.
This means: The city has made a slave of you.

7. *Onimitzpanti, onimitzteteuhti*
I have given you your flag and strips of paper.[36]
This is said when someone has reached the point of despair. Finally he says to the other: *"I have given you your flag and strips of paper."* (. . . which are carried by those on their way to death on the sacrifical stone. **CGN:** 346. *Ed.*)

8. *In muztla, in uiptla*
Tomorrow, the day after tomorrow.
This means: We shall be seeing each other in just a short time.

9. *In ye quauhtica, in ye mecatica tanotihui*
When you are already behind bars and tied in ropes.[37]
This means: I am starting to warn you now, but when you are already tied up, can I go and say something to you? Will it still be opportune? (What does my counsel serve when you are held in prison? **CGN:** 346. *Ed.*)

10. *Ixtlapal, nacacic*
On the side, on the sly.
This was said when someone was admonished many times over but turned a deaf ear and regarded it with disdain. When he was tied up and taken away, these words were said to annoy him: *Do not glance at me obliquely and askance, for I have done my duty.* (Don't look for me, or even look at me sideways, for you will be judged. You wouldn't hear my counsel in time. **CGN:** 346. *Ed.*)

11. *In ye tlecuilixcuac, in ye tlamamatlac*
Now in front of the fire, now in front of the step.
This was said about those who were to be sacrificed and were taken up the pyramid to die, or were placed before the fire when the moment came for them to die. Previously they had been counseled so that this should not happen to them.[38]

12. *In ye techinantitlan, in ye tequiyaoac*
    Now beside the walls of strangers, now in the doorway of strangers.
    With these words they instructed either children or com-
    moners to keep them from doing what they should not do,
    from doing something bad, so that they would not be ban-
    ished, not forced to live beside the walls of strangers, in the
    doorways of strangers. The person was told: "If you do
    something and are banished, you shall pass your life *beside
    the walls of strangers, in the doorways of strangers.*" We also
    say this: *You shall be forced to live in others' cities; you no longer
    shall live in your own city.*

13. *Tzonpachpul, cuitlanexpul: vel[39] achi itzoncal tictlalilia*
    Unkempt and filthy; or, Straighten your wig a little!
    This is said of a person who derides his king or ruler, or
    makes an accusation against another, or ridicules his father
    or mother. He does not want to live the way his father or
    grandfather lived. Thus he is reprimanded and told:
    Straighten your wig a little! Or, *You are making your father or
    grandfather live unkempt and filthy!* (You are dirtying and
    messing the hair [honor] of your ancestors. **CGN:** 347. *Ed.*)

14. The person who ridiculed his father and mother, or his king
    or governor, was also told and thus reprimanded: *Do not
    stand the king, or the throne, or your father, on their heads!* (Don't
    hold your superiors up to ridicule. **CGN:** 347. *Ed.*)

15. *Tzonhueztli, tlaxapuchtli neuiuixtoc in ixpan petlatl, icpalli*
    The snare and the trap are aflutter in the presence of the throne.
    This was said to someone who made an accusation against
    another before the king, or to someone close to the king.
    He was told: *Be careful! Before the throne,* meaning the king,
    the snare and the trap are aflutter.

16. *Coloyotoc, tzitzicazzotoc*
    Full of scorpions, full of nettles.
    This was told to the person who made accusations against
    others before the king, or someone who went about in the
    company of the king: "Be careful!" They told him, "For the
    king deals out punishment as well as favors."

17. **Teuhyo, tlazolo**
Full of dirt, full of filth.
This phrase is said about a person who becomes king by usurping the throne, or someone who acquires goods by chicanery or becomes rich by thievery. Such a person was told: "Have you become king in the proper way? Have you acquired wealth or the things you eat in the proper way? Your kingship—or the food you eat—is *full of dirt, full of filth!*"

18. **Mitzoalixtlapalitztica, mitzoalnacazitztica**
They are looking at you out of the corner of their eyes, they are looking sidelong at you.
This was said of the principal ruler or the high priest. By being king, he was like a great cypress, a great ceiba, because the people put their trust in him.[40] (This was said about a governor or a high priest, who could not be looked at directly. **CGN:** 348. *Ed.*)

19. **Mixtitlan, Ayauhtitlan**
From out of the clouds, from out of the mists.
This was said about people very illustrious and very great, who cannot be looked at, who had never been known, who had never been beheld anywhere. And so when the Spaniards came here, throughout all Mexico it was said: *Out of the clouds, out of the mists.* It was also said about those who were highly esteemed and very rich.

20. **Poctli, ayauitl: tenyotl, mauizyotl**
Smoke and mist: fame and glory.
This was said about a king not long dead whose *smoke and mist,* meaning his *fame and glory,* had not yet vanished; or, about someone who had gone far away but whose fame and glory had not faded.

21. **Tehuatl, tlachinolli**
The vast sea,[41] *the conflagration.*
This was said when a great war or a great pestilence occurred. They said: *Sea and fire* have overcome us, have swept over us. This means pestilence or war itself.

22. *Ocelopetlatl, quappetlatl*
    The jaguar mat, the eagle mat.[42]
    This means where the strong and valiant are, whom no one
    can vanquish. For this reason they say: "*The eagle mat and
    the jaguar mat* are laid out there." And they also said: "There
    stand *the jaguar wall and the eagle wall*, which protect the
    city," which means *water and mountain.*[43]

23. *Cuitlapilli, in atlapalli*
    The tail and the wing.
    This means the common people. For this reason the subjects
    are called *tails and wings*, and the king, lord of the *tails and
    wings.*

24. *In atzopelic, in ahautac*
    Disgusting, stinking.
    This is said about a person who is ungrateful, or a commoner
    who is banished. He is told: "Be off! Leave the city! It regards
    you as *foul-tasting and stinking!*" Or, a ruler is told: "You are
    not regarded as savory, you are not regarded as fragrant."

25. *In auitzyo, in ahuayo*
    Is it not full of thorns, is it not full of briars?
    This was said of a ruler or noble who was very august. No
    one could get close to him as he was thought of as a wild
    beast. For this reason one was told not to misprize the king.
    "Do you not think that the king or the throne has *thorns*?
    When you bring your disputes before him, or when accu-
    sations are forever being made against others, do you not
    think he *has briars*? He is disgusted!"

26. *Tzopelic, ahuiyac*
    Sweet and fragrant.
    This was said about a city where there was prosperity and
    joy, or about a king who brought joy to the people.

27. *Tetzon, teizti, teaoayo, tetentzon, teixquamul, tetzicueuhca,
    tetlapanca*
    *Someone's hair, nails; someone's thorns, briars; someone's beard,
    eyebrows, a chip off the block, and sliver from the same stick.*

This means someone born of nobility, of a noble family. He was also designated as, *Someone's blood, someone's red ink.*

28. **Teix, tenacaz**
Someone's eyes and ears.
This phrase was said of a royal emissary or ambassador, who bore the king's orders to other regions. The emissary was told: "It may be true that the king himself has not come. You have come and you are the *eyes*, you are the *ears* of the king. You are his hearing and his sight."

29. **Teixptla, tepatillo**
Someone's image and surrogate.
This was said of the king's emissaries. It was also said of the king's son when his father died, for in his son the king left his *image*, the son was acting as his *representative*.

30. **In itconi, in mamaloni, in tecuexanco, in temamaloazco yetiuh**
Borne in the arms and on the back, carried in the mantle and cradled in the arms.
This was said of the common people, the subjects, those who are governed. They said: "The people are *carried in the mantle and borne in the arm and on the back.* They are led, they are governed, they are *carried in the cradle of the arms;* they do not lead themselves."

31. **Texillan, tecozcatlan oquiz**
From someone's entrails, from someone's throat, he came forth.
This was said about the person who comes from nobility.[44]

32. **Ihiyo, itlatol**
His breath, his words.
This was said only about the words of kings. They said: "The king's *venerable breath*, his *venerable words.*" It was not said about anyone else's words, only "*the illustrious breath, the illustrious words* of our lord."

33. **In tlauilli, in ocotl, in machiotl, in octacatl, in coyaoca tezcatl: mixpa nicmana**
I set before you a light, a torch, an example, a measuring rod, a great mirror.

The phrase was said of a lord who spoke to the people and placed before them fine words. He told them: "What I raise before you is *a torch, a light,* and what I hold before you is *a mirror.*" Or, "What I offer you is *an example for you, your measuring rod.* You shall take it as *a model,* you shall take it as an *example,* so that you may live properly, or that you may speak well."

34. *Toptli, petlacalli*[45]
A basket, a coffer.
These words were said about someone who could keep a secret, who was closemouthed; or if some wrongdoing happened before his eyes, he did not reveal it to anyone. He was just like *a basket, a coffer.* They said: "He guards words or another's life perfectly."

35. *Xicoti, pipiyolti*
Being a hornet, being a bumblebee.
This was said of those who eat and drink at the expense of the nobles of the city, either asking for it or being given it. They are then told: "Do not put on airs because of this, do not be presumptuous, as you are *just bumblebeeing,* you are *just horneting,* sipping at the expense of the city or the king."

36. *Nextepeoalli, otlamaxalli nicnonantia, nicnotatia*
I have made my mother and father of the garbage heap, of the crossroads.
This was said of the women or men who congregated on the roads. It was not the wish of their mothers and fathers that they should end up like this; it was by their own choice that they congregated on the roads. They took themselves there.

37. *Anitlanammati, anitlatamati*
I think nothing of my mother, I think nothing of my father.
This phrase was said of someone who was admonished over and over but did not listen, he disregarded the admonition. It was expressed in this way: "He regards his mother and father as if they were nothing. He just wants to live as he pleases."

38. *Mixtlaza, motlantlaza*
    You are stepping on your face, you are stepping on your teeth.
    This was said about a king or noble who said something
    that was not proper and mortified someone, something that
    he ought not to have said. He was told: "Be still! Be prudent!
    You are *stepping on your face.*" This means: "You have dis-
    graced yourself." And he was also told "You dirty yourself,
    you dishonor yourself, you mar your life and your words."

39. *Moteyotia, mitauhcayotia*
    He makes himself famous, he makes himself celebrated.
    This was said of the person who did something estimable
    either in war or by fashioning something well. Therefore it
    was said: *He made himself famous, he made himself celebrated,*
    and thus the memory of his fame, renown, honor, and glory
    shall remain.

40. *Mixtilia, momauiztilia*
    He regards himself highly, he holds himself in great esteem.
    This phrase is said of the person who is not friendly in
    speaking to others. He also loves his own words very much
    and he does not lower himself by smiling or bantering.
    Therefore they said: *He regards himself highly, he holds himself
    in great esteem.*

41. *Cuix topyo, cuix petlacallo*
    Could it be put in a basket, could it be put in a coffer?
    This phrase is said of women who do not safeguard them-
    selves, whether they have gone astray or not. Thus it was
    said: "Perhaps they have gone astray, perhaps not. *Are they
    basketable, are they cofferable?* Gold is something that can be
    kept in a coffer, it can be kept in a basket; it is able to be
    protected. But not women, they cannot be protected."

42. *Uel chalchiuhtic, uel teuxiuhtic, uel acatic, uel ololiuhqui*
    Fine jade, rich turquoise, long as reeds and very round.
    This was said of a royal orator who counseled the people
    very well. They said: "He spoke magnificently—*with jades,
    turquoises*—and his words sounded as precious stones, *long
    as reeds and very round.*"

43. *Ontetepeoac, onchachayaoac*
There was a sowing, there was a scattering.
This was said of a royal orator who counsels the people
well. After he spoke, after the sermon had been preached,
they understood its truth and they told him: "The people
have been enriched, they have become wealthy. *There has
been a sowing, there has been a scattering* of precious jades,
etc."

44. *Oton motlamachti, otonmocuiltono: opopouh, onixtlauh
inic monantzin, inic motatzin*
*You have become rich, you have become wealthy; with this your
mother and father have discharged their duty, have fulfilled their
obligations.*
This was said of the commoners collectively and it can also
be said of one person. When people have been advised they
are told: "You, the people, *have become rich, you have become
wealthy.* With this that you have heard—meaning the
speech—*your mother and father,* or the city, or the authorities,
have discharged their duty, have fulfilled their obligations."

45. *Itzuitequi, acamelaoa*
Obsidian blades, hardened arrows.[46]
These words were said about one person who hated another
and was constantly plotting to do something monstrous to
him. He went about saying: "How can I do something to
that scoundrel?" He was always looking for a way to do
something sinister, to do something evil to another.[47]

46. *Ontlatepeuh, intlachayauh in petlapan, in icpalpan*
He flung something, he spilled something on the mat and seat.[48]
This meant a commoner who brought an accusation against
another before the king, or perhaps offended the king in
some way. They said the commoner *flung, he spilled something
before the king,* which meant he offended or displeased the
king.

47. *Ontlaxamani, ontlapoztec*
She smashed it, she broke it.
This phrase was said of a wetnurse or midwife when she

suckled the child of a noblewoman and the child died. For this reason it was said: *She smashed it, she broke it.* Or when a doctor wanted to cure someone and the patient died under his care, he was told: *You smashed him, you broke him.*

48. **Tezo, teuipana**
He threads people, he arranges people in order.
This means a person well versed in genealogy of the nobles. Thus it was said: *He threads people, he arranges people in order.* And nobles and sons of nobles were called: *Someone's necklace, someone's quetzal feather plumage; someone's princes.*

49. **Tecuic, tetlatol**
Another's song, another's words.
This is meant of a person who did not speak his own words but the words of the elders or of nobles. And when it was a commoner who made a speech he was told: "Is this *your song, are these your words* that you speak? It is not appropriate for you to say them!"

50. **Pipillo, coconeyo, iuincayotl xocomiccayotl**
Childishness and puerility, drunkenness and inebriation.[49]
These words were said about a person who did something poorly, or by a person who did something well or spoke well but was modest. When someone did something well, or spoke well, he did not say: "I did something very well, or spoke well." He said: "What I did was *childish, puerile, drunken, and inebriated.*" Or, "It was witless and senseless." Or, "I may or may not have done it, I may or may not have said it." (This was also a form of modesty that was used to refer to something that one had done or expressed well. **CGN:** 353. *Ed.*)

51. **Tlachpanaliztli, tlacuicuiliztli nicchioa**
I sweep, I gather up the sweepings.
This was said of someone who performs a task or service for the city or the temple. It was said thus: Before our Lord or the city[50] one just *sweeps and gathers up the sweepings.*

52. **Aompa nicquixtia, aompa nicnacaztia**
Nowhere do I hit the mark, nowhere have I been fully heard.

This is a phrase that was said when someone accused another before the king and if the accusation was false, then a protest was made before the king. As a result the king was humiliated; because he had been challenged he was mortified. Therefore they said: "This person has humiliated the king. *Nowhere did he hit the mark, nowhere was he well heard.*" This means that he did not hear straight and he did not see straight. (One who had humiliated the king expressed his clumsiness in this way. **CGN:** 353. *Ed.*)

53. *Iztlactli, tenqualacatli*
Saliva, spittle.
These words mean falsehood and untruth. It was said to the king or noble who believed all the lies he heard.

"Do not tell lies and falsehoods in the presence of the king," the liar was told. "Investigate it thoroughly, look at it closely."

And they said to the king: "Oh Lord, do not listen to *saliva and spittle.* Be so good as to look sharply and listen to the words carefully; as you are believing, you are taking in lies."

54. *Ye otimalihui, ye ompa onquiza in toneuiztli*
It has now swelled, it has reached the point of affliction.
This means that my heart and body are sorely afflicted. I have nothing, as nothing is my food and nothing are my rags. (This expresses poverty. **CGN:**353. *Ed.*)

55. *Netloc, nenaoac, netzitzquilo, nepacholo*
Together, side by side, clasping and embracing.
These words are said of nobles or rulers who serve each other and love each other very much. Thus it is said: "The nobles and rulers are *together, side by side, clasping and embracing.*"

56. *Anezcalicayotl, xolopicayotl*
Ill breeding, stupidity.
This means a person who is not well bred, not well spoken, and whatever he is ordered to do he does poorly. He per-

severes in *ill breeding and stupidity*. (Someone who consistently does poorly what he is ordered to do. **CGN: 353.** *Ed.*)

57. *Oc xonmotlamachti, oc xonmoculltono*
May you continue rich, may you continue prosperous.
This phrase is said to a person who is very illustrious, or someone who has all the necessities of life. For this reason, they say to him: "*May you continue rich, may you continue prosperous* with the help of our Lord, Lord of the Endless and Boundless."

58. *In uel patlaoac, in uelxopaleoac quetzalli*
A very broad and very green quetzal plumage.
This was said of the king, or a noble, or a royal orator. The person who was counseled was told: "May you capture the words. They are the *quetzal's plumage, very wide and precious green*. The Lord king has done you a service."

59. *In popocatiuh, in chichinauhtiuh*
He is smoking, he is sizzling.
This was said of a person who reprimanded others in very harsh words, words that stung. He did not speak calmly and everyone was very frightened. He did not speak clearly so that everyone could understand.

60. *Taueuetl, in tipochotl motlan moceoualhuiz, moyacaluiz, in maceoalli*
You are a great cypress and a ceiba; under you the people shall have cover, they shall have shade.
This is said of the rulers. They are thought of as great *cypress and ceibas*; under them *there is cover, there is shade*. (This was said of the lords who protected their subjects. **CGN: 354.** *Ed.*)

61. *Motenan, motzacuil*
Your wall, your enclosure.
This was said of those who served in some capacity, such as tribute collectors or captains. Or it was said of a king or a noble who governed the people, as he was like their *wall and enclosure*, encircling and surrounding them. For what-

ever would befall the people would first befall the king or noble.

62. ***In ye imecac, in ye iquauic in totecuyo, in zan ticamatlapul, in zan tixtlapul***
Now in the ropes, now in the stocks[51] *of our Lord, your mouth in the earth, your face in the mud.*
These words are understood as sickness, for it is as if our Lord binds us fast. For this reason they say: "May you continue to enjoy yourself, may you continue to be happy, may you continue to eat and drink. Later, perhaps tomorrow or the day after, when you eat you may take sick, you may be stricken by illness. Then you will be in the *stocks and ropes of our Lord;* you will lie in the clutches of sickness, *your mouth in the earth, your face in the earth.*"

63. ***In ticicatinemi in timeltzotzontinemi: in iuhqui mixitl, in iuhtlapatl otiquic***
You are panting and beating your breath as if you had drunk a potion of jimsonweed.[52]
This is said of someone who no longer wishes to listen to admonition. He is just like a drunkard, like someone who is maddened with jimsonweed. He lives without recalling anything that has been told. As he does not come to his senses, he is reprimanded in this way: "What devil have you taken, what the devil have you been sucking on? Nothing stays with you, nothing remains fixed in your heart. You spurn, you reject all admonition!"

64. ***In tamoyauatinemi,***[53] ***in tecatocotinemi***
You are borne by the water, carried by the wind.
This was said of a person who just wandered from place to place. He did not settle down anywhere, he did not make his home anywhere but just went from house to house. "What are you up to? What are you doing?" They said to him: "It is as if you were *carried by the wind, borne by the water.* Settle down somewhere, do not be wandering about!"

65. ***In otitochtiac, in otomazatiac***
You have turned into a rabbit, you have turned into a deer.

This was said about someone who no longer lived at home.
He no longer paid attention to his father and mother but
ran away when they wanted to correct him. He did not stay
at home but went away, spending his days elsewhere, sleeping elsewhere. He had become *like a rabbit, like a deer.* And
so he was told: "*You have turned into a rabbit, you have turned
into a deer.* You have become a fugitive and a savage. You
have taken the road of the rabbit and the road of the deer."
(You have become a savage; you no longer obey your parents; you have fled your home. **CGN:** 355. *Ed.*)

66. *Azoc uel achic, azoc cemiluitl in ipaltzinco in totecuyo*
    *Perhaps a few moments, perhaps even a day, with the help of our
    Lord.*
    These words were said to the ruler, to the person who gov-
    erned, whereby he was exhorted, fortified, and given cour-
    age. He was told: "It is now that you must glorify our Lord
    in some way and *perhaps you shall have one more day, perhaps
    a few moments more* on our Lord's earth. If not then the sticks
    and stones shall soon come." This means sickness, pestil-
    ence, or death. And he was told that his renown and glory
    could decline and disappear.

67. *In atl itztic, in atl cecec topan quichioa in totecuyo*
    Our Lord dashes cold water, icy water upon us.
    This is said when our Lord causes some misfortune to hap-
    pen to us, such as a disaster, pestilence, or famine. At this
    time it is said: "*Our Lord dashes cold water, icy water upon us.*
    He is pinching our ribs and pulling our ears.[54] Or like a
    thorn, like a needle, our Lord pricks us and punishes us."

68. *Otimatoyaui, otimotepexiui*
    *You hurled yourself into the water, you flung yourself from a
    precipice.*
    This means that you have gotten yourself into difficulties,
    no one else put you there. Someone does something wrong,
    such as committing murder, or something dangerous or
    frightful that he should not do.

69. **In amoyaoalli, in tlamatzoalli**
    The jug holder; the tortilla folder.[55]
    This is said to a king or noble who is beset by sorrow. They told him: "Do not grieve so, do not turn away from the *straw base of the jug and the folded tortilla.* Take a little, take something. Do not neglect yourself, as your grief may turn into sickness." (This signifies food and drink. **CGN:** 355. *Ed.*)

70. **In youalli, in ehecatl in naoalli in totecuyo**
    The Night, the Wind; the Sorcerer, Our Lord.
    These words were said of the idol, *Tezcatlipoca.* They said: "Do you think that *Tezcatlipoca* and *Huitzilopochtli* speak to you like humans? They are invisible as *the night and the wind.* Do you think that they speak to you like human beings?"

71. **Tlaalaoa, tlapetzcaui in ixpan petlatl, icpalli aquineuhian, aquixoaian**
    It is slick and slippery before the throne; there is no door, no way out.
    This means that in the presence of the king no one finds salvation, it is no place of refuge.

72. **Iuian, yocuxca ximonemilti: ma motolol, ma momalcoch, in tetloc, in tenaoac**
    Live tranquilly and peacefully with others and with others keep your head lowered, your head bowed.
    This was said to the nobles or children of nobles. In this way they were exhorted and told: "You must *live tranquilly and peacefully with others and beside others.* You must not be arrogant, you must not be presumptuous; arrogance is not proper, it is not right. One does not live with others in this manner. It is proper to live with *one's head bowed, one's head lowered.*"

73. **Iiztitzin quitlanlquatinemi, imatzin quimocozcatitinemi**
    They are chewing their nails, they are flapping their arms around themselves.
    This was said of those who live in misery, of the poor. They said: "Have pity on the needy, on the poor, who go about

chewing their nails, and hugging themselves. They pass their lives beside the walls of others and in the doorway of others."[56]

74. ***Atitlanonotzalli, atitlazcaltili, atitlauapaoalli, atimuz-calia, atitlachia***
You are undisciplined, coarse, unseemly, uncouth, and senseless.
These words are said to the person who had no upbringing and no sense. He was stupid and understood nothing. They said to him: "Assuredly your mother and father did not instruct you and teach you how to live. *You are undisciplined, coarse, unseemly.*"

75. ***Uel ixe, uel nacace***
Possessed of good eyes, possessed of good ears.
This means a person who is very knowledgeable, who sees and understands everything clearly. He is said to *possess good eyes and good ears.* He does not believe any lies but only accepts absolute truth.

76. ***Iuian tecuyotl, iuian tlatocayotl***
A gentle reign, a gentle rule.
This is said of someone who governs well and who is a benign ruler and noble. He is exceedingly wise, discerning, and cultivated. He loves the people greatly and respects them very much. He is not contemptuous of such unfortunates as the blind, those with maimed hands and crippled legs; or the unkempt and the ragged, the poor who have nothing for supper and breakfast[57] and who have nothing to put around their waists and hang on their shoulders; or those who lean against the walls of others and in the doorways of others; or those who are in the doorways of others, and beside the houses of others, holding out their hands; those who go nowhere and arrive nowhere.

77. ***Yollotl, eztli***
Heart and blood.
These words were said of chocolate because in the past[58] it was precious and rare. The common people and the poor

did not drink it. For this reason it was said: *Heart and blood,
worthy of veneration.*[59] They also said it was deranging and
it was like the mushroom, for it intoxicated people,[60] it made
them drunk. If a commoner drank it it was considered scan-
dalous. In the past the rulers or great warriors, or the commander of the army or the commander of the arsenal, and
perhaps two or three people who were rich drank it; it was
considered something grand. They drank chocolate in small
amounts, it was not drunk immoderately.

78. *Quauhyotica, oceloyotica*
With the valor of eagles, the ferocity of jaguars.
This was said about combat because the nobles did not gain
renown and honor if they did not go to war, if they were
not brave and valiant captains and did not capture prisoners.
It was the same for the common people also; only *as eagles,
and jaguars*[61] did they achieve honor and renown. And it
was the same for the rich or wealthy person who sacrificed
slaves. He was also celebrated, though he was not a captain.
He earned his esteem by his riches because he often invited
people to banquets and regaled them with gifts. (Only with
the valor of the eagle and the jaguar can one attain riches
and renown. **CGN:** 357. *Ed.*)

79. *In tetloan in apaztli*
The cup and the bowl.
This means *pulque* and these words were said to someone
who was drinking, such as a child—a boy or a girl—not an
old man or woman.[62] He was reprimanded and told: "Stop
drinking, young man or young woman! Beware of the *cup
and the bowl* (meaning pulque), which will make you drunk.
Are you an old man? Are you an old woman? You are just
a stripling!"

80. *Otontlalililoc in uel chamaoac, in uel tetziliuhqui*
You have been strongly and tightly bound.
This was said either to a noble or a commoner who was
admonished and thus given courage. He was told: "You
have now been given, you have now received very precious

advice. You have been tightly bound, you have had a rope wound around your shoulders.''[63] (Admonitions fortify you as if you were a bundle tied up and reinforced with ropes. **CGN:** 357. *Ed.*)

81. *Pollocotli, zacaqualli*
Chaff and straw.
This means lies, which are something bad, something wrong. It was said to someone who was rotten, who was a disturber of the peace, and deceitful. "Lies, which are evil and wrong, have stuck to you like *chaff and straw.*" To someone who dedicated and devoted himself to lying, they said: "*Chaff and straw* are what you feed on, you liar, you agitator!"

82. *Acan atl ic timaltiz, ic timochipaoaz*
There is no water anywhere with which you can wash and cleanse yourself.
This was said to someone who committed an offense, such as stealing or adultery. They said to him: "Now, what are you going to do? Your crime is known. *Is there water anywhere with which you can wash and cleanse yourself?* What shall become of you? What shall you do? You are ruined!"

83. *Toyomotlan, tonacaztitech mopipiloa in totecuyo.*
Our Lord is pinching our ribs and pulling our ears.[64]
This was said when our Lord caused some such thing to befall us as a frost that ravaged the crops, or a famine. For this reason it was said: *Our Lord has pulled our ears and pinched our ribs.*

84. *In tlacaquimilli in tlacacacaxtli, oitlan tonac otoconmama*
A bale of people, a cargo of people, you have taken upon you and loaded on your back.
This phrase was said of someone who had been installed as king and ruler. He was told: "*You have taken upon you and loaded on your back, a bale of people, a cargo of people.* You shall become fatigued, you shall become weary because of the people. You have loaded on your back, you have taken upon

you a great burden. What shall be the will of our Lord tomorrow or the day after? Shall it be sticks and stones?"[65]

85. **Tetl oatococ, quauhuitl oatococ**
The sticks and stones have been carried off by the water.[66]
This was said of arduous work and toil, and affliction. The labor oppressed the people greatly, it brought misery and perhaps pestilence.

86. **Intlil, intlapal in ueuetque**
The black and the red of the ancients.[67]
This was said of the traditions of the ancients, the way of life they established. One lived by it, or perhaps did not live by it. Therefore it was said: "Do not let *the red and the black of the ancients perish!*" This means the traditions. Or, "Why do you destroy the way of life, the *black and the red of our grandfathers, the ancients?*"

87. **Intlacouh, in zacapech in ueuetque**
The beds of twigs and straw of the ancients.
This was said about the ancient Chichimeca when they first arrived. It was still forest and open plains when they laid down *their beds of twigs and of straw.* It was said: "There our ancestors, our grandfathers, the Chichimeca, first laid down their *beds of straw, their beds of twigs.*" When they settled themselves in the forest and on the open plains it was full of cactus and magueys.

88. **Teizolo, Tecatzauh**
Something that mars and soils people.
This was said about a way of living and speaking that was wrong. It was said if some noble or lord spoke rashly or snapped at people savagely like a dog. He was reprimanded and told: "Hold your words! do not speak vulgarly. What you say *mars and soils people.*" Or perhaps someone committed a sin, or adultery. The person who did this was admonished and told: "It is unseemly for you to do this, for *you mar yourself, you soil yourself.* One should not live like this, one should not be like this—it is not right, it is

not proper. Stop this! The ancients did not live like this, they did not leave you this way of life. They lived peacefully and tranquilly, and that is what they left to you and all the people."

89. *Nopuchco, nitzcac nimitztlaliz*
I shall put you on my left in my black sandals.[68]
This was said when a king exhorted someone. He said: "You noble, or lord, stand close to me, *at my left, in my black sandals.*" (Or, "You shall put me *at your left*, you shall put me *in your black sandals.*")[69] "Be cautious, conduct yourself well, live properly, and put yourself *at my left, in my black sandals.*" And also when someone spoke for the king, he was told: "You stand *at the king's left, in his black sandals.*" This means he assists the king and speaks for him; he gives his orders and delivers his words.

90. *Inamox, intlacuilol*
Their books, their writings.
This means the same as *their black and their red.*[70]

91. *Mitzayani in ilhuicatl, tentlapani in tlalli*
The heavens rip open, the earth rends apart!
These words were said about something extraordinary that happened, something that did not happen very often, such as when the body of our Lord is received.[71] This is what they said: "A miracle is happening; *the heavens rip open, the earth rends apart!*" No one could laugh or be merry. Everyone was awestruck and frightened because of it. They quivered and trembled in the presence of the divinity, the king.[72]

92. *Xomolli, Tlayoualli ticmotoctia*
You hide yourself in the corner, in the dark.
This was said when some able person, perhaps an experienced and renowned noble or official, perhaps he had lost his good name. He just went off somewhere and no longer sat down with the nobles or rulers. He no longer showed himself anywhere but kept himself hidden. A person who did this was told: "Why do you go away? You no longer

show yourself anywhere. *Why do you hide yourself in the corner, in the dark?"* This means: "You keep yourself hidden and no longer appear among people. You do not show yourself anywhere in order to be sent on a mission, to perform a service for the city. You of your own accord, destroy your glory. You are being an imbecile just lying *in the corner in the dark!"*

2

The Metaphors from the
Orations of Fray Andrés de
Olmos[1]

ALTHOUGH SULLIVAN NEVER FINISHED WORK on the
metaphors of Olmos, those that she did translate are quite different from the metaphors of Sahagún. The nearly one hundred
metaphors in Olmos's grammar form a "Manual of Metaphor."
An example is given in Spanish and then a long listing of metaphoric terms that can be applied to that situation follows. This
is quite different from the more expansive explanations of the
metaphors given by Sahagún.

In her copious notes on the Olmos vocabulary, which she
apparently did not think was a very significant work when she
started editing it, there are constant references to the metaphors
that she did not translate before her death, as well as to the
Huehuetlatolli of Olmos. She obviously had intended to finish
the translation of both the metaphors and the *Huehuetlatolli*. The
metaphors, as they are presented here, are a translator's notes,
which were immediately added to her translator's dictionary for
future reference.

The Manners of Speech of the Elders in Their Ancient Orations

The following manners of speech are metaphorical, for there is one sense to the meaning of the word to the letter and another sense to the expression or the sentence. Although some follow the sense as they are glossed, others contain an additional meaning that goes well beyond that.

1. *Here, on behalf of God, I open and reveal the heart.*
   Here I open the chest, the coffer. The jades, the turquoises are scattered, are strewn about. They gleam, they glisten, they are beneficial, they are true, they emanate from the only God.[2]

2. *Father, mother, ruler, captain, governor, who is like a tree that gives cover.*
   Mother, father, foundation, protector, a great silk tree, a great bald cypress, that gives shade, that gives cover, that gives shelter. He is like a great tree filled with branches, a great tree filled with leaves.

   He has a lap in which he holds one, he has arms in which he cradles one. Calmly, tranquilly, he strings things together, he arranges things in order and thus he carries them in his hands, he bears them on his back, he carries in his arms. Truly possessed of a back, truly possessed of shoulders, he bears people, he leads them along the way, he governs people, he guides people.

   A jade, a turquoise, a jewel, a quetzel feather, he is the water, the mountain, the city, the ruler, he is the mat and the seat, the authority. He is a light, he is a mirror, he is a torch, a flaming torch, he is a model, a measuring rod, he is a stamp, he is the arm's length measure, he is a supporting arch, he is like a round jade bead, a long reedlike jade bead, very green, he is very brilliant, he sets the example of the black and the red inks of tradition. He is like a great tree full of branches, a great tree full of leaves, thus he rules over people.

3. *Farmer or person of low estate.*
   Eagle, jaguar, tail, wing, woodcutter, tiller of the soil.

4. *Rootstock, or first father, or originator of a family line, ruler or governor.*
   Hair of the head, rope, entrails, nourishment, root, someone's hair, someone's grandfather.

5. *People's kinsmen, those who descend from the same stock.*
   He who is someone's thorn, he who is someone's prickle, he who is someone's fragment, he who is someone's shard, he who has someone's blood, he who has someone's red ink, he who has someone's legs, he who is someone's chips, he who is someone's slivers, he who is someone's eyebrows, he who is someone's beard, he who is someone's buttocks, he who has someone's quetzal feather plumage, he who has someone's heels, he who has someone's bits, he who has someone's pieces, he who has kinsmen, he who has second kin, he who has third kin, he who has kinsfolk, he who has another's liver, he who has another's entrails, all who came out of someone's belly, someone's throat.

6. *A child is born, lovely as an adornment of cast gold.*
   He is something that is cast of gold, something that is perforated like jade, something that is polished like jade or gold. He was cast of gold, perforated like jade, polished as a piece of jade or gold. He is shown off like a gold necklace.

7. *He awakens, he comes to life, he is prudent, [or] he is guided by reason.*
   He is a cornstalk that blooms, an ear of corn that starts to form, a plant that puts out a shoot, a tree that puts out leaves. He is prudent, he is wise, he blooms, he blossoms. It is as if he burst into bloom, as if he burgeoned, as if he went about carrying, as if he dispatched at a glance, a heart met, as if he were prudent, guided by reason, as if he were possessed of eyes, as if he were possessed of ears that were intelligent.

8. *A dearly beloved son or child, compared to beautiful and precious birds.*
A roseate spoonbill, a troupial, a quetzal bird. The great spoonbill, the brilliant troupial, the Mexican trogon, the lovely cotinga, a princely feather, a precious child.

9. *A person or a ruler who shows compassion, or gives alms, or comforts an unhappy person.*
Weeping, sighing, tears, compassion, commiseration, a spoonful of something, a doubled-over tortilla, a handful of something. He covers him with, he puts on him, chalk, feathers, with black, red, and yellow paint, he soothes the person, thus he caresses him, he comforts him. He paints the person white, he plasters him with feathers, he paints him red, he paints him yellow, thus he puts bells on him, thus he clothes him, he comforts him.

10. *Someone's servant, self, or vassal.*
He who possesses someone's hand, who possesses someone's tumpline, who possesses someone's back, who possesses someone's carrying frame, who possesses someone's land, who possesses someone's branches.

11. *To open someone's eyes by punishment, or to chastise him.*
I shall inflict scorpions, nettles, thorns, bodkins, cold water on someone. In addition, I give, I strengthen someone with, I serve someone with, stones, sticks, a tumpline, an axe, thus I punish someone.

12. *God punishes by inflicting death, or the king or a judge passes the death sentence.*
He hurls, he casts, green stones, green sticks at someone. In addition he cuts off people's hands, also, he puts someone in a noose, in a pit, in a snare, thus God or the king hurls someone into the water, hurls someone from a cliff.

13. *For the sin of disobedience, God sends plagues or bad times.*
Because the jaguar, the commoner, walked, stepped on the hair, the head of God, in this way he kicked his mat and seat. Hence, great sticks, great stones fall on someone and the heavens rend and the earth shakes.

14. *I live, I pass my life in misery, in want; I go about in need.*
    I am in need, I am in want, thus I eat at myself, my heart.
    My supper, my breakfast, are not apparent, are not visible.
    I suffer want in the corners of others' houses, beside others'
    walls.

15. *A father, a mother, or a king admonishes, reprimands.*
    He shatters something, he breaks something in two, he casts
    something into the water, he hurls something from a cliff.
    Someone's father, someone's mother, a lord, the king,
    washes someone's face with blood and tears, makes some-
    one exude them. Hard rocks, icy water, issue forth from his
    belly, from his throat.

16. *I heed someone's counsel.*
    I make someone's countenance, someone's heart, my
    mother and father. I cover myself with another's blood, an-
    other's red ink, I cover myself with another's crimson feath-
    ers, with another's shards.

17. *I do not want a father or mother, but to take any lover that appeals
    to me.*
    I do not need maternal words, I do not need paternal words,
    but I take as my mother and father the crossroads, a heap
    of ashes. I wish to be without a face,[3] a countenance, a
    body, a heart.

18. *Arrogant, one who holds no one in esteem, who debases others
    and who is disdained.*
    He walks on people's faces, people's heads, he treads on
    people, he tramples people underfoot. He rises up against
    people, he sits on people, he places another on the mat and
    seat,[4] he is aggressive. He insists on being honored, insists
    on being respected. He respects no one, he goes about with-
    out respect for anything, but walks on the face, on the head
    of his name, his honor. He is arrogant, he kicks people's
    mat and seat, hence respects nothing.

19. *To stir up disputes by means of which people kill or massacre each
    other.*

I go between people, in the middle of people. I go stirring up dirt, filth, and ashes. I close people's eyes with burning things, with sharp things, I sow discord, thus I go about giving people pulque and mushrooms to drink and eat exciting them, thus I misguide them, I provide them with clumsy feet, mouths, hands. Thus I go back and forth sold from one to another, I talk out of both sides of my mouth, I am two-faced, I am fork-tongued. I make myself seem good to both sides, I go about as a "bracelet snake,"[5] a ladderbacked woodpecker,[6] I go about making people drink blood and eat hearts, bewitching people, thus I go about stirring up people.

20. *The ruler or governor ruins the country by ruling badly, or by becoming prideful with power.*
He stirs things up, he creates disturbances, he raises dust, he confuses, he misguides people.[7] He demolishes things, he tears things down, he breaks things, he hacks things to bits, he casts things into the river, he hurls things from the cliffs, he puts people in dangerous places, he puts people in the mud. He kicks things, he scatters things about, his father is hurled down, his mother is hurled down, he goes about crazed, he is panting,[8] in this way he rules his city. He brings shame upon, he degrades, the mat and seat. He casts lots, he practices sortilege on the face, on the head of his lordship, of his nobility, thus he puts people on the plains, in the forest.

21. *The slave.*
He who is an axe, a tumpline, the earth, the mud, the stones, the wood, who has heron feathers and a jacket of ropes, whose place of being, whose dwelling place is the urinal, the dung heap.

22. *Lazy, an idler, ill-bred, shameless, one who does not want to work.*
He plays with piles of dirt, he plays with piles of shards, he makes little piles of garbage, he amuses himself in the mud pile, he amuses himself in the dirt like a child. He just wants to run around, he goes around like a madman, he

does not want to do anything, he has no desire to do anything, he has dead feet, he has dead hands, he dupes people, his supper and breakfast is in the homes of others.

23. *The holy teachings that come from the heart should be revered and not disdained.*
The box, the coffer is untouchable, unseizable, untakeable, it is a thing not to be reviled because the good teachings of the elders that flow, that issue from someone's heart are not worthy of being hurled to the ground.

24. *He exposed himself to danger and madly, or in desperation, he attacked his adversaries, or he placed himself in such a position that there is no way out, like a moth into the flames.*
Like a moth he hurled himself into the flames. He thought nothing of his breast, his head, he scorned them. He exposed himself to dangers, he crashed into them, madly he fell on them. The fire is roaring and like a moth he crazily hurls himself into it.

25. *A valiant or brave person.*
A man, a brave man, red-faced, angry and fierce, glorious-faced, yellow-footed, yellow-lipped, he proves to be a great mountain lion, a great bear, he distinguishes himself as a great eagle, a great jaguar.

26. *He goes about like a scoundrel, following the road of the beasts, deranged, senseless.*
Now he is sweating, he is deranged, he is unhinged. He does not go out at the exit, he does not enter at the entrance, he only follows the road of the deer, of the rabbit. He is uncultivated, wild as the field, he is devastating, he is an animal. He goes like a madman, he goes like a rabbit, he goes like a deer, he goes about like a fool, he goes about deranged, he is without hands, he is without feet. He is mad; not alive, he is not human, he is drunk on mushrooms, he is drunk on jimsonweed, he is a deer-footed oaf, he is crude. He has seen the road of the rabbit, the road of the deer. He is agitated, his eyes do not see, his ears do not hear.

27. *I reprimand him for his language.*
    I fling him down on his head, on his skull, on the top of
    his head. I make him walk on his forehead, on his knees.
    I fortify him with sticks and stones. I kick his toes, his
    elbows, his knees and legs.

28. *Gossip, evil-tongued scandalmonger.*
    Cleft lip, chipped lip, strong-lipped, evil-mouthed, bad-
    mouthed, evil, hatred. Nowhere is he looked at, is he spoken
    to, is he heard, is he regarded.[9] Thus he is, thus he lives.
    He chomps madly, he invites himself to human conversa-
    tion, he speaks senselessly.

Abbreviations

A&D   Anderson and Dibble translation of the Florentine Codex

C.G.N.   Sullivan's *Compendio de la gramatica Náhuatl*

F.C.   Florentine Codex, facsimile edition, 1979

Hist. Gen.   Garibay's 1956 edition of Sahagún's *Historia general de las cosas de Nueva España*

P.M.   The *Primeros Memoriales*, facsimile edition by Francisco Paso y Troncoso

R.S.   Rémi Siméon's *Dictionnaire de la langue nahuatl ou mexicaine*.

All additions to Sullivan's original notes to the texts are marked *ed.*

Sources and Readings

The sources that Sullivan drew on for her translations of Classic Aztec were voluminous and it is not my intention to either provide a summary of all of them here, for interested scholars can refer to her original publications for these materials, or a bibliography of the source material for Classic Aztec literature, as the subject is far too broad and the manuscripts are of limited interest outside the rarefied air of scholarly circles. Sullivan's own publications have been adequately treated in a memorial volume edited by her colleagues Karen Dakin and J. Kathryn Josserand, entitled *Smoke and Mist: Mesoamerican Studies in Memory of Thelma D. Sullivan*, (Oxford: British Archaelogical Review), 2 vols. pp. 7–11. What follows is rather a listing of sources and materials that may help clarify the texts plus a few general works on the Aztecs.

There is also a short listing of the dictionaries and grammars that she used in her work. Her own grammar, the *Compendio de la gramatica Náhuatl*, lists most of her primary sources on Classic Aztec grammar.

THE AZTEC WORLD OF ANCIENT MEXICO

Notes

1. Motecuzoma is the Aztec spelling of the name of the leader better known as Montezuma or Moctezuma.

2. Classic Aztec, or Nahuatl, is the language reduced to Western alphabetic writing by friars and scribes in the sixteenth century and spoken in the heart of the Aztec empire, Tenochtitlan.

3. The "Black and the Red" is a metaphor for knowledge in Aztec. Their painted books were also called books of "the Black and the Red" (see IV, 1 and 2).

4. For information on human sacrifice, see Michael Harner (1977), "The Ecological Basis for Aztec Sacrifice," *American Ethnologist*, 4:117–35. Also see Barbara J. Price's rejoinder (1978), "Demystification, Enriddlement, and Aztec Cannibalism: A Materialist Rejoinder to Harner," *American Ethnologist*, 5:98–115. Christian Duverger (1978), *La Fleur Létal: Économie du sacrifice aztèque*, Paris: Éditions de Seuil. Robert C. Padden (1967), *The Hummingbird and the Hawk*, Columbus: Ohio State University Press. Woodrow Borah and Shelburne F. Cook (1963), *Aboriginal Populations in the Valley of Mexico on the Eve of the Spanish Conquest*, Berkeley: University of California Press. Inga Clendinnen (1991), *Aztecs: An Interpretation*, Cambridge, England: Cambridge University Press.

5. See J. Gines de Sepúlveda (1951), *Democrates Alter*, Spanish translation, *Democrates secundo: De las justas causas de la guerra contra los Indios*, Madrid: Instituto F. de Vitoria; and Bartolome de las Casas (1967), *Apológética historia summaria cuanto a las cualidades, disposición, cielo y suelo destas tierras*, 2 vols., edited by Edmundo O'Gorman, Mexico City: UNAM. See also *Apologia*, English translation, *In Defense of the Indians*, Dekalb: Northern Illinois University Press, for the details of this debate.

6. Charles Wicke and Fernando Horcasitas (1957) reported a personal communication from Robert H. Barlow indicating that sacrifices had taken place on Mount Tlaloc within recent memory. See the article "Archaeological Investigations on Mount Tlaloc, Mexico," *Mesoamerican Notes*, 5:83–97; and T. J. Knab (1992), "Geografía del Inframundo," *Estudios de la Cultura Náhuatl*, 21:31–58.

7. Thelma D. Sullivan (1980), "Tlatoani and Tlatocayotl in the Sahagún Manuscripts," *Estudios de la Cultura Náhuatl*, 14:225–238, specifically p. 235.

8. See Yólotl Gonzalez Torres (1972), "El concepto de tona en el México antiguo," *Boletín de la INAH*, 19, secunda época, pp. 13–16; Alfredo López Austin (1980), *Cuerpo humano e ideología: Las concepiones de los antiguos Nahuas*, 2 vols. Mexico City: UNAM; English translation by Thelma Ortiz de Montellano and Bernard Ortiz de Montellano (1988), *The Human Body and Ideology: Concepts of the Ancient Nahuas*, 2 vols., Salt Lake City: University of Utah Press; and Davíd Carrasco (1990), *Religions of Mesoamerica*, New York: Harper & Row.

9. Susan D. Gillespie (1989), *The Aztec Kings*, Tucson: Arizona Press.

10. Nahuas is a global term for all Aztec peoples, i.e., all peoples speaking dialects of the Nahuatl language. Alfredo López Austin (1980), *Cuerpo humano e ideología: Las concepiones de los antiguos Nahuas*, 2 vols. México City: UNAM; English translation by Thelma Ortiz de Montellano and Bernard Ortiz de Montellano (1988), *The Human Body and Ideology: Concepts of the Ancient Nahuas*, 2 vols., Salt Lake City: University of Utah Press, p. 7.

11. John Bierhorst, trans. (1992), *The History and Mythology of the Aztecs: The Codex Chimalpopoa*, Tucson: Arizona Press, p. 4.

12. Among those who have recognized the reinterpretations of realities are Rudolph Van Zantwijk (1985), *The Aztec Arrangement: The Social History of Pre-Spanish Mexico*, Norman: University of Oklahoma Press; Susan M. Kellog (1986), "Kinship and Social Organization in Early Colonial Tenochtitlan," in *Ethnohistory: Supplement to the Handbook of Middle American Indians*, vol. 4, Austin: University of Texas Press; and Susan D. Gillespie (1989), *The Aztec Kings: The Construction of Rulership in Mexica History*, Tucson: University of Arizona Press. Some of the basic histories that show this process are: Nigel Davies (1973), *The Aztecs: A History*, New York: G. P. Putnam's Sons; and Burr Cartwright Brundage (1979), *The Fifth Sun: Aztec Gods, Aztec World*, Austin: University of Texas Press; and perhaps the most widely known history of the Aztecs, that of William H. Prescott (1871), *History of the Conquest of Mexico*, edited by John Foster Kirk, 2 vols., Philadelphia: Lippincott.

13. Davies, *op. cit.*, and Brundage, *op. cit.*, both note this, as does Prescott, *op. cit.*

14. Clendinnen, *op. cit.*, p. 8.

15. Davíd Carrasco, *op. cit.*; and (1991) "Introduction: Aztec Ceremonial Landscapes," in *To Change Place: Aztec Ceremonial Landscapes*, Davíd Carrasco, ed., Boulder: University of Colorado Press.

16. Edward Calnek (1978), "The City State in the Basin of Mexico," in *Urbanization in the Americas from Its Beginnings to the Present;* see also R. P. Schaedel, J. E. Hardoy, and N. Scott Kinzer, The Hague: Mouton; and (1979) "Tenochtitlan in the Early Colonial Period" in *Actes du Congrès International des Américanistes*, Congrès du Centenaire, Paris, 2–9 September 1976, pp. 35–40.

17. Richard F. Townsend (1979), *State and Cosmos in the Art of Tenochtitlan*, Studies in Pre-Columbian Art and Archaeology no. 20, Washington, D.C.: Dumbarton Oaks, pp. 17–21.

18. Many years ago Sullivan pointed out that Tlaloc was an earth deity and probably a very ancient member of the pre-Columbian pantheon. Thelma D. Sullivan (1972), "Tlaloc: A New Etymological Interpretation of the God's Name and What It Reveals of His Essence and Nature," in *Atti del XL Congresso Internazionale Degli Americanisti*, II, pp. 213–19.

19. Johanna Broda (1991), "Sacred Landscape of the Aztec Calendar Festivals: Myth, Nature and Society," in Davíd Carrasco, ed., *To Change Places: Aztec Ceremonial Landscapes*, Boulder: University of Colorado Press, pp. 74–120.

20. Clendinnen, *op. cit.*, p. 240.

21. Davíd Carrasco (1987), "Myth, Cosmic Terror and the Templo Mayor," in *The Great Temple of Tenochtitlan*, J. Broda, D. Carrasco, E. Matos M., eds., Berkeley: University of California Press, p. 156.

22. T. J. Knab (1984), "Metaphors, Concepts and Coherence in Aztec," in *Mesoamerican Symbolism*, G. Gossen, ed., Albany: State University of New York, pp. 45–55.

23. Daniel G. Brinton (1887 and 1890), *Ancient Nahuatl Poetry*, and *Rig Veda Americanus: Sacred Songs of the Ancient Mexicans, with a Gloss in Nahuatl*. Nos. 7 & 8, Philadelphia: Library of Aboriginal American Literature.

Readings

Bierhorst, John. 1985. *Cantares Mexicanos: Songs of the Aztecs*. 2 vols. Stanford: Stanford University Press.

Brinton, Daniel G. 1887 and 1890. *Ancient Nahuatl Poetry*, and *Rig Veda Americanus: Sacred Songs of the Ancient Mexicans, with a Gloss in Nahuatl*. Nos. 7 and 8. Philadelphia: Library of Aboriginal American Literature.

Broda, Johanna, Davíd Carrasco, and Eduardo Matos M., eds. 1987. *The Great Temple of Tenochtitlan*. Berkeley: University of California Press.

Carrasco, Davíd. 1990. *Religions of Mesoamerica*. New York: Harper & Row.

Clendinnen, Inga. 1991. *Aztecs: An Interpretation*. Cambridge, England: Cambridge University Press.

Dakin, Karen, and Doris Heyden. 1988. "Introduction: Thelma D. Sullivan." In *Smoke and Mist: Mesoamerican Studies in Memory of Thelma D. Sullivan*. 2 vols. Karen Dakin and J. Kathryn Josserand, eds., Oxford: BAR, pp. 3–11.

Davies, Nigel. 1973. *The Aztecs: A History.* New York: G. P. Putnam's Sons.

Díaz del Castillo, Bernal. 1956. *The Discovery and Conquest of Mexico.* Translated by A. P. Maudsley. New York: Farrar, Straus and Giroux.

Garibay K., Angel María. 1971. *Historia de la Literatura Náhuatl.* 2 vols. Mexico City: Editorial Porrúa.

———. 1961. *Llave del Náhuatl.* Mexico City: Porrúa.

———. 1964–1968. *Poesía Náhuatl.* 3 vols. Mexico City: UNAM.

Karttunen, Frances. 1983. *Analytical Dictionary of Nahuatl.* Austin: University of Texas Press.

López Austin, Alfredo. 1980. *Cuerpo humano e ideología: Las concepciones de los antiguos Nahuas.* 2 vols. Mexico City: UNAM. English translation by Thelma Ortiz de Montellano and Bernard Ortiz de Montellano. 1988. *The Human Body and Ideology: Concepts of the Ancient Nahuas.* 2 vols. Salt Lake City: University of Utah Press.

Molina, Fray Alonso de. 1571. *Vocabulario en lengua Castellana y Mexicana y Mexicana Castellana.* 1970, 4th edition. Mexico City: Porrúa.

Sahagún, Fray Bernardino de. 1979. *Historia general de las cosas de Nueva España; Códice Florentino.* 3 vols. Mexico City: Secretaría de Gubernación. (Facsimile edition of the entire Florentine Codex.)

———. 1956. *Historia general de las cosas de Nueva España.* Edited by A. M. Garibay K. 4 vols. Mexico City: Porrúa.

Siméon, Rémi. 1885. *Dictionnaire de la langue nahuatl ou mexicaine.* Paris: Imprimerie Nationale.

Soustelle, Jacques. 1955. *La vie quotidienne des Aztèques en la veille de la conquête espagnole.* Paris: La Club de Meilleur Livre. English translation by Patrick O'Brian. 1964. *The Daily Life of the Aztecs on the Eve of the Spanish Conquest.* London: Pelican Books.

Sullivan, Thelma D. 1971. "The Finding and Founding of Mexico Tenochtitlan." *Tlalocan,* VI:312–36.

———. 1972. "Tlaloc: A New Etymological Interpretation of the God's Name and What It Reveals of His Essence and Nature." In *Atti del XL Congresso Internazionale Degli Americanisti,* II:213–19.

———. 1976. *Compendio de la gramatica Náhuatl.* Mexico City: UNAM.

———. 1986. "A Scattering of Jades: The Words of the Aztec Elders." In *Symbol and Meaning beyond the Closed Community: Essays in Mesoamerican Ideas.* Edited by G. Gossen. Albany: State University of New York, pp. 9–17.

———. 1986. *Vocabulario de la lengua Náhuatl del padre Andrés de Olmos.* Mexico City: UNAM.

Todorov, Tzvetan. 1982. *La conquête de l'Amérique: La question de l'autre.* Paris: Editions du Seuil. English translation by Richard Howard. 1984. *The Conquest of America.* New York: Harper and Row.

Whorf, Benjamin Lee. 1946. "The Milpa Alta Dialect of Aztec." In Harry Hoijer, ed., *Linguistic Structures of Native America.* Viking Fund Publication No. 6. New York: The Viking Fund, pp. 367–97.

Translating the Aztec World: Thelma D. Sullivan

Notes

1. Benjamin Lee Whorf (1946), "The Milpa Alta Dialect of Aztec," in Harry Hoijer, et al., *Linguistic Structures of Native America*, Viking Fund Publications in Anthropology, No. 6, New York: The Viking Fund, pp. 367–97.

2. Her "etymological method" is best illustrated in her paper on the meaning of Tlaloc, where she showed that rather than being a rain god the fundamental nature of Tlaloc is as an earth deity. Thelma D. Sullivan (1972), "Tlaloc: A New Etymological Interpretation of the God's Name and What it Reveals of His Essence and Nature," in *Atti del XL Congresso Internazionale Degli Americanisti*, II, pp. 213–21. Her translator's dictionary, now at Dumbarton Oaks, also amply indicates the fruitfulness of this method in Nahuatl.

The Aztec World: I, 1

The manuscript on which this section is based was found among the papers of Sullivan at Dumbarton Oaks, folder VIII, Codex Chimalpopoca. It is apparently a fragment of a larger translation, perhaps of the entire manuscript. It was used in her speaking script for her Dumbarton Oaks lecture, "A Scattering of Jades," and it was referred to in other notes and letters among her papers. Perhaps this is the only section of the translation that she was sufficiently pleased with to have typed up.

The manuscript has been edited in accordance with Sullivan's notes for her Dumbarton Oaks presentation and the indications from her correspondence and other files. It was clear from her notes and correspondence that Sullivan had intended to complete work in the same style that she had used for the Mexicayotl in the following chapter.

Notes

1. There is some fragmentary evidence that it may have been read from an earlier pre-Columbian-style painted manuscript. Although there is little evidence concerning its actual composition, it was part of the collection of historical manuscripts assembled by Caballero Lorenzo Benaduci de Boturini and had originally formed a part of the collection of Fernando de Alva Ixtlixochitl, a descendant of Aztec nobility.

2. Sullivan's notes from unpublished works on the Ancient Suns and the *Huehuetlatolli*, Words of the Ancients, along with the speaking script she used for her final lecture at Dumbarton Oaks, show quite clearly her notion of this piece as a vital collection of narratives in the Aztec tradition. In order to put these selections in a coherent context I have kept the chronological order and some of the historical and calendric materials that thread the narratives together, however vaguely they are organized. John Bierhorst has recently completed a translation of the entire manuscript, which is forthcoming from the University of Arizona Press.

3. *Huitztlampa*, "South," in the text, but logically it should read *Cihuatlampa*, "West." The cardinal points were read counterclockwise.

4. Xiuhtecutli is the old fire god. Tozpan, Ihuitl, and Xiuhnel represent the three hearth stones that support the griddle on the fire. [In modern Aztec towns in the Sierra de Puebla the three stones are viewed as supporting the earth, *talticpac*, with the fires of the underworld below and the clouds of smoke of the sky above. *Ed.*]

5. *Cemiztetl, cemiztitl*, "one fingernail span," i.e., the span from the thumbnail to nail of the index finger.

6. *Telpochtli*, "the youth," one of the names of Tezcatlipoca.

7. The Nahuatl greeting of welcome, which roughly means "You have troubled yourself in coming."

8. F. C., Book XII, Chapter IV, gives a good description of both the mask and the headdress, *apanecayotl*. Also see plates II and IV of the Codex Boturini in which the hieroglyph *apanecatl* is in the form of a feathered headdress, presumably the *apanecayotl*.

9. These could also be bee hives. [In Tlaxcala, in Modern Aztec, the gourds used to collect the sweet juice of the maguey, *agua miel*, that upon fermentation becomes pulque, an agave beer, are called "honeyjars." In the Sierra de Puebla stingless native bees are kept in jars rather than Western-style hives. *Ed.*]

10. [This is a way of testing the quality and strength of pulque. One-finger pulque is very fresh; two-finger pulque is called such because it takes two fingers to lift the slimy liquid to the mouth. *Ed.*]

11. The fifth drink was considered the one that caused drunkenness. See F. C., Book X, Chapter XXIX, f. 210; A&D, Book X, p. 193.

12. Before drinking pulque the Aztecs would pour a cup of the drink around the four sides of the hearth. See Codex Matritence, 245v; A&D, Book II, p. 182; F. C. II, f. 243. [In the Sierra de Puebla this is an offering to the fire dogs, the three stones that hold the *comal*, or griddle; these are the same as the three who guarded the old fire god, Mixcoatl, Tozpan, and Ihuitl, mentioned above. *Ed.*]

13. [In Modern Aztec in the Valley of Puebla this phrase implies having sexual relations with someone. *Ed.*]

14. [Sullivan found this song problematic and left it untranslated. *Ed.*]

Readings

Anderson, Arthur J. O., and Charles Dibble, trans. 1952–1982. *Florentine Codex*. 12 vols. Salt Lake City: University of Utah Press.

Bierhorst, John. 1992. *The Codex Chimalpopoca: The Anales de Cuauhtitlan and Legend of the Suns*. Tucson: University of Arizona Press.

Boturini Benaduci, Caballero Lorenzo. 1746. *Idea de una nueva historia general de la América septentoral*. Madrid.

Brasseur de Bourborg, Charles Etienne. 1859. *Histoire des nations civilisées du Mexique et de l'Amérique-Centrale*. Paris: Bertrand.

Chimalpopoca Galicia, Faustino. 1885. *Anales de Cuauhtitlan. Noticias historicas de México y sus contornos*. Mexico City: Anales del Museo Nacional, Escalante.

Codex Boturini. 1958. Mexico City: Vargas Rea.
Sahagún, Fray Bernardino de. 1979. *Historia general de las cosas de Nueva España; Códice Florentino.* 3 vols. Mexico City: Secretaría de Gubernación. (Facsimile edition of the entire Florentine Codex.)

————. 1905–1907. *Edición parcial en facsímile de los códices matritenses que se custodian en las Bibliotecas del Palacio Real y de la Real Academia de la Historia.* Edited by Francisco Paso y Troncoso. 3 vols. Madrid: Hauser y Menet. (This is a facsimile edition of the manuscript known as the *Primeros Memoriales.*)

Velázquez, Primo Feliciano. 1945. *Codice Chimalpopoca: Anales de Cuauhtitlan y Leyendu de los soles.* Mexico City: UNAM.

THE AZTEC WORLD: I, 2

This section is based on Sullivan's 1972 article for *Tlalocan*, vol. VI, pp. 312–36, of the same title. It was also published, and slightly updated, under the title "The Aztec Migration Myth," in *The New World Journal*, vol. 4, Bob Callahan, ed., by Turtle Island Press, Berkeley, California, for the Netzhualcoyotl Historical Society, in 1979. Alterations to the original are those indicated in Sullivan's notes at Dumbarton Oaks.

Notes

1. The original introduction that Sullivan wrote for this piece was far more extensive than the published version, explaining exactly how she viewed the text and what she had done in her translation to make it conform to her view of it. For this reason I will cite extensively her original introduction to this piece.

2. The original manuscript of this work is in the Bibliothèque National de Paris, MS No. 311, entitled *Crónica Mexicana.* [Sullivan worked from a photocopy made by Francisco del Paso y Troncoso in the Archivo Histórico of the Museo Nacional de Antropología e Historia in Mexico City marked Paquete No. 21. The text is almost unreadable and I have checked every section against the photocopy that Sullivan worked from. What she left out of the translation was as important as what she included. The translation does not follow the text word for word. Minor sections were excised to conform to our notion of a good narrative and a readable text. *Ed.*]

3. [Here Sullivan disagrees with Anderson and Dibble's translation of *tlaquetzqui* as entertainer, and also with Garibay's translation, for actors were storytellers and vice versa. As she states, "Only we, who have no storytellers in our culture, need to have this explained." *Ed.*]

4. Various versions of the text exist in the post-Columbian codices, MS 1528, Codex Aubin, Chimalpain, Durán, Codex Raimírez.

5. *Teochichimeca,* "The Great Chichimeca," or "The True Chichimeca." *Chichimeca,* "People of Chichiman," "Place of Dogs." *Azteca* or *Aztlan tlaca,* "People of Aztlan," "Place of Herons." *Mexitin,* etymology undetermined. *Chicomoztoca,* "People of Chicomoztoc," "The Place of the Seven Caves," the place of origin of the Aztecs and their predecessors.

6. ". . . their insignias as Knights . . . were two or three feathers, green

or blue, bound to their hair with red ties . . . from these hung as many tassels as the number of feats and exploits they had performed in war. . . ." (Durán, *Historia*, V. II, p. 363; see also Durán, *The Aztecs*, p. 204).

7. *In tlien intlapial, in intlequimilol*, literally, "that which is guarded, that which is wrapped up," a metaphor for the idol they carried on their backs in a shawl-like cloth, the way some Indian women to this day carry their babies. (See *Crónica Azcatitlan*, plates V, VI, VII; *Códice Boturini*, plates II, IV.)

8. *Izca in imitacauhca in michoaque: amo momaxtlatiya, zan maxauhtineca: zan yehuatl ic motlapachoaya incicuil, in mitoa inixcol: zan huel iuhqui in huipilli conmaquiaya . . . n cihua: zaniyo mocuetiaya, atle inhuipil catca. . . .* "These are the defects of the people of Michoacan. They [the men] only cover themselves with shirts called *xicolli* [a sleeveless jacket]. They put it on like a *huipil* [over the head]. . . . The women only wore skirts, they did not have *huipiles*. . . ." (P.M. f. 190v; C.F., Book X, f. 139r; A&D, Book X, p. 189.)

9. [In Sullivan's published text this line reads "I shall provide the people with food" and is followed with this note: "Although I have translated the text as it reads, I believe that it was meant here that he will provide the gods with food and drink via the sacrifice of captives. In the F.C., Book VI, f. 71v. is the statement: '. . . *yehuatl tonatiuh inan ita mochihua, yehuatl teatlitia, tetlamaca in teopan, in mictlan. . . .*' He [the warrior] becomes the mother and father of the sun. He provides drink, he provides food for Those Above and in the Region of the Dead." In the manuscript "people" is corrected in this line and the one above it to read "the gods," for the "people" of Huitzilopochtli at this time were in fact the gods, or at least deified ancestors, which I feel is the proper reading. *Ed.*]

10. ". . . They [the Toltecs] sowed and harvested cotton of every color . . . also Quetzalcoatl possessed an abundance of *cacao* plants ["Bushes" in the original, they are actually trees. *Ed.*] of different colors . . ." (*Hist. Gen.*, Book III, p. 279). Chocolate was mixed with herbs and spices, which altered its color.

11. *In atlauhtli, in tlamimilolli*, the metaphor for ravine, is, literally, "the ravine, the cliff," the bottom and sides that form a ravine.

12. *Axolotl, Ambystoma trigrinum, Ambystoma* sp., a salamander-like amphibian.

13. *Ephydra californica* Torrey, possibly also *Corixa* sp. Both are water insects whose eggs were eaten.

14. *Izcahuitli*, small red aquatic worms that were eaten. They were also used to increase lactation in nursing mothers (*Hist. Gen.*, V. III, pp. 177, 263).

15. *Cassidix* sp. (A&D, Book XI, pp. 50, n.1).

16. In Muñoz Camargo's account of the civil war between the Chichimeca of Poyauhtlan, who later settled in Tlaxcala, and the Tepaneca and Culhuaca, the future Tlaxcalans killed so many of their adversaries that blood flowed in streams to the edge of the lake and turned the water crimson. In commemoration of this victory, says the text, they ate the red *izcahuitli* worm. (Muñoz Camargo, *Historia de Tlaxcala*, Mexico City, 1892, p. 33.) Apparently the Aztecs shared this myth, and numerous others,

with their traditional enemies the Tlaxcaltecans, both of whom, it is safe to assume, inherited them or adopted them from earlier peoples.

17. *Tlaxotecayotl*, "Song in the style of the people of Tlaxotlan"; *Tecuilhuicuicatl*, "Song of the Festival of the Lords." This was sung in *Panquetzaliztli*, the festival to Huitzilopochtli (C.F., Book II, f. 83r; A&D, Book II, p. 130; *Hist. Gen.*, V. I, p. 206).

18. *Centzonhuitznahua*, "The Four Hundred Southerners," symbolic of the innumerable stars in the southern skies whose light is obscured (killed) by the round vigorous sun, Huitzilopochtli.

19. Bright yellow, also called *pilnechihualli*. This is thought to be an allusion to his youth, to his role as the young sun (A&D, Book III, p. 316; Seler, *Borgia*, V. I, p. 55; Spence, p. 66).

20. In the myth of the birth of Huitzilopochtli, recorded in the Madrid and Florentine Codices of Sahagún, Coyolxauhqui appears as his sister. His mother is Coatlicue. (C.F., Book III, f. 1r; A&D, p. 1; P.M., V. VII, f. 132v; *Hist. Gen.*, V. I, p. 71.)

21. "On top of Texcaltepetl," Lava Rock Mountain.

22. [Although Sullivan translates this as Copil was a greater sorcerer than his mother, the actual text, though slightly ambiguous in reference, appears to be that he was not as great a sorcerer as his mother. *Ed.*]

23. *Itztapaltetl*, "flagstones."

24. There is some confusion as to his name. As will be seen further on, he is called Quauhtlequetzqui, or Quauhcoatl.

25. According to this text this was still in 1299.

26. "Enemy Woman," or, "Woman of Discord."

27. "This is the same woman that henceforth the Mexicans worshipped as the mother of the gods . . . called *Toci* . . ." (Durán, *Historia*, V. II, p. 42). She was sacrificed and flayed in the festival of Ochpaniztli.

28. *Tlacatlacualli*, a food offering. This could be translated as "fast food." ["Man's food" or tacos "to go" would work here too, for *tlacua*, "something to eat," is where our word *taco* comes from. *Ed.*]

29. These are words of welcome and should not be read literally. [To become ill in this case is to overeat due to one's host's generosity. *Ed.*]

30. A spear with a barbed tip.

31. "Among the Rushes," "Among the Reeds," respectively.

32. The Aztecs came from *Aztlan*, "The Place of the Herons," a white aquatic bird, hence white was a symbolic color for them. Also there is an expression in Nahuatl, *Noyollo iztaya*, "my heart becomes white," which means that one is joyful because a longed-for desire has been fulfilled.

33. *Tleatl*, "Water of Fire" and *Atlatlayan*, "the place where the water blazes." *Matlalatl*, "blue water," and *Tozpalatl*, "yellow water."

"Again they came upon a spring . . . and they saw that the water which had been clear and lovely the day before, that day was red. The water divided into two streams and the second stream, at the point at which it divided, was so blue and thick, it was frightening." (Durán, *Historia*, V. II, p. 48; almost identical is the text in the Códice Ramírez, p. 37.)

A spring called *Tozpalatl* is mentioned in the Florentine Codex as located within the ceremonial center of Tenochtitlan (*Hist. Gen.*, V. I, p. 241; A&D, Book II, p. 178).

These springs appear to be symbols for *Teoatl, Tlachinolli*, "The Vast Waters, the Conflagration," a metaphor for the ritualistic wars staged for the purpose of taking captives for sacrifice to the gods.

Matlalatl and *Tozpalatl* were considered purifying waters; for example, in the oration on the bathing of the newborn baby, the midwife says, *"Ma ximocalque, ma xontemo in matlalac, in topalac* (sic): *ma mitzmopapaquili, ma mitzmahaltili in tloque nahuaque,"* "Enter, go down into the blue water, into the yellow water. May the Lord of all, the Supreme Lord, cleanse you, purify you" (F. C., Book VI, f. 150r). Also, the father instructing his sons on their roles as ruler says, *". . . Imac quimanilia in matlalatl, in toxpalatl, inic altilo in cuitlapilli, in atlapalli,"* "In his hands he [the Lord of All] places the blue water, the yellow water with which the people are cleansed . . . ," that is, with which people are punished for their crimes. (F.C., Book VI, f. 71v.)

An analysis of these concepts, too lengthy for a footnote, will appear at some future time. [Unfortunately the analysis was never published, but there are extensive notes on the springs and waters. *Ed.*]

34. *Opuntia ficus-indica* (L). A cactus that produces a red fruit.

35. A serpent.

36. [This section that describes the founding of the Great Temple of Tenochtitlan was not included in Sullivan's original publication. *Ed.*]

37. See Molina's dictionary, "cerro," hill, or small mountain. This was also a term for a small pyramid or shrine.

Readings

Anderson, Arthur J. O., and Charles Dibble, trans. 1950–1982. *Florentine Codex*. 12 vols. Salt Lake City: University of Utah Press.

Codex Azcatitlan. 1949. Paris: Société des Américanistes.

Codex Boturini. 1958. Mexico City: Vargas Rea.

Díaz del Castillo, Bernal. 1956. *The Discovery and Conquest of Mexico*. Translated by A. P. Maudslay. New York: Farrar, Straus and Giroux.

Durán, Fray Diego. 1967. *Historia de las Indias de Nueva España y Islas de Tierra Firme*. 2 vols. Mexico City: Porrúa.

———. 1964. *The Aztecs: The History of the Indies of New Spain*. Translated and edited by Doris Heyden and Fernando Horcasitas. New York: Orion Press.

———. 1971. *The Book of the Gods and Rites and The Ancient Calendar*. Translated and edited by Doris Heyden and Fernando Horcasitas. Norman: University of Oklahoma Press.

Garibay K., Angel María. 1953. *Historia de la Literatura Náhuatl*. Mexico City: Porrúa.

León, Adrián, trans. 1949. *Crónica Mexicayotl de Fernando Alvarado Tezozómoc*. Mexico City: UNAM.

Molina, Fray Alonso de. 1571. *Vocabulario en lengua Castellana y Mexicana y Mexicana Castellana*. 1970, 4th edition. Mexico City: Porrúa.

Muñoz Camargo, Diego. 1892. *Historia de Tlaxcala*. Mexico City: Secretaría de Fomento.

Codex Ramírez. 1944. *Relación del Origin de los Indios que Habitan Esta Nueva España según sus Historias.* Mexico City: Leyenda.

Sahagún, Fray Bernardino de. 1979. *Historia general de las cosas de Nueva España; Códice Florentino.* 3 vols. Mexico City: Secretaría de Gubernación. (Facsimile edition of the entire Florentine Codex.)

———. 1956. *Historia general de las cosas de Nueva España.* Edited by A. M. Garibay. 4 vols. Mexico City: Porrúa.

———. 1905–1907. *Edición parcial en facsimile de los códices matritenses que se custodian en las Bibliotecas del Palacio Real y de la Real Academia de la Historia.* Edited by Francisco Paso y Troncoso. 3 vols. Madrid: Hauser y Menet. (This is a facsimile edition of the manuscript known as the *Primeros Memoriales.*)

Seler, Eduard. 1963. *Comentarios al Códice Borgia.* 2 vols. Mexico City: Fondo de la Cultura Económica.

Spence, Lewis. 1923. *The Gods of Mexico.* London: T. Fisher Unwin.

Sullivan, Thelma D. 1963. "Náhuatl Proverbs, Conundrums, and Metaphors Collected by Sahagún." *Estudios de la Cultura Náhuatl.* VI:93–177.

The Aztec World: I, 3

These two short chapters from Sahagún's history are from Sullivan's as yet unpublished translation of the Spanish of the Florentine Codex. It is among her earliest works, prepared for a volume edited by Patricia Fuentes, yet as with all of her translations, she continued to revise it.

Notes

1. [The Spanish text of Sahagún's work is in fact an independent document of great import rather than simply a rough approximation of the Nahuatl text. Sullivan translated the entire Spanish text of the Florentine Codex, but unfortunately was never able to find a publisher. Hopefully, someday her translation in its entirety will find a farsighted publisher. Her translation of the *Historia* was her first foray into the vast Sahaguntine corpus, which occupied her for most of the remainder of her life, and it remains among the best of her unpublished translations.

[Sullivan worked when she started out on the project from the version of the manuscript that her teacher Fray Garibay had prepared for Porrúa's publication. Realizing the problems with this version, she sought a microfilm of the Florentine Codex. Although the School for American Research had copies of the microfilm they were of little help to her, and she finally obtained a copy from her Mexican colleagues. Mexican academics recognized in her a superb scholar long before her American colleagues took notice of her work. Perhaps if more of her work had been published in her lifetime she would have received wider recognition as the superb translator and scholar that she was. *Ed.*]

2. [The translation that follows is from the Spanish text of the Florentine Codex, which provides a better view of the stark realities of the surrender of the empire to its new masters. The Aztec text in this case dwells on particular points, such as the nature of the capes worn, that would be

important to the Aztec reader, using the flourishes of Aztec rhetoric such as multiple parallelisms and metaphors. In this particular case the Spanish text reveals far better the fundamental clash of the two cultures by what it leaves out, as well as what it dwells on. *Ed.*]

3. [This is the only example that Sullivan translated of a piece composed for the written page; all other translations from Aztec still have the voice of the spoken word. Sullivan realized that even wills and other documents, despite the dry scribal format they were forced into, were initially dictated. *Ed.*]

4. The text here reads "Tres Casas" and gives the day sign in Nahuatl as *Ce Coatl*, 1-Serpent, which corresponds to August 13, 1521.

Readings

Anderson, Arthur J. O., and Charles Dibble, trans. 1952–1982. *Florentine Codex*. 12 vols. Salt Lake City: University of Utah Press.

Cortéz Hernán. 1970. *Cartas de relación de la conquista de México*. Madrid: Espasa Calpe.

———. 1963. *Cartas y Documentos*. Mexico City: Porrúa.

Díaz del Castillo, Bernal. 1956. *The Discovery and Conquest of Mexico*. Translated by A. P. Maudslay. New York: Farrar, Straus and Giroux.

Fuentes, Patricia. 1963. *The Conquistadores*. New York: Orion Press.

García Granados, Rafael. 1952–1953. *Diccionario biográfico de la historia antigua de Méjico*. Mexico City: UNAM.

Sahagún, Fray Bernardino de. 1979. *Historia general de las cosas de Nueva España; Códice Florentino*. 3 vols. Mexico City: Secretaría de Gubernación. (Facsimile edition of the entire Florentine Codex.)

———. 1956. *Historia general de las cosas de Nueva España*. Edited by A. M. Garibay. 4 vols. Mexico City: Porrúa.

———. 1982. *Historia general de las cosas de Nueva España*. Edited by Alfredo López Austín and Josefina García Quintana. 2 vols. Mexico City: Fomento Cultural, BANAMEX. (This is a direct transcription of the Spanish from the Florentine Codex.)

LIFE AND DEATH IN ANCIENT MEXICO: II, 1

This section consists of translations used by Sullivan in her numerous works on ancient Mexico, as well as some translations she prepared for friends and colleagues. What follows is a brief summary of the sources. All of the translations have been checked against her own notes at Dumbarton Oaks.

Notes

1. This may mean tortillas made from corn that came from Toluca, which he mentions in a previous chapter in discussing the corn vendor: "Each variety of corn he sells separately . . . the corn from Toluca and that of other regions. . . ." (C.F., Book X, 18, f.136.)

2. *Motonalchicaoa*, literally, "his day sign was fortified." [In Modern Na-

huatal of the Sierra de Puebla this means to become well, strong, or lucky.
Ed.]

3. See Molina's dictionary. *"Resucitar, levantarse,"* to resuscitate or raise
up from the dead, is one of the meanings of *nino, quetza.*

Readings

Anderson, Arthur J. O., and Charles Dibble, trans. 1950–1982. *Florentine
Codex.* 12 vols. Salt Lake City: University of Utah Press.
Bittman Simmons, Bente, and Thelma D. Sullivan. 1978. "The Pochteca."
In *Mesoamerican Communication Routes and Cultural Contacts.* Thomas A.
Lee Jr. and Carlos Navarrete, eds. NWAF Paper No. 40, pp. 211–18.
Ixtlilxochitl, Fernando de Alva. 1976. *Obras Historicas.* 2 vols. Mexico City:
UNAM.
Kennedy, Diana S. 1972. *The Cuisines of Mexico.* New York: Harper & Row.
———. 1975. *The Tortilla Book.* New York: Harper & Row.
Sahagún, Fray Bernardino de. 1979. *Historia general de las cosas de Nueva
España; Códice Florentino.* 3 vols. Mexico City: Secretaría de Gubernación.
(Facsimile edition of the entire Florentine Codex.)
———. 1905–1907. *Edición parcial en facsimile de los códices matritenses que se
custodian en las Bibliotecas del Palacio Real y de la Real Academia de la Historia.*
Edited by Francisco Paso y Troncoso. 3 vols. Madrid: Hauser y Menet.
(This is the manuscript known as the *Primeros Memoriales.*)
Sullivan, Thelma D. 1972. "Tlaloc: A New Etymological Interpretation of
the God's Name and What It Reveals of His Essence and Nature." In
Atti del XL Congresso Internazionale Degli Americanisti, II: 213–19.
———. 1974. "The Rhetorical Orations, or *Huehuetlatolli,* Collected by
Sahagún." In *Sixteenth Century Mexico: The Work of Sahagún.* Munro S.
Edmonson, ed. Albuquerque: University of New Mexico Press, pp.
79–98.
———. 1976. *Compendio de la gramatica Náhuatl.* Mexico City: UNAM.
———. 1980. "Tlatoani and Tlatocayotl in the Sahagún Manuscripts." *Estudios de la Cultura Náhuatl,* V, 14: 225–38.
———. 1982. "Tlazolteotl-Ixcuina: The Great Spinner and Weaver." In *Art
and Iconography of the Late Post Classic Period in Central Mexico.* A Conference at Dumbarton Oaks, October 22 and 23, 1977. Washington, D.C.:
Dumbarton Oaks/Harvard University, pp. 7–35.
———. 1986. "A Scattering of Jades: The Words of the Aztec Elders." In
*Symbol and Meaning beyond the Closed Community: Essays in Mesoamerican
Ideas.* G. Gossen, ed. Albany: State University of New York, pp. 9–17.

LIFE AND DEATH IN ANCIENT MEXICO: II, 2

All of the texts contained in this section are from the Florentine Codex.
They were first published in *Estudios de la Cultura Náhuatl.* Sullivan later
prepared a more directly rhetorical version for the journal *Alcheringa.* The
final version of these texts is the *Alcheringa* version to which I have added
some of the material from the *Estudios* publication, including notes that
were not incorporated into the text of the final version. Sullivan's copious

notes and her files on pregnancy and childbirth practices throughout Mesoamerica were valuable in preparing the final version of these pieces. The volume of material that she had collected on the role of women, pregnancy, and childbirth practices in Mesoamerica was truly astounding.

Notes

1. [This draft was prepared for *Alcheringa*, a journal of ethnopoetics, many years after her first version appeared in *Estudios de la Cultura Náhuatl*. For the *Alcheringa* version of her translation Sullivan left out the footnotes and the introduction, often incorporating this material into the text, both for the sake of readability and also to emphasize the ability of the text to stand on its own as literature. I have replaced some of the original notes for the interested reader where there might be confusion, as had Sullivan in her notes. *Ed*.]

2. [In Sullivan's files in the folder containing her final version of this text is a wealth of materials on childbirth practices, both in modern and ancient Mexico, which show that the knowledge and ideology of the Aztec woman was never conquered. Nearly five hundred years after the conquest of Mexico and decimation of its population from plague, pestilence, and forced labor, the Aztec woman, and especially the midwife, remains a paragon of her society. *Ed*.]

3. [All of these texts are to be found in F.C., Book VI, ff. 128v–151r. *Ed*.]

4. *Xochicalli*, or "House of Flowers," is a metaphorical name for the bathhouse. The bathhouse, or *temazcalli*, was shaped like an igloo and was an architectural personification of the warm, moist womb of the mother goddess. Exercising its powers on the sick and on the pregnant, it not only symbolized regeneration in the most obvious sense; as can be seen in the *Tonalamatl*, Books of Destiny, such as the *Borgia, Borbonico, Vaticanus B, Aubin* and the like, the flower is the symbol for blood, the essence of life, and the precious nourishment of the Sun. [The flower is also the ultimate aesthetic achievement of plants, and thus a powerful metaphor, but in this context the four-petaled flower, which is a sort of road map to the underworld, *Tlalocan*, is most probably what is meant. *Ed*.]

5. *Yohualticitl*, "Midwife of the Night." This is one of the numerous names of the Mother Goddess. Her male counterpart is Yohualtecutli, and their realm is called *Yohuayan*, "the Region of the Night." They represent the primordial god and goddess, *Ometecutli* and *Omecihuatl*, in their aspect of rulers of the night, here symbolic of the procreative force, sexual activity being associated with night. *Hist. Gen.*, V. II., 38, p. 210.

6. *Eagle, Jaguar* as used here is a metaphor for "young man," or, "young buck."

7. *Mictlantecutli*, "Lord of the Region of the Dead," of the netherworld.

8. In the corresponding Spanish text Sahagún translates this as "fathers of the nation, our lords . . . ," that is, rulers, who were considered the mothers and fathers of the people. However it is more in accord with the text's theme of birth that the reference be to the very old heads of the families.

9. *Oxomoco* and *Cipactonal* were the first man and woman to be created, from whom all mankind descends. The accounts differ as to which is male and which is female. They were considered the inventors of the 260-day calendar of divination, the art of divination, the interpretation of dreams, the division of time into days, hours, and years, etc. They were also the originators of medicine and the first herbal doctors. Among the Mexicas, they were held to be the first leaders of their people after their arrival in the mythical *Tamoanchan,* or "Place of Origin." See *Historia de los Mexicanos por sus Pinturas* in *Teogonia e Historia de los Mexicanos,* Mexico City: Porrúa, 1965; *Hist. Gen.,* V. I, p. 319; V. II, pp. 186, 208, 209; *Códice Chimalpopoca,* Mexico City: UNAM, 1945, p. 3.

10. In the corresponding Spanish text, Sahagún translated *pitzina* to mean the breaking of the water. *Pitzina* means "to break, smash, shatter, pierce." This translator believes the word is used here metaphorically and means the child will be damaged, or killed, as in the metaphor *ontlaxamani, ontlapoztec,* "she smashed it, she broke it," referring to a midwife, or wet nurse, or physician, when a child or patient died.

11. One of them speaking on behalf of all.

12. One of the names of the Mother Goddess. From *quilitl,* "edible plant," and *-huaztli,* an instrumental suffix, the name meaning that which generates plants. She is the generating force.

13. Sahagún clarifies this in his corresponding text, explaining that in the bathhouse it was customary to beat the back with corn leaves that had been cooked in the bathwater, that is, the water they threw on the stones to create steam. Clavigero, in his excellent description of the *temazcalli,* says that the leaves were merely moistened with the water, which is more likely. *Hist. Gen.,* V. I, p. 174; Clavigero, *Historia Antigua de México,* Mexico City: Porrúa, 1958, V. II, pp. 323 ff.

14. [The Huichol follow the same practice today with the dying, in cases where death is considered inevitable, sealing them in a room until death removes them from this world. *Ed.*]

15. "Warrior Woman" or "Valiant Woman." Plural, *Mocihuaquetzque.* These were the women who died in childbirth with the unborn child still in the womb, and the women who were immolated. These women became the *Cihuapipiltin* or *Cihuateteo,* the deified women. If a woman died after the child was born or after the child was removed from the womb, as described above, she did not become a *Mocihuaquetzqui,* a warrior woman; what made her a warrior woman was having died in the battle of childbirth with a captive, the child, still in her womb.

16. The *Mocihuaquetzque* were not cremated, as were the warriors who went to the House of Sun, or for that matter most of the dead.

17. The text says *diblome,* "devils," a Nahuatlization of the Spanish word. This is occasionally found in the texts collected by Sahagún and the reference is always to a god or an idol. [Quite a difference in attitude between Fray Bernardino's and Sullivan's translation of the term as goddesses. *Ed.*]

18. The young warriors.

19. *Tlamamacapalitotique* (plural), literally: "Those who make others

dance in the palms of their hands." [This incorporates one of the terms for the sorcerer Tezcatlipoca. *Ed.*]
   20. The land of the dead.
   21. [This apparently refers to Tezcatlipoca. *Ed.*]
   22. [This may be the origin of the Llorona stories of the ferocious weeping woman in modern Mexico. *Ed.*]
   23. A term of endearment for the dead. It means owl.

Readings

Anderson, Arthur J. O., and Charles Dibble, trans. 1950–1982. *Florentine Codex*. 12 vols. Salt Lake City: University of Utah Press.
Codex Aubin. 1576. *Colección de documentos para la historia de México*. 1903. Mexico City: Antonio Peñafiel.
Codex Borbonicus. 1576. Faksimile, 1974. Karl Nowotny, ed. Gratz, Austria: Akademische Druck und Verlagsanstalt.
Codex Vaticanus B. 1972. Faksimile. Gratz, Austria: Akademische Druck und Verlagsanstalt.
Garibay K., Angel María, ed. 1965. *Teogonía e historia de los Mexicanos: tres opúsculos del siglo XVI*. Mexico City: Porrúa. (This contains the *Historia de los Mexicanos por sus pinturas*.)
Sahagún, Fray Bernardino de. 1979. *Historia general de las cosas de Nueva España; Códice Florentino*. 3 vols. Mexico City: Secretaría de Gubernación. (Facsimile edition of the entire Florentine Codex.)
———. 1969. *Historia general de las cosas de Nueva España*. Edited by A. M. Garibay. 4 vols. Mexico City: Porrúa.
Seler, Eduard. 1963. *Comentarios al Códice Borgia*. 2 vols. Mexico City: Fondo de la Cultura Económica.
Sullivan, Thelma D. 1966. "Pregnancy, Childbirth, and the Deification of Women Who Died in Childbirth." *Estudios de la Cultura Náhuatl*, VI: 64–95.
———. 1969. "Embarazo y parto: costumbres, supersticiones, y técnicas prehispánicas de los aztecas y su supervivencia en México." *Anuario Indigenista*, XXIX: 285–93.
———. 1972. "Tlaloc: A New Etymological Interpretation of the God's Name and What It Reveals of His Essence and Nature." In *Atti del XL Congresso Internazionale Degli Americanisti*, II: 213–19.
———. 1980. "O Precious Necklace, O Quetzal Feather!" *Alcheringa*, IV, 2: 38–52.
Velázquez, Primo Feliciano. 1945. *Códice Chimalpopoca: Anales de Cuauhtitlan y Leyenda de los soles*. Mexico City: UNAM.

PRAYERS AND SONGS OF THE GODS: III, 1

The *Prayer to Tlaloc*, though slightly revised by Sullivan in her notes, is essentially the same as the piece she published in *Estudios de la cultura Náhuatl*.

Notes

1. This prayer is found in Book VI, the book of "Rhetoric, Moral Philosophy, and Theology of the Mexican Peoples," in the eighth chapter, ff. 28r to 33r, of the Florentine Codex.

2. Tlalocan, or the Region of Tlaloc, God of Rain (from *Tlalli*, "earth"; *onoc*, "to be lying or stretched out on" [This was one of Sullivan's earliest translations. She later concluded, on the basis of a different etymology, that Tlaloc was in fact an earth deity and that the association with rain and water was a secondary function (Sullivan, 1972). *Ed.*]) was a place of infinite abundance and perpetual verdure to which went those who had died by drowning or were struck by lightning, or those affected by such diseases as leprosy, venereal disease, various skin ailments, gout, and dropsy. They were the dead who were buried; all others were cremated. (*Hist. Gen.*, V. I, p. 297.)

3. *Yauhtli: Tagetes lucida* or *florida*. Pulverized, it was used as an incense exclusively in the propitiation of Tlaloc and as an anesthetic sprinkled on the faces of those to be sacrificed by burning [This was also a potent muscle relaxant (Díaz, 1976). *Ed.*]. It was employed medicinally for a variety of ailments. (*Hist. Gen.*, V. I, pp. 121, 167; V. III, p. 326.)

4. An aromatic resin produced by trees of the *bursceraccae* family, it was used as incense on religious as well as nonreligious occasions. (*Hist. Gen.*, V. I, p. 242.)

5. In religious rites, rubber was liquified and spattered on papers, figures of gods were molded from it, and balls for the sacred Game of the Ball were made of solid rubber. It was also highly regarded as a curative for a wide range of ailments. (*Hist. Gen.*, V. I, pp. 167–70; V. III, pp. 150, 286.)

6. *Maquiztli*: literally "armlet," figuratively jewels and adornments.

7. *Chicomecoatl*, 7-Serpent, was the goddess of all the fruits of the earth. Sister to the Tlaloque (plural of Tlaloc), the multiple gods of rain [Sullivan later recognized that the Tlaloque included all the earth deities, male and female, associated with Tlaloc and Tlalocan. *Ed.*], she was totally dependent on them for her fertility, symbolizing not only the earth's dependence on rain but also the principle of duality at the core of all Nahuatl concepts; 7-Serpent was also the date in the 260-day astrological calendar that fell in the thirteen-day period ruled by the sign Ce Quauhitl, 1-Rain, the day on which the goddess was celebrated. It was an auspicious sign. (*Hist. Gen.*, V. I, pp. 47, 50, 150, 337.)

8. *Cuitlapilli, atlapilli*: literally "tail and wing"; figuratively, the common people.

9. Infants were tightly bound and lashed to boards or frames made of slats and stood against the wall or were hung from a rafter. This served the double purpose of keeping them out of mischief and making, so it was believed, their backs strong.

10. *Zaquan: Gymnostinops montezuma; quecholli: Ajaja ajaja*. They were prized for their plumage.

11. *Xochcocoyotl* is given by Sahagún as one of the names for dog. (*Hist. Gen.*, V. III, p. 232.) It might, however, be a species of dog. Dogs were

widely kept as pets, used for food on certain occasions, and special tawny-colored dogs were bred to be cremated with their masters at the time of death in order to carry them across a wide body of water, the last lap of the arduous, four-year journey to Mictlan, the Region of the Dead.

12. *Ayauh tonan: Cuphea jorullensis* HBK; *tzitziquilitl: Erigeron pusillus* Nutt.; *Itzmiquilitl: Portulaca rubra* (?); and *tepicquilitl: Mesembryan-themum blandum* L are all edible plants. (*Hist. Gen.*, V. IV, pp. 324, 366; A&D, Book XI, p. 137.)

13. The Nahuas believed that the Fifth Sun, or age, in which they were living would end in cataclysm as did the four suns before it. The fifth sun, *Nahui Olin*, 4-Motion, created and put into motion when the gods sacrificed themselves in a great fire in Teotihuacan [There is now archaeological evidence that the great fire of Teotihuacan was an actual historical fact. *Ed.*], had to be kept in motion (i.e., alive) by being constantly nourished with human blood—the blood of warriors who died in battle, the blood of captives and sacrificial victims, and blood drawn in various acts of autosacrifice. However, these acts only postponed what they believed to be the inevitable fate of the world as described in this text. (*Códice Chimalpopoca*, Mexico City: Imprenta Universitaria, 1946, f. 2; *Hist. Gen.*, V. II, p. 293; Muñoz Camargo, *Historia de Tlaxcala*, Mexico City, 1892, p. 154; Torquemada, *Monarquía Indiana*, Mexico City: Chavez Hayhoe, 1943, V. II, p. 271.)

14. The god and goddess of corn.

15. A noble or commoner who died of a disease other than those that would consign him or her to Tlalocan, and did not die in battle, went to Mictlan, the Region of the Dead. A cup of water was placed under his shroud before he was cremated, and periodically food was set out where his ashes were buried in the courtyard of his house, apparently to sustain him on his journey. (*Hist. Gen.*, V. I, p. 296; Motolinía: *Memoriales*, Mexico City, 1903, p. 245; Torquemada, *Monarchía Indiana*, p. 523.)

16. All epithets of the sun. The Eagle Ascendant and Precious Child refer to the rising sun; the Valiant One and Brave Warrior to his triumph in his battle with the night.

17. Like the gods who hurled themselves into the fire to put the sun into motion, the blood of warriors gloriously consumed by the fire of battle provided the richest nourishment for the sun so that it could make its daily journey through the skies and be victorious in its combat with the night. Those slain in battle joined the sun in heaven, accompanying it on its course from dawn to midday. The women who perished in the battle of childbirth took over and accompanied the sun on its downward course to the west. Offerings of food were placed near the buried remains of the cremated warriors to sustain them in heaven for four years, after which they were transformed into hummingbirds, other birds of rich plumage, and butterflies, and they nourished themselves on the nectar of the manifold flowers in that paradise. (*Hist. Gen.*, V. I, p. 298.)

18. *In itconi, in mamaloni, in tlamamalli*; literally, "he who is carried, he who is borne on the back, the burden."

19. Rattles and rattleboards, the latter being a board with rattles inserted into it, were used in the feast of *Etzalqualiztli*, dedicated to Tlaloc, to imitate

the sound of rain and thunder. It was believed that the Tlaloque, the numerous helpers of Tlaloc, poured the rain out of great jars, and that when they beat the jars with sticks and broke them, they caused thunder and lightning. (*Hist. Gen.*, V. I, p. 164; *Historia de los Mexicanos por sus Pinturas*. Mexico City: Chávez Hayhoe, 1941, p. 235).

Readings

Anderson, Arthur J. O., and Charles Dibble, trans. 1950–1982. *Florentine Codex*. 12 vols. Salt Lake City: University of Utah Press.

Historia de los Mexicanos por sus Pinturas. 1941. Mexico City: Chávez Hayhoe.

Motolinía, Fray Toribio de Benavente. 1903. *Memoriales de Fray Toribio de Motolinía, manuscrito de la colleción del Señor Don Joaquín García Icazbalceta*. Mexico City: Luis García Pimentel, Casa del Editor.

Muñoz Camargo, Diego. 1892. *Historia de Tlaxcala*. Mexico City: Secretaría de Fomento.

Sahagún, Fray Bernardino de. 1979. *Historia general de las cosas de Nueva España; Códice Florentino*. 3 vols. Mexico City: Secretaría de Gubernación. (Facsimile edition of the entire Florentine Codex.)

————. 1956. *Historia general de las cosas de Nueva España*. Edited by A. M. Garibay. 4 vols. Mexico City: Porrúa.

Siméon, Rémi. 1885. *Dictionnaire de la langue nahuatl ou mexicaine*. Paris: Imprimerie Nationale.

Sullivan, Thelma D. 1966. "A Prayer to Tlaloc." *Estudios de la Cultura Náhuatl*, V: 39–55.

————. 1972. "Tlaloc: A New Etymological Interpretation of the God's Name and What It Reveals of His Essence and Nature." In *Atti del XL Congresso Internazionale Degli Americanisti*, II: 213–19.

Torquemada, Juan de. 1943. *Monarquía Indiana*. Mexico City: Chávez Hayhoe.

Velázquez, Primo Feliciano. 1945. *Códice Chimalpopoca: Anales de Cuauhtitlan y Leyenda de los soles*. Mexico City: UNAM.

PRAYERS AND SONGS OF THE GODS: III, 2

Although this was one of the few selections that Sullivan published from the vast corpus of Classic Aztec poetry, these were certainly not the only pieces that she had translated. While working with Father Garibay, she recounted, she had disagreed with him on many occasions over the exact meaning of various passages from Classic Aztec poems and had translated many of them herself to show him. Unfortunately this work was not among her papers at Dumbarton Oaks.

Readings

Bierhorst, John. 1985. *Cantares Mexicanos: Songs of the Aztecs*. Stanford: Stanford University Press.

Garibay K., Angel María. 1951. *Historia de la Literatura Náhuatl*. 2 vols. Mexico City: Porrúa.

―――. 1964–1968. *Poesía Náhuatl*. 3 vols. Mexico City: UNAM.

Peñafiel, Antonio. 1904. *Cantares en idioma mexicano: Reproducción facsimilaria del manuscrito original que existe en la Biblioteca Nacional*. Mexico City: Secretaría de Fomento.

Sullivan, Thelma D. 1963. "Songs of Ancient Mexico." *Mexico This Month*, VIII, 12: 26.

―――. 1976. *Compendio de la gramatica Náhuatl*. Mexico City: UNAM.

PRAYERS AND SONGS OF THE GODS: III, 3

These are probably the most difficult of all the texts that Sullivan translated in her lifetime, and unfortunately she never lived to finish her work on them. I will cite a few of the many attempts at translating these difficult pieces and some of the more general work on Classic Aztec poetics.

Notes

1. [In preparing this volume I have relied primarily on a version that Sullivan gave me shortly before her final journey to Houston where she died a month later. The version that I was given was intended for translation into Spanish for a literary publication of the National Autonomous University of México where she had been working up until her death. This was not meant as a final version, as it contained only the translations of the first ten of the twenty songs. In a note on our draft proposal for this book Sullivan indicated that the final version of these songs would be the one she was preparing as a part of the *Primeros Memoriales* translation that she was working on at the time of her death.

[There was an outline for an introduction in the version that Sullivan gave me shortly before her death that she had intended to write in Spanish covering Sahagún's commentaries on this genre, the archaisms common in them, and borrowings from other Mesoamerican languages, as well as some general observations on the style and metaphors that made them so difficult to translate. Had she lived, it was her intention to include these and several other pieces from the *Cantares Mexicanos* and *Romances* manuscripts together with selections from Sahagún's *Psalmodia*, a collection of Classic Aztec songs from which Sahagún had purged all pre-Columbian references, in a general piece on Classic Aztec poetics.

[This was to have been part of an anthology of Classic Aztec literature that she had intended for a scholarly audience with selections from her translations of all the major genres of Classic Aztec literature. Her translations ranged from dry wills and testaments to the highest forms of poetry, such as these pieces. Sullivan considered these songs among the most difficult pieces that she had ever translated and had been working on them on and off since her first few attempts at translating Classic Aztec poetry were published in the early 1960s. Despite the great difficulties that these pieces presented, Sullivan always maintained that, while these pieces were "very, very tricky," they were nevertheless translatable. My own early experience with them led me to believe otherwise.

[The version that I received from Sullivan was far from a final draft, and thanks to H. B. Nicholson, Arthur J. O. Anderson, Wayne Ruwet, and Sullivan's literary executor Rita Wilenski, I obtained a more complete version of the manuscript done shortly before her untimely death. The version presented here is based on both the draft for translation into Spanish, and the final manuscript left at the time of her death. This version is as close as possible to a final literary translation that Sullivan left before her death. It incorporates elements of both drafts, taking into account her "etymological method" of work and the styles that she had indicated in both drafts.

[Arthur J. O. Anderson, working with the drafts produced just before her death, completed Sullivan's work for inclusion in her translation of Sahagún's *Primeros Memoriales* being edited by H. B. Nicholson. The posthumous publication of this monumental work by the University of Oklahoma Press will be the first complete version of these early texts of Sahagún ever published in English. The version prepared by Arthur J. O. Anderson for inclusion in the translation of the *Primeros Memoriales* must be considered the final version, if there can be a final, or definitive, version of such texts, for it is in fact a collaboration of two of the finest Nahuatlatos working in English in this century. *Ed.*]

2. [In 1570, after spending nearly three years in the Convento de San Francisco in Mexico City examining and reexamining all of his writings, support was withdrawn from his work and his manuscripts were impounded. Sahagún's work was considered suspect once the Inquisition had taken firm hold in New Spain. Five years later when the good friar was again allowed to collect his manuscripts and begin the final task of composing and editing what would become the Florentine Codex, the spiritual climate in the New World had changed. It was in this new climate that Sahagún decided to omit any attempt at translation of the songs of the gods from his history of all things of New Spain. See Luis Nicolau D'Olwer, 1952, *Fray Bernardino de Sahagún*, Mexico City: Instituto Panamericano de Geografía e Historia. *Ed.*]

3. [The glosses that Sahagún included in his early drafts of these pieces, while useful to the scholar and translator, do little to illuminate these obscure pieces and are appended to the text more as a translator's notes. In fact, they appear repetitious and redundant. I have not, for this reason, included Sullivan's translations of Sahagún's clarifying notes to these songs, and have not included her copious notes on each of these pieces. The notes will no doubt be of great interest to scholars, who will find them in her full translation of the *Primeros Memoriales*, now being edited by H. B. Nicholson. In order to clarify these difficult pieces, each of the first ten songs is followed by a short set of commentaries summarizing both Sahagún's notes, as well as Sullivan's notes and clarifications. The commentaries are arranged so that each paragraph corresponds to a distinct stanza. *Ed.*]

Readings

Anderson, Arthur J. O., and Charles Dibble, trans. 1950–1982. *Florentine Codex.* 12 vols. Salt Lake City: University of Utah Press.

Bierhorst, John. 1985. *Cantares Mexicanos: Songs of the Aztecs.* Stanford: Stanford University Press.

Brinton, Daniel G. 1890. *Rig Veda Americanus: Sacred Songs of the Ancient Mexicans, with Gloss in Nahuatl.* Philadelphia: Brinton's Library of Aboriginal American Literature, No. 8.

Brotherston, Gordon. 1979. *Image of the New World: The American Continent Portrayed in Native Texts.* Translated with Ed Dorn. London: Thames & Hudson.

García Granados, Rafael. 1952–1953. *Diccionario biográfico de la historia antigua de Méjico.* Mexico City: UNAM.

Garibay K., Angel María. 1958. *Veinte himnos sacros de los Nahuas.* Mexico City: UNAM.

———. 1951. *Historia de la literatura Náhuatl.* 2 vols. Mexico City: Porrúa.

———. 1964–1968. *Poesía Náhuatl.* 3 vols. Mexico City: UNAM.

León Portilla, Miguel. 1969. *Pre-Columbian Literatures of Mexico.* Norman: University of Oklahoma Press.

Molina, Fray Alonso de. 1571. *Vocabulario en lengua Castellana y Mexicana y Mexicana Castellana.* 1970, 4th edition. Mexico City: Porrúa.

Sahagún, Fray Bernardino de. 1583. *Psalmodia Christiana.* Mexico City: Pedro Ocharte.

———. 1979. *Historia general de las cosas de Nueva España; Códice Florentino.* 3 vols. Mexico City: Secretaria de Gubernación. (Facsimile edition of the entire Florentine Codex.)

———. 1905–1907. *Edición parcial en facsimile de los códices matritenses que se custodian en las Bibliotecas del Palacio Real y de la Real Academia de la Historia.* Edited by Francisco Paso y Troncoso. 3 vols. Madrid: Hauser y Menet.

Seler, Eduard. 1904. *Die religiösen Gesänge der alten Mexicaner.* Berlin.

Sullivan, Thelma D. 1982. "Tlazolteotl-Ixcuina: The Great Spinner and Weaver." In *Art and Iconography of the Late Post Classic Period in Central Mexico.* A Conference at Dumbarton Oaks, October 22 and 23, 1977. Washington, D.C.: Dumbarton Oaks/Harvard University, pp. 7–35.

———. 1986. *Vocabulario de la lengua Náhuatl del padre Andrés de Olmos.* Mexico City: UNAM.

———. *The Primeros Memoriales.* A translation completed by Arthur J. O. Anderson and edited by H. B. Nicholson, with notes. In preparation. Norman: University of Oklahoma Press.

Velázquez, Primo Feliciano. 1945. *Códice Chimalpopoca: Anales de Cuauhtitlan y Leyenda de los soles.* Mexico City: UNAM.

Wasson, Gordon R. 1980. *The Wondrous Mushroom: Mycolatry in Mesoamerica.* New York: McGraw-Hill.

WORDS OF JADE: IV, 1

Although the metaphors were among her earliest publications, Sullivan was constantly revising her translations of them. Her *Compendio de la gra-*

matica Náhuatl contained some of her revisions, but she had intended to revise them completely. On her copy of the manuscript at Dumbarton Oaks it was evident that she had been making revisions even while completing her translation of the *Primeros Memoriales*. This version incorporates all of the revisions that were available.

Notes

1. [This piece was one of Sullivan's first publications. She placed it in *Estudios de la Cultura Náhuatl*, a journal founded by Father Garibay, as a homage to him. Her introduction is a testament to Father Garibay, her mentor, and also provides a fine way to view these gems of Classic Aztec literature.

[The original introduction to this translation that Sullivan provided not only reveals her sincere reverence for Father Garibay, but even at this early stage in her study of the Nahuatl language a profound understanding of its complexities. The metaphors were later revised and appended to her *Compendio de la Gramatica Náhuatl*. The modifications were minor, but in her own copy of the *Compendio* she continued making further notes for a later revision of the text. There were also many additions to the manuscript in her files that aided in preparing this version. The entire translation has been checked against a reproduction of the Florentine Codex, as well as published and unpublished versions of her translation, incorporating only the changes she indicated. The short explanations of the metaphors that she added for clarity to the version in the *Compendio* have been added where needed. They are cited as C.G.N. Had she lived, Sullivan contemplated a complete revision of this piece for her proposed anthology of Nahuatl literature. I have not done such a complete revision, because both her original version and her further notes make this unnecessary. Sullivan was such a careful translator that she would revise endlessly, but having checked this text against the original there is little that I would change. All of this material is from the Florentine Codex, Book VI, ff. 183r–215v. *Ed.*]

2. ". . . others kill others while drunk, and all these consequences are attributed to the god of wine and to the wine, not to the drunkard, as they say that he did not do it but that the god did . . . they did not regard as a sin anything they did while drunk." Sahagún, *Hist. Gen.*, V. I, p. 75.

3. [This implies to have flowered, fruited, fallen to earth, and rotted. The verb ending carries the meaning. It is a metaphor for a man's life in Modern Aztec. *Ed.*]

4. I.e., something that is thrown away. There is a play on words here: *xictli*, "umbilical cord," and *xictia*, "to look down upon someone."

5. *Nahualli*, "magician, sorcerer, conjuror," etc. The above, however, probably refers to Tezcatlipoca, one of whose names was Nahuapilli, Lord Sorcerer or Magician.

6. [This implies pulling up something delicate, destroying something that deserves to be nurtured. *Ed.*]

7. The amaranth has spikes that are covered with seeds, which, if they are not picked at a certain time, simply blow away. *Tzontli*, "hair, head,"

and *huauhzontli,* "amaranth," form a play on words that roughly means "my head droops like an amaranth whose seeds have dried and fallen."

8. Like my nose, I shall never lose him.

9. *Mollanilztia,* "to boast," and *tlaniiztli,* "shin," are from the same root. Less protected than the rest of their bodies, the warriors probably received more wounds on their legs.

10. In Nahuatl the number 400 figuratively means an incalculable number of anything and is used the way we use a thousand or a million.

11. After a captive had been sacrificed the flesh was distributed. The captor did not eat the flesh of his own captive, since the captive was considered his alter ego and the sacrifice of himself. However some of the bones were returned to him and kept as trophies.

12. A play on words. *Ix-,* from *ixtli,* "face." *Nextli* means "ashes." The verb *nextia* means "to show, to reveal."

13. Literally, "Now it has been."

14. *Tlalticpac,* which means "the earth, the world," also means "the penis."

15. [This implies that I can hold sensitive information or secrets well, for to scrape corn from someone's belly means to rip them open and tear out their entrails. In a modern context it is to gut an animal. *Ed.*]

16. This implies that one falls to earth.

17. That is, "Weren't we friends?"

18. Pulque is the fermented juice of the maguey or agave. The *Centzontotochtin,* the Four Hundred (or innumerable) Rabbits, were the gods of wine. They also represented the innumerable types of drunkenness. For a lively description of many types of drunkenness, see Sahagún, *Hist. Gen.,* V. I, p. 324.

19. Should read: *Tlacayotl eoa.*

20. There was a spring in Chapultepec where Motecuzoma bathed, and was therefore considered *ne plus ultra.*

21. The text reads *nicaci,* which would make this read "I catch," but this does not appear to fit the context.

22. That is, scribes.

23. A play on words. *Compaxoa* means "to bite, to eat something," and also "to evaluate something."

24. This is to arrange one's feeling, or have or feel something deeply.

25. The text ends abruptly here. The second meaning of the proverb, when applied unfavorably, of course is implicit.

26. *Tzotzocolli* is a water jug and also the manner in which distinguished warriors dressed, their hair pulled up on the sides into a top knot and resembling a water jug.

27. A horn instrument, a forerunner of the slide trombone, post-Columbian.

28. The granaries had straw roofs. They are still constructed in this way all over Mexico.

29. The musical instrument.

30. Portable shelves in a frame.

31. A variety of tomato that is green in color when ripe and is encased in a thin yellow outer covering; the "tomatillo."

32. Shaped like a poppy.

33. The distaff was sometimes set in a clay vessel and thus danced around when the thread was being spun.

34. Jade and quetzal feathers were the two most valued objects and therefore synonymous with anything precious.

35. When a slave was purchased he was given a headpiece of white heron feathers to indicate that he was sold. Both words are synonyms for slave and servitude.

36. The captive went to be sacrificed carrying a flag and strips of paper. The figure of speech roughly means "I have talked and talked and now I am through."

37. Here, "sticks" or "bars" are synonymous with jails, which were cagelike affairs made of thick timbers. When they caught a culprit, they bound him in ropes and then took him off to jail. See Durán, *Historia de las Indias de Nueva España*, Mexico City: Editorial Nacional, 1951, V.II, p. 222.

38. The Nahuas had several forms of capital punishment, one of which was the sacrifice of the offender to the gods. This took place at the top of a pyramid; however, sometimes they threw the victim into the fire first, and when he was half burned, took him out and removed his heart.

39. This is from Latin: "or."

40. The people were not permitted to look directly into the face of the king, hence their great expectation; they looked at him out the corner of their eyes. The king was thought of as a cypress and ceiba, huge trees that provide shade and protection.

41. Blood.

42. "And for those who unaided took four captives . . . from then on they could sit on the mats they used and ycpalles [seats] in the hall where the other captains and valiant men sat." Eagle and Jaguar were high ranks in the army, a king of knighthood. Sahagún, *Hist. Gen.*, V. II, p. 332.

43. *Altepetl*, the word for "city," is compounded of *atl*, "water," and *tepetl*, "mountain."

44. This is the opposite of the previous metaphor. The entrails sustain the organism, the throat gives the orders. The nobles sustained and directed the people.

45. *Toptli* is a basket with a handle. *Petlacalli*, literally "a container of straw," is a deep basket with a cover, in which things were stored.

46. The arrow shafts were straightened and hardened over a fire.

47. [These are the same words that are used even today to describe witchcraft in the Sierra de Puebla and in the Valley of Puebla. *Ed.*]

48. *Mat and seat* is a metaphor for throne.

49. *Xicomiccayotl* means inebriation induced by drugs or mushrooms.

50. That is, the nation.

51. Prisoners of war, criminals, and slaves were put in wooden collars and bound in ropes. The wooden collars jutted straight out in back and there were holes in the ends through which a stick passed. Another stick was laid above the holes and the two sticks were lashed together. The collar was so devised that a person could not reach the lashed ends with

his hands. See Motolinia, *Memoriales,* p. 325; Durán, *Historia de las Indias de Nueva España,* V. I, p. 458.

52. [This a perfectly accurate description of the effects of jimsonweed poisoning, for having taken the drug one remembers nothing of what has been said to him. *Ed.*]

53. Probably: *Tamatoyauatinemi.*

54. See metaphor No. 83.

55. Synonyms for food and drink that rhyme in Nahuatl. I have literally translated them, though it sounds clumsy in English, as it reveals a certain delicacy of expression characteristic of the Nahuatl language.

56. See metaphor No. 12.

57. The Nahuas ate only twice a day, about 9 A.M. and after sundown when the day's work was done. A metaphor for the sustenances of life.

58. I.e., before the conquest.

59. Like the heart and blood of the sacrificed man, which nourished the sun, they thought chocolate gave strength and courage to those who drank it.

60. [There is apparently no basis to this claim. After considerable research, both in the field, and in the laboratory, it was found that the alkaloid theobromine was contained in such small quantities as to cause no effect. In the field, the only preparation found with any effect was a fermented beverage made from the pulp of the fresh cacao in the Soconusco region of Chiapas. This beverage could be the basis for the intoxicating qualities of cacao, as it is quite pleasant when prepared properly. It should also be noted that the Aztecs most valued green cacao from which this drink could be made. *Ed.*]

61. Like the valiant warriors who were elevated to the ranks of Eagle and Jaguar, a kind of knighthood, by risking their lives in combat, the commoner could also achieve honor through his efforts. The merchant, who traveled far and wide exposing himself to danger, could not capture slaves but could buy them and earn the esteem of others with his largess.

62. Drinking was forbidden except on certain religious occasions and during pregnancy, and drunkenness was punishable by death. Only the old were permitted to drink as much as they wished.

63. They bound the infants tightly to give them strength. *Mecatl,* which means "rope," also signifies discipline.

64. A naughty child had his ribs pinched and his ears pulled, a custom that persists in Mexico today.

65. See metaphor No. 66.

66. Meaning that the punishment was over.

67. Red and black were the inks used in writing and signified wisdom. By extension in this case they mean a code of conduct. More profoundly, however, the colors red and black symbolize light and darkness, day and night, life and death, the active and the passive, male and female, etc.— the concept of duality that pervades all Nahuatl religion and philosophy. It is a divine duality and therefore wisdom implies a knowledge of, or contact with, a universal and divine truth.

68. *Códice Matritence de la Real Academia,* f. 21v. . . . *quac yancuican quicui in cactli, amo tlamachyo, amo cuicuiltic, zan tliltic, in icuetlazmecayo azo uitz-*

tecutli, anozo chichiltic cuetlaztli. "At the time he [the person who had risen to high rank] began wearing sandals that were not tooled, that were not figured, but plain black ones with orange and red laces."

69. The informant also gives an example of *opochtli*, "left," and *itzcactli*, "sandals."

70. See metaphor No. 86.

71. This can refer to either Holy Communion or the eating of the flesh of a sacrificial victim.

72. The king was considered the representation of the deity.

Readings

Anderson, Arthur J. O., and Charles Dibble, trans. 1950–1982. *Florentine Codex.* 12 vols. Salt Lake City: University of Utah Press.

Durán, Diego. 1951. *Historia de las Indias de Nueva España.* Mexico City: Nacional.

Sahagún, Fray Bernardino de. 1979. *Historia general de las cosas de Nueva España; Códice Florentino.* 3 vols. Mexico City: Secretaría de Gubernación. (Facsimile edition of the entire Florentine Codex.)

———. 1969. *Historia general de las cosas de Nueva España.* Edited by A. M. Garibay. 4 vols. Mexico City: Porrúa.

———. 1905–1907. *Edición parcial en facsimile de los códices matritenses que se custodian en las Bibliotecas del Palacio Real y de la Real Academia de la Historia.* Edited by Francisco Paso y Troncoso. 3 vols. Madrid: Hauser y Menet.

Sullivan, Thelma D. 1963. "Nahuatl Proverbs, Conundrums, and Metaphors Collected by Sahagún." *Estudios de la Cultura Náhuatl,* IV: 93–177.

———. 1976. *Compendio de la gramatica náhuatl.* Mexico City: UNAM.

———. 1985. *Thelma D. Sullivan's Compendium of Nahuatl Grammar.* Translated by Thelma D. Sullivan and Neville Stiles. Edited by Wick R. Miller and Karen Dakin. Salt Lake City: University of Utah Press.

———. 1986. *Vocabulario de la lengua Náhuatl del padre Andrés de Olmos.* Mexico City: UNAM.

———. *The Primeros Memoriales.* A translation completed by Arthur J. O. Anderson and edited by H. B. Nicholson, with notes. In preparation. Norman: University of Oklahoma Press.

WORDS OF JADE: IV, 2

Sullivan apparently prepared these while working on the Olmos vocabulary. Some of the modifications to her understanding of metaphors were incorporated into her translations of the preceding metaphors of Sahagún but not all.

Notes

1. Rémi Siméon, ed., *Arte para aprender la lengua Mexicana,* Paris, 1875, p. 211ff.

2. Probably in the original *Totecuyo, in tloque, in nahuaque,* "Our Lord of the near and the nigh."

3. *Amo niquitta,* "carecer del uso de una cosa." R.S. To no longer have the use of something or no longer see it.

4. He conceals another's crime; see R. S.

5. "Two-faced": The *maquizcoatl* was said to have a head at both ends, A&D, XI, p. 79.

6. "A sower of discord, contentious." Ibid, p. 52.

7. *Ixtia, te-,* "to awaken"; *tlachialtia, te-,* "to show, to instruct."

8. He is intoxicated as if with jimsonweed. *Ed.*

9. He is looked upon, spoken to, heard, regarded without respect.

Readings

Anderson, Arthur J. O., and Charles Dibble, trans. 1950–1982. *Florentine Codex.* 12 vols. Salt Lake City: University of Utah Press.

Molina, Fray Alonso de. 1571. *Vocabulario en lengua Castellana y Mexicana y Mexicana Castellana.* 1970, 4th edition. Mexico City: Porrúa.

Sahagún, Fray Bernardino de. 1979. *Historia general de las cosas de Nueva España; Códice Florentino.* 3 vols. Mexico City: Secretaría de Gubernación. (Facsimile edition of the entire Florentine Codex.)

Siméon, Rémi. 1875. *Arte para aprender la lengua mexicana, compuesto por Fray Andres de Olmos.* Facsimile edition with introduction by Miguel León Portilla. 1972. Guadalajara, Mexico: Edmundo Aviña Levy.

———. 1885. *Dictionnaire de la langue nahuatl ou mexicaine.* Paris: Imprimerie Nationale.

Sullivan, Thelma D. 1986. *Vocabulario de la lengua Náhuatl del padre Andrés de Olmos.* Mexico City: UNAM.

INDEX